THE BIG CIGAR BOX GUITAR SONGBOOK

3 STRING CGB IN G

Thomas
Balinger

Thomas Balinger
The Big Cigar Box Songbook, 100+ Songs for 3 string CBG in G

thomasbalinger@gmail.com

ISBN: 9798616360779

PREFACE

Hello fellow players,

and welcome to my collection of classic tunes, arranged for easy **C**igar **B**ox **G**uitar. These songs cover a wide musical range—I'm sure there's something in here for every musical taste.
All songs have been arranged for **three-string CBG in G tuning (G-D-G)** with the beginning player in mind. I added chord symbols, chord diagrams and melody tab to the standard notation to make playing as easy and straightforward as possible. There's also a strumming pattern suggestion for most songs. You can use these as a starting point to change and modify according to your own taste.

There's a short section on **tuning** your CBG, reading **CBG tablature** and the **basic CBG chords**. I also included some **easy strumming and picking patterns** you can either use on their own or as a starting point to create your own accompaniments.

For those of you interested in playing the Blues (and who isn't?), I added a few pages covering some of the most important **Blues basics**. This is no replacement for a method book, of course, but intended to provide you with a starting point for your exploration of the Blues.

Have fun with this great instrument!
Thomas Balinger

CONTENTS

SONGS

THE CIGAR BOX GUITAR

Sometimes called "the poor man's guitar", cigar box guitars have been around for quite some time. Illustrations of cigar box instruments date as far back as the middle of the 18th century. Their simple design and cheap materials made them ideal DIY projects which they still are today.

While the earliest CBGs only had one or two strings, modern designs typically have three, four or more strings and are often equipped with pickups.

Popular CBG tunings are G-D-G and A-E-A for three-string models and G-D-G-B or A-E-A-C# for four-string CBGs.

Any playing technique used on a "normal" guitar can be used on a CBG as well, with bottleneck playing being a favorite.

If you're interested in more details on the CBG, check out the very informative "One man's Trash: A history of the cigar box guitar" by William Jehle.

Last not least, if you ever happen to be in Alabama, visit the annual **Cigar Boy Guitar Extravaganza**, held in Huntsville (or simply watch the movie *Songs inside the box*, a documentation about the modern CBG revival well worth viewing for all CBG aficionados).

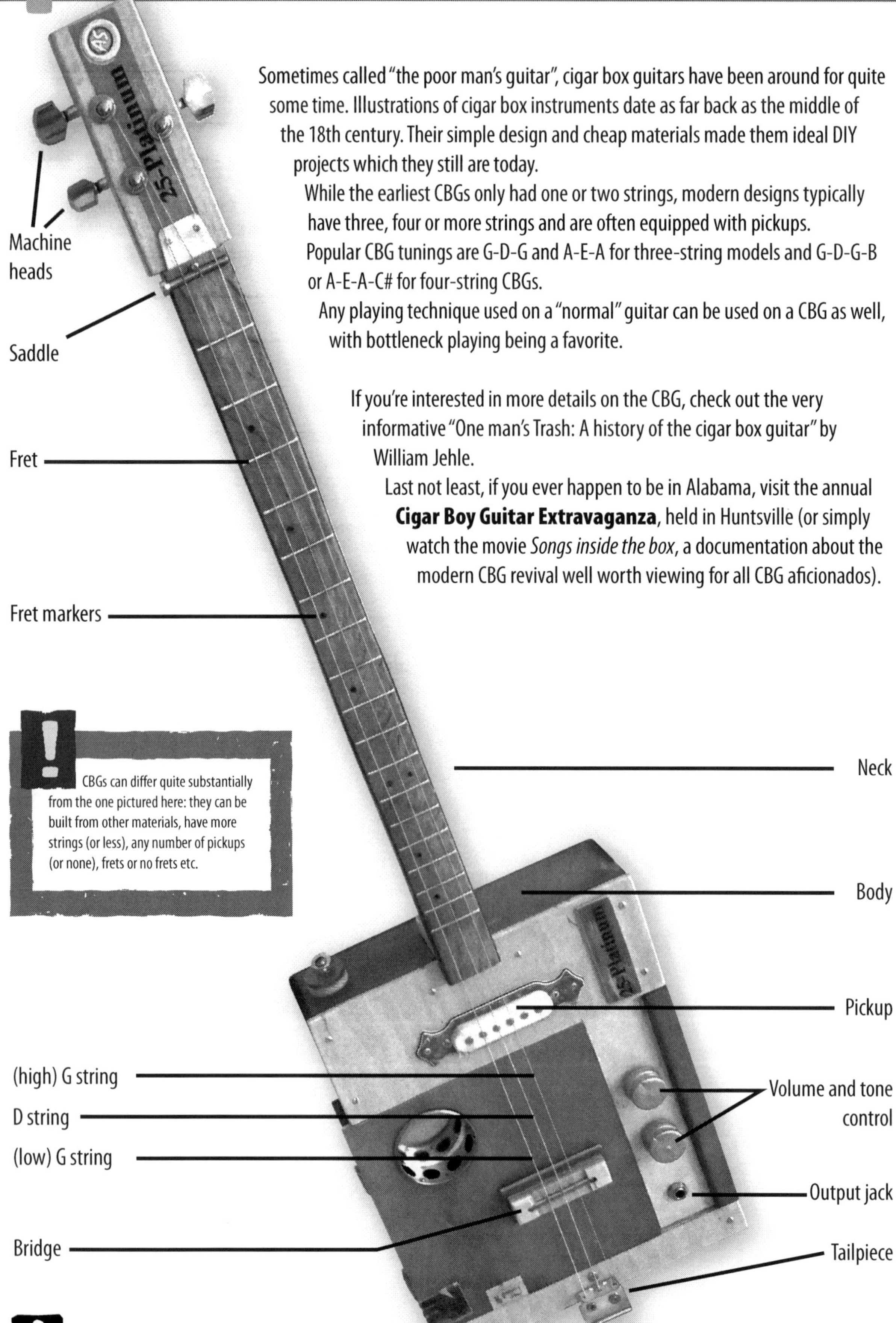

CBGs can differ quite substantially from the one pictured here: they can be built from other materials, have more strings (or less), any number of pickups (or none), frets or no frets etc.

PLAYING TECHNIQUE

When playing in a sitting position simply rest your CBG on your thigh. Standing up, use a guitar strap (available at your local dealer or on the internet).

Right hand playing technique

You can pick the strings with your finger(s) a pick (or plektrum) or even a combination of both. Try and see what feels best to you. By the way, you don't have to play with your fingers or a pick exclusively–many players simply use both, switching between fingers and pick depending on the desired sound and playing feel.
When playing with your fingers you can start by using the thumb or index finger to pick the strings. It's way more comfortable and economic, however, to simply alternate index and middle finger (picking with the index finger, followed by the middle finger, the index finger again and so on). You'll be using thumb, index finger and middle finger of your picking hand eventually to play picking patterns or more complex accompaniments.

The pick is a little piece of plastic or felt, held between thumb and index finger of the picking hand. Every player has his own pick size and pick material preferences. Try different picks to find your own pick of choice. There are whole books on playing with a pick, but the basic principle is simple: you can play using downstrokes (picking in the direction of the floor) or upstrokes (picking in the opposite direction). Especially efficient is a playing technique called alternate picking. This simply means alternating downstrokes and upstrokes and allows effortless, fast and clean playing by minimizing movement.

Left hand playing technique

The basic principle here is using one finger per fret and to fret right behind the fret wire, not in the middle between two adjacent frets. Use enough pressure to get a clean tone, not more. You can use your thumb on the backside of the CBG neck as a kind of „counterweight" to the other fingers.

There are two options available for left-handed players:

1. Holding your CBG exactly like a right-handed player. Your „strong" hand will be fretting the strings while you pick with the right hand.
2. Playing „mirror-inverted" and re-stringing your CBG (eventually requiring modifications to the saddle).
   Try it and see what feels best to you.

TUNING YOUR CIGAR BOX GUITAR

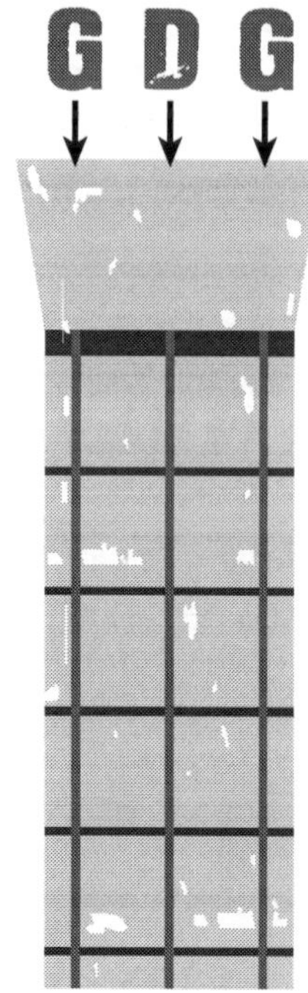

The songs in this book are arranged for CBG in standard G tuning:

- G (melody string).
- D (middle string)
- G (bass string)

Just like its stringed brothers your CBG has to be tuned on a regular basic. Besides sounding horrible, playing a CBG out of tune makes it impossible to play along with other instruments or a recording.

Most beginners experience the traditonal tuning method aka „tuning by ear" as a arduous and often frustrating task, because it requires you to be able to hear if two notes have exactly the same pitch.Your sense of hearing has to adapt to this new task. This is a very fast process for a lucky few humans, but can take as long as a few months for most others.

To avoid losing all the fun in playing CBG during this period, I'd suggest buying an electronic tuner. One of these indispensable little helpers can be bought for just a few dollars and save you a lot of trouble and frustration. There's a plethora of different models available but a simple clip-on tuner will do just fine. This kind of tuner is simply clamped to the CBG's headstock, detecting the pitch of the vibrating string and telling you whether to tune up or down. There's one small drawback, though: you'll have problems tuning a CBG that is heavily out of tune because the tuner can't detect which string is played.

When shopping for a tuner look for a big and easily readable display. Many clip-on tuners feature a rotatable display which allows optimal adjustability.

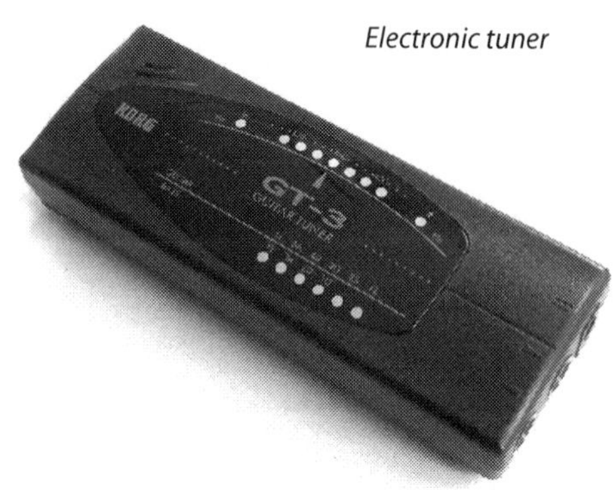

Electronic tuner

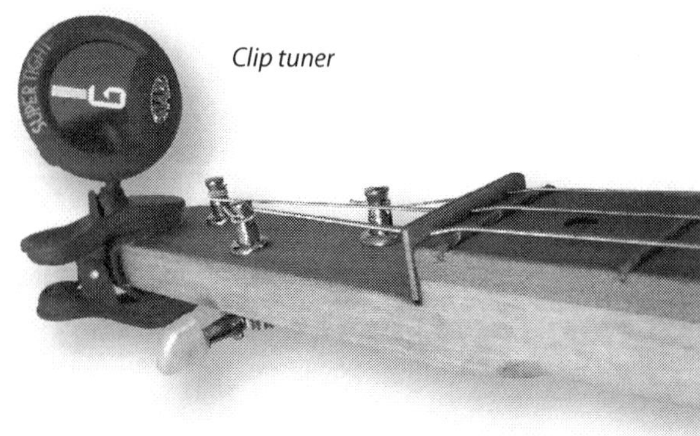

Clip tuner

Cigar Box Guitar Tablature

I've notated the songs' melodies in standard notation and tablature.
If you don't want to read music, simply use the tablature. Here's how it's read:

- Horizontal lines represent the strings, vertical lines the bar lines.
- Numbers indicate the frets.
- Open strings are indicated by an "0".

So the passage below (the first bar of "When the saints go marchin' in") reads:

- first play the D string (open string),
- followed by the D string (4th fret),
- then the high G string (open string)
- and the high G string (2nd fret).

G	D	G
G#	E♭	G#
A	E	A
B♭	F	B♭
B	F#	B
C	G	C
C#	G#	C#
D	A	D
E♭	B♭	E♭
E	B	E
F	C	F
F#	C#	F#
G	D	G

The notes on the Cigar Box Guitar fretboard.

! Enharmonically equivalent chords and note names (e.g. C# = D♭, D# = E♭, F# = G♭, G# = A♭ and A# = B♭) are listed in the more commonly used version only.

Bottleneck Playing

The bottleneck is a small round tube (originally made from the neck of a bottle, hence the name) of glass, plastic, ceramic, metal or (cow) bone worn on a fretting hand finger. Most players wear it on the middle or ring finger but try and see which finger works best for you.

When playing bottleneck the string you're playing is not pressed down on the fretboard. Instead, the bottleneck glides along the string(s) **without touching the frets or the fretboard**.

To get a clean tone use your free finger(s) to dampen any unwanted string noise behind the bottleneck (behind in this case means in the direction of the headstock). The correct pitch for any note is not where you'd normally fret but instead right above the fret wire (or where the fret would be when you're playing a fretless CBG). It will take a little bit of practice to hit the correct pitch(es) when playing bottleneck (of course, you can also play pitches "in between" the notes, but that's another story). A good way to hone your bottleneck skills is to play songs you've already played "regular" style (like the ones in this book) with a bottleneck before venturing farther out. From low-down gritty Blues to ethereal and haunting wailing, the bottleneck does it all–at least in the hands of a master player. Listen to Billy Gibbons' rendition of *Billy the Kid* for a prime example.

Bottleneck (guitar) players worth checking out are Johnny Winter, Duane Allmann (still my favorite), Warren Haynes and Sonny Landreth, to name just a few.

Here are some further variants on the "worn on a finger of the fretting hand" theme you may find worth checking out:

The **thumb slide** (or spoon slide), which is worn on the **thumb** of the fretting hand.

Lap steel bar in action

Slide bar

Some players prefer **slide bars** (as used by lap steel players). Due to their mass, those have a pretty "fat" tone and allow you to "bend behind the bar" (a lap steel playing technique).

There are also bottlenecks designed to be worn like a **ring**, leaving your fingers free to fret. These are great if you want to play normally, but insert a little bottleneck in your playing from time to time. There are countless variations on the "bottleneck theme" and I'd suggest you experiment with as many as you like–it's lots of fun!

> **!** Bottleneck playing is easier (and sounds better) with heavy gauge strings and a high action. Having your CBG set up this way will hamper normal playability, though.
> Unless you can afford having two CBGs set up for bottleneck and normal playing, respectively, you'll have to find a compromise.

Fretless CBG

The fretless CBG is a very special beast. As the name suggests, it has no frets (most fretless CBGs have "frets" painted on the fretboard, though, to help you find your way around the neck). Fretless CBGs are mostly played with a bottleneck. Playing bottleneck you really don't need the frets, so why install them in the first place?
It takes some time to learn to play the correct pitch(es) on a fretless CBG, but in return you'll get a whole new musical world to explore "between the frets".

SPICE UP YOUR SOUND

These playing techniques take a little bit of practice but they're well worth the effort and will bring you a big step closer to sounding like a proficient player–furthermore, they're key elements of playing the Blues. And although the Blues is all about feeling they will greatly help you in achieving an authentic sound and feel.
These few paragraphs are not meant to replace a good teacher or a method book, but to help you on your way to becoming an accomplished Blues player. Playing the Blues can be a life-long enjoyment (and learning experience, too).

Last not least, it's always a good idea to listen to (and have a closer look at) the players you like to see how they do it and to emulate their playing to develop your own style.

Hammer on

The basic idea of this playing technique is to play two (or more) consecutive notes but to pick just the first one. Have a look at the following example:

You fret the note E (D string, 2nd fret) with your index finger then pick it and "hammer" your ring finger on the D string at the 4th fret, close to the fret wire. Aim for a smooth effortless "hammer" and an even loudness of both notes.

Hammer ons can also be played using open strings.
In this example, you pick the G, D and high G string and hammer on with your index finger to the 2nd fret on each string. Aim for a smooth sound and even loudness of both notes.

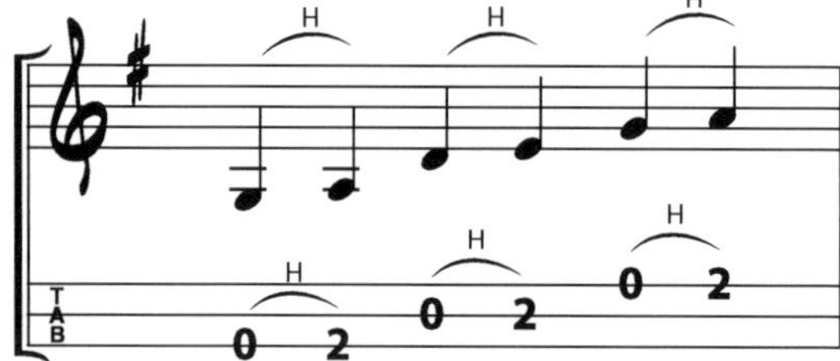

Pull off

The pull off is the opposite of the hammer on. Here, you fret both notes, picking the first one and "flicking" your fretting finger with a fast motion off the string, sounding the second note.
As with the hammer on, aim for even loudness of both notes. To master a good pull off can take quite a bit of practice, so don't be disappointed if at first you don't succeed.

Slide

When playing a slide you fret a note, pick it and slide your finger along the fretboard to the target tone with a smooth even motion–without losing contact to the fretboard.
You can play the slide slow, with clearly identifiable pitches between start and target note, or faster, "blurring" the notes between start and target tone. Experiment with different forms of sliding and see what you like best.
A slide is notated like this (sometimes abbreviated sl):

Bending

String bending is one of the most expressive playing techniques. Bending is executed by fretting a note and pushing the string perpendicular (sideways) across the fretboard, thus raising its pitch. Bending is easiest with the middle or ring finger, because you can use the other fingers to support the bend (you're effectively using two or three fingers to bend).

The most common bends are half step (1 fret) and whole step (2 frets) bends, but some players like to bend 1 1/2 steps or even more (listen to Gary Moore, Robin Trower and, of course, Jimi Hendrix for some prime examples of dramatic bends).

Take some time to practice bending to the exact pitch because nothing sounds worse than a bend gone wrong. A good method to develop your ear is to play the note you plan to bend to as a fretted note, keeping its pitch in mind (or even singing it) and then bending to it from a lower note.

You can also "pre-bend" the string before picking, pick it and gradually release it to the original pitch (called a release bend). This will take a bit of practice because you can't hear the exact pitch you're bending to until you pick the string. You'll need to develop a feeling for the strings' tension and the resulting pitch.

The thinner your strings, the easier you'll find bending them. Heavy string gauges have a fatter tone, though, so I'd recommend trying different string gauges to find your personal compromise.

Vibrato

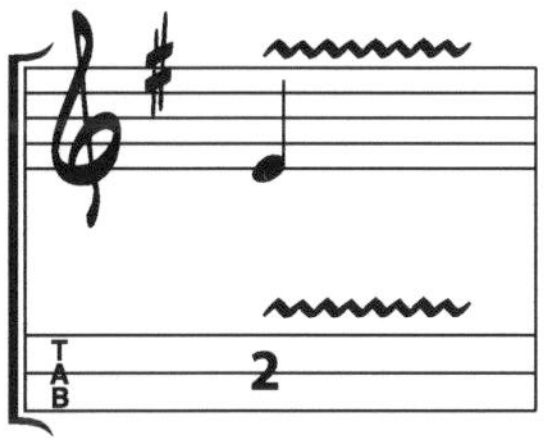

Vibrato means changing the pitch of a note in a regular and even fashion. On the guitar, this is done by very slightly bending the string, releasing it to the original pitch, bending it once again, releasing it to the original pitch etc. You can play a slow or a fast vibrato. Take some time to study the vibrato of Blues masters like B.B. King to get an idea of what a good vibrato can add to your own playing.

Blues chords and rhythm playing

You could write a whole book on this topic and would just be scratching the surface, but I hope the following ideas will get you started in playing the Blues.

Many Blues songs are based on the 12-Bar Blues chord progression (*chord progression* simply meaning a certain sequence of chords). In the key of G (the key your CBG is tuned to) these are the chords G, C and D. In Blues and related styles, these chords are often played as so-called "seventh" chords, notated by a "7" behind the chord symbol.

If this sound greek to you, don't worry–I've notated the Blues chords for the most common keys used in western music on the following pages. So the next time someone calls for "A Blues in A", simply flip to 16 page and start playing (spoiler: the chords in this case are A, D and E).
You can play these chords as major chords (chord symbol: capital letter) or as seventh chords (symbol: capital letter, followed by a small "7") to add a little extra color.
For starters, try playing the chords using some of the picking and strumming patterns on pp. 190-192 (Since the Blues is almost exclusively in 4/4 time, only those with the time signature 4/4 will work here).
Once again, listening to the players you like and trying to emulate their sound will teach you more about Blues rhythm than I could ever hope to write down.

There's another very effective way to play Blues rhythm I'd like to show you. Have a look at this tablature (the first part of a Blues in G). And here's how it's done:
The complete example is played with a pick, using only downstrokes (hitting the string in the direction of the floor).

- Using a pick, play the open G and D strings two times, counting "one-and".
- Now, play the open G string and the D string, 2nd fret two times, counting "two-and".
- Repeat the above, counting "three-and" and "four-and") and voila–you've just played the first bar of a 12-bar Blues in G.

To play a complete 12-bar Blues, you'll need to adapt the Rhythm you just played to the other chords. This is easily done by barring across all strings of your CBG with your index finger:

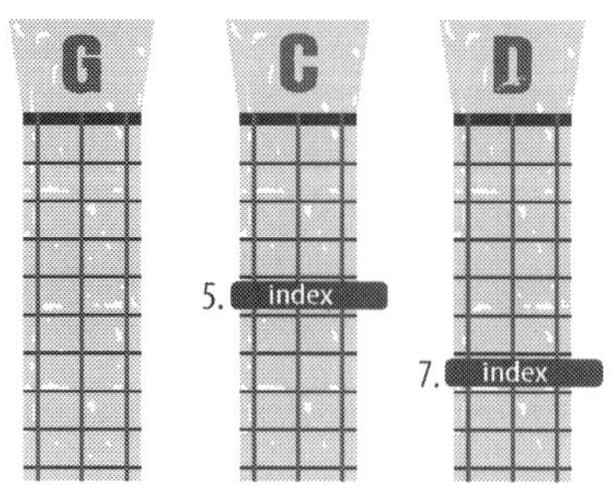

Below, I've notated a complete 12-bar Blues in G—have fun playing!

Speeding this up a little you're right in Chuck Berry territory—many of his songs use this kind of rhythm playing or some variant thereof. There's a popular variant of this rhythm you may have heard:

These few short pointers won't make you a proficient Blues player, of course (it takes time, careful listening and practice to become one), but I hope you can use them as starting points on your own musical journey.

The most common Blues progressions

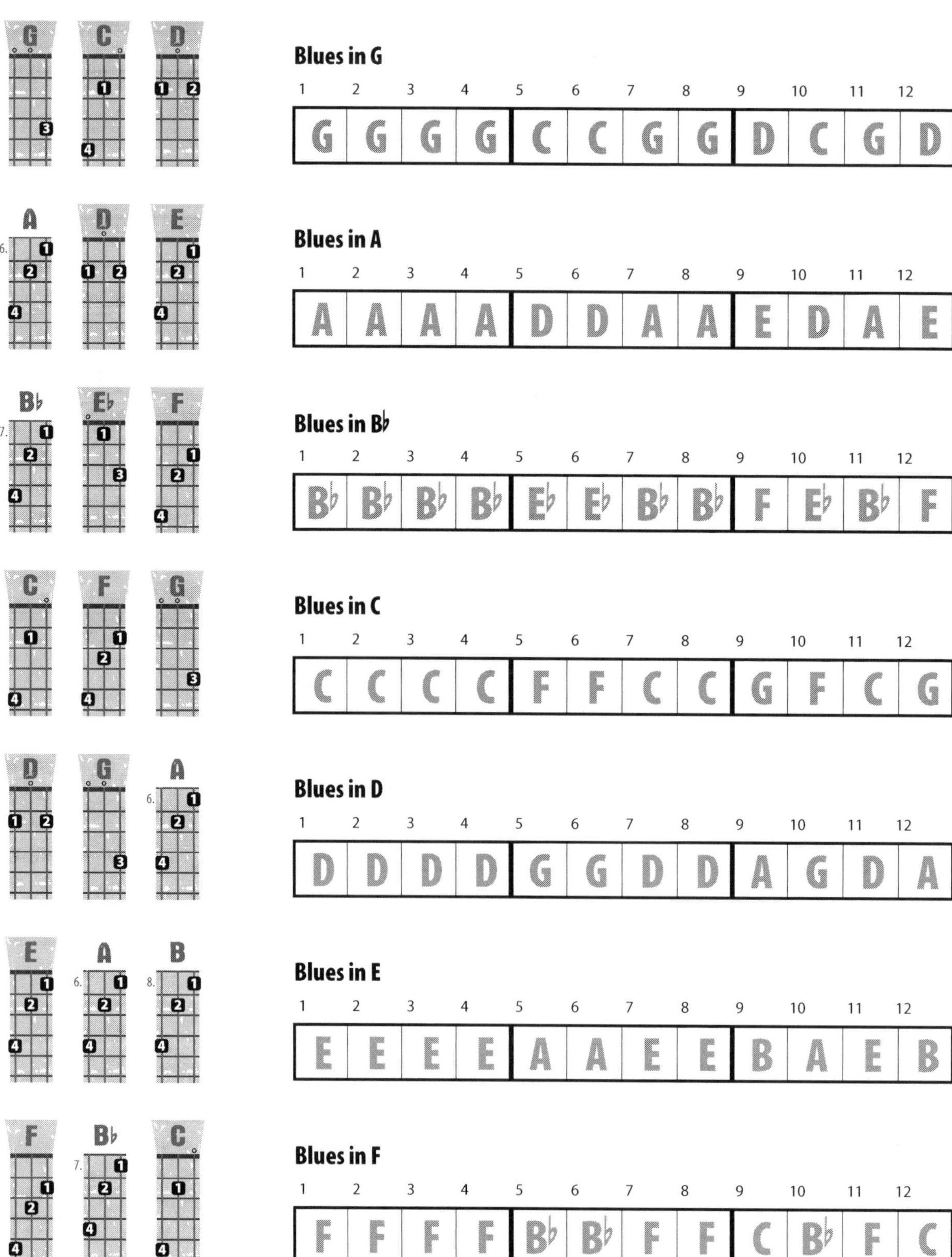

Blues in G

1	2	3	4	5	6	7	8	9	10	11	12
G	G	G	G	C	C	G	G	D	C	G	D

Blues in A

1	2	3	4	5	6	7	8	9	10	11	12
A	A	A	A	D	D	A	A	E	D	A	E

Blues in B♭

1	2	3	4	5	6	7	8	9	10	11	12
B♭	B♭	B♭	B♭	E♭	E♭	B♭	B♭	F	E♭	B♭	F

Blues in C

1	2	3	4	5	6	7	8	9	10	11	12
C	C	C	C	F	F	C	C	G	F	C	G

Blues in D

1	2	3	4	5	6	7	8	9	10	11	12
D	D	D	D	G	G	D	D	A	G	D	A

Blues in E

1	2	3	4	5	6	7	8	9	10	11	12
E	E	E	E	A	A	E	E	B	A	E	B

Blues in F

1	2	3	4	5	6	7	8	9	10	11	12
F	F	F	F	B♭	B♭	F	F	C	B♭	F	C

USING AN AMP

Playing with a dynamic drummer or a band the acoustic sound of your CBG just won't be loud enough. You'll need an **amp** (short for **amplifier**).
There are literally thousands of amps available, each with its own advantages and disadvantages and spanning a price range from a few to hundreds or even thousands of dollars. I won't recommend any particular amp because every player has different needs and aims for a different sound. Finding out what amps your favorite players are using is always a good start. You may start with a simple, affordable amp and upgrade to a bigger one when you've outgrown your smaller amp. Many of the smaller amps are battery-powered which is a great plus if you're planning to play your CBG outdoors. Some amps also feature extra inputs to connect a smartphone or an MP3 player. This way you can play or practice with your favorite musicians any time you like. And of course, you can use all the great effect pedals for guitar ...

By the way, there's an interesting option if you're more the DIY type: just build your CBG amp yourself. Depending on your abilities with a few simple tools and a soldering iron you can either start from scratch or put together any of a number of amp kits readily available.

Last not least: Your CBG needs a **pickup** to be played with an amp, so if it doesn't have one already (many CBGs come factory-equipped with a pickup), have one installed or buy a CBG with a pickup.

Jolly Good Fellow

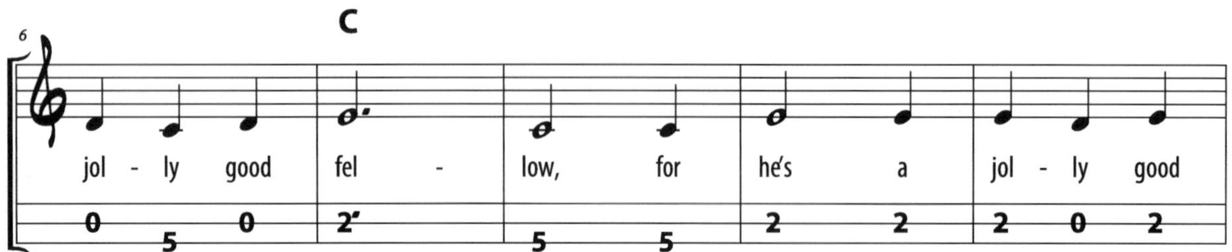

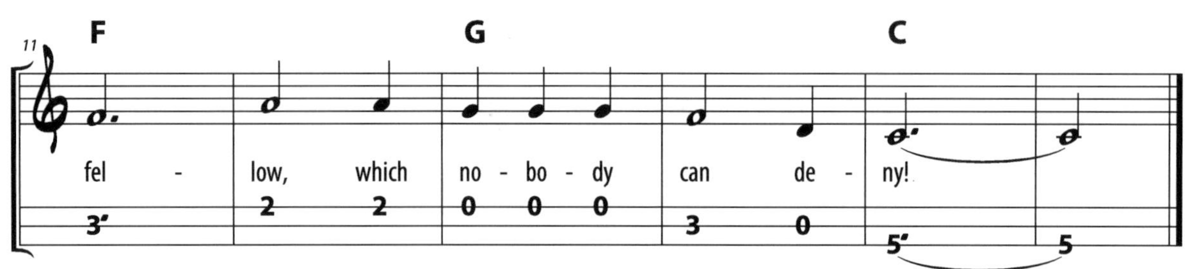

2 We won't go home until morning, (3x)
'till daylight doth appear.
'Till daylight doth appear,
'till daylight doth appear.
We won't go home until morning, (3x)
'till daylight doth appear.

Strumming Pattern

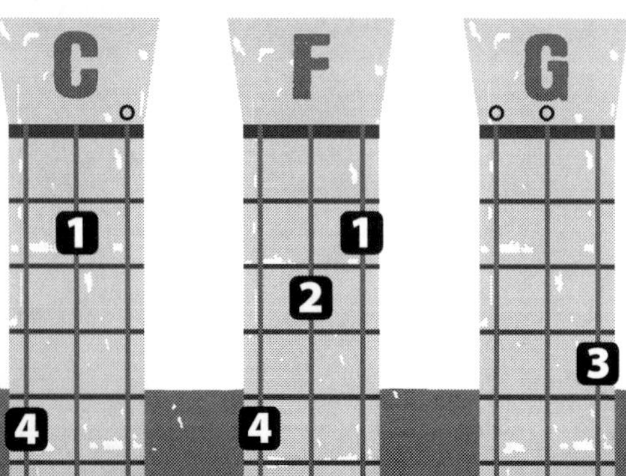

When the Saints Go Marchin' In

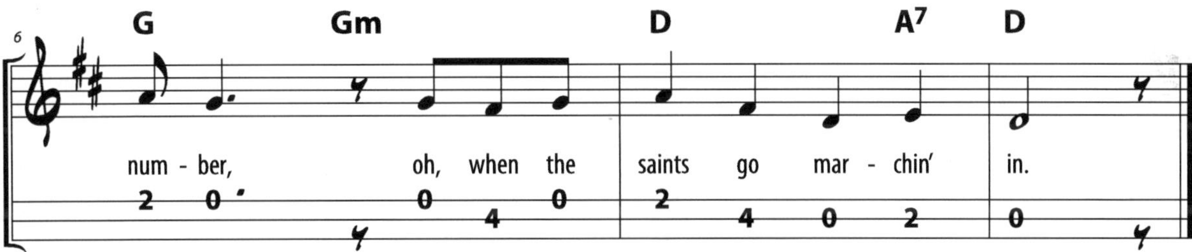

2 And when the stars begin to shine ...

3 When Gabriel blows in his horn ...

4 And when the sun refuse to shine ...

5 And when they gather round the throne ...

6 And when they crown him King of Kings ...

7 And on that halleluja-day ...

Strumming Pattern

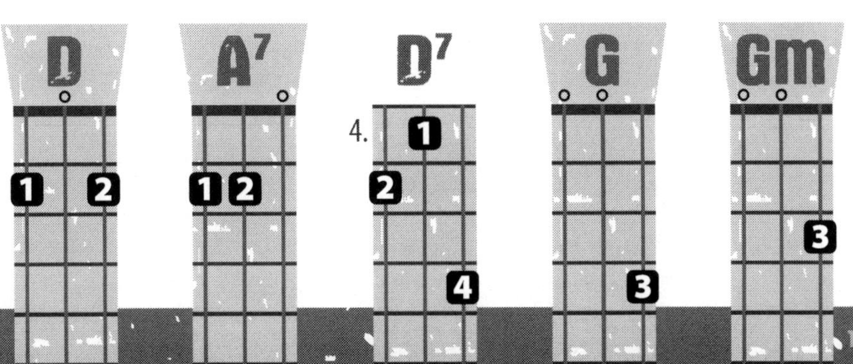

DOWN BY THE RIVERSIDE

2 I'm goin' to lay down my sword and shield ...

3 I'm goin' to put on my travelin' shoes ...

4 I'm goin' to put on my starry crown ...

5 Gonna put on my golden shoes ...

6 Gonna talk with the Prince of Peace ...

7 Gonna shake hands around the world ...

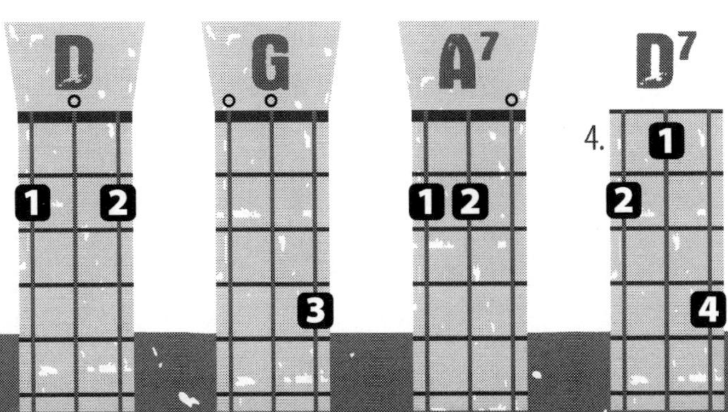

AURA LEE

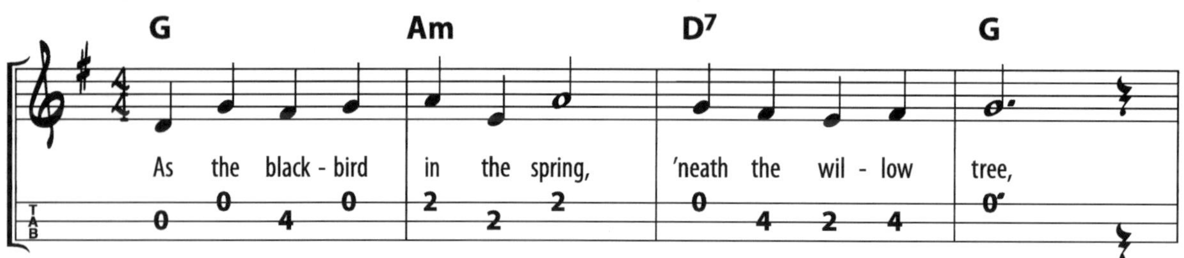

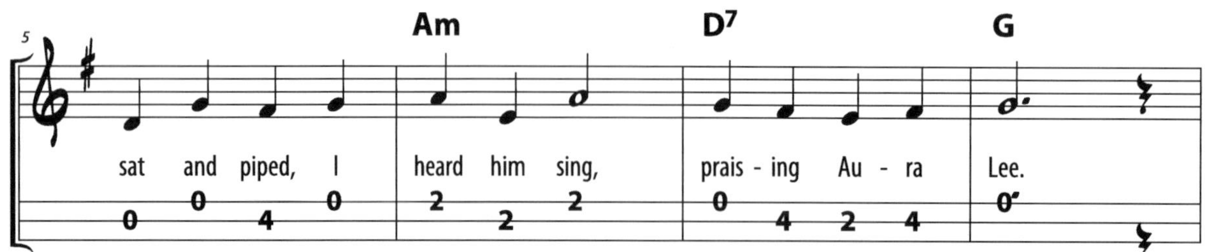

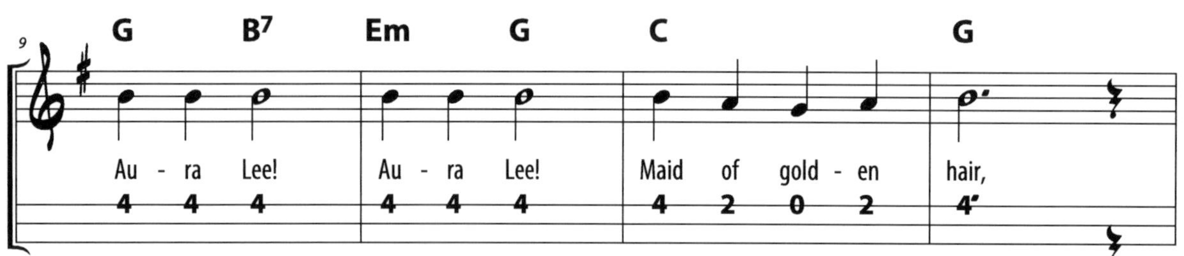

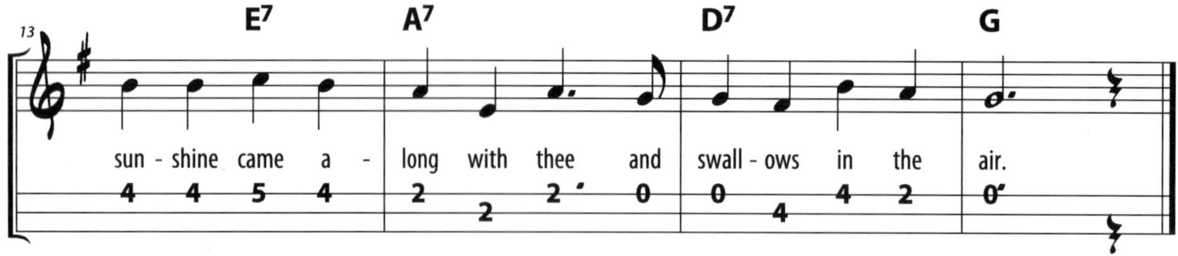

G

Am

D7

4.

B7

2 In thy blush the rose was born,
music, when you spake,
through thine azure eye the morn,
sparkling seemed to break.
Aura Lee, Aura Lee,
birds of crimson wing,
never song have sung to me,
as in that sweet spring.
Aura Lee! Aura Lee! ...

3 Aura Lee, the bird may flee,
the willow's golden hair,
swing through winter fitfully,
on the stormy air.
Yet if thy blue eyes I see,
gloom will soon depart;
for to me, sweet Aura Lee
is sunshine through the heart.
Aura Lee! Aura Lee! ...

4 When the mistletoe was green,
midst the winter's snows,
sunshine in thy face was seen,
kissing lips of rose.
Aura Lee, Aura Lee,
take my golden ring;
Love and light return with thee,
and swallows with the spring.
Aura Lee! Aura Lee! ...

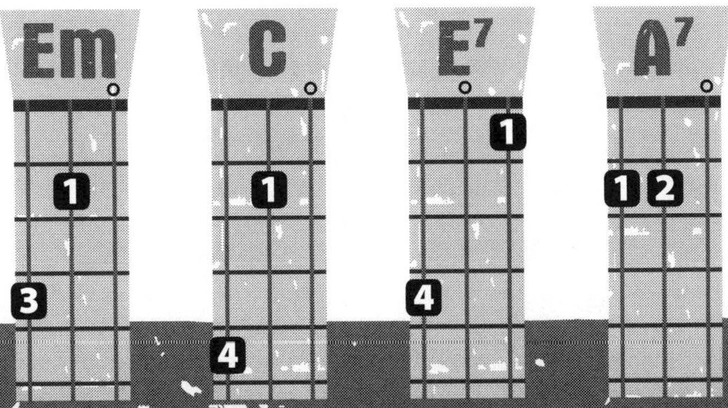

BEAUTIFUL BROWN EYES

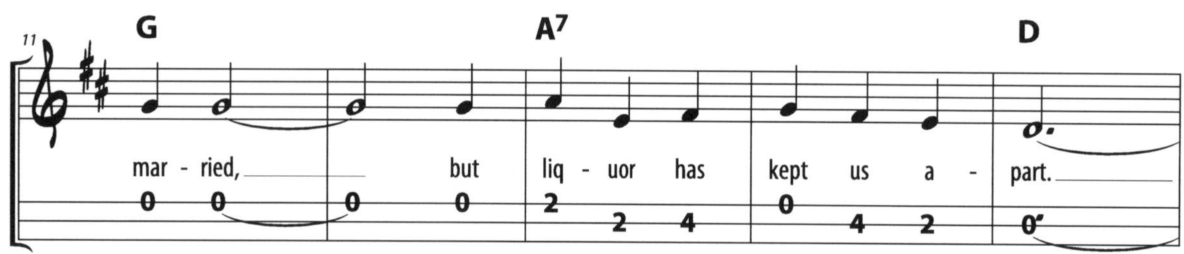

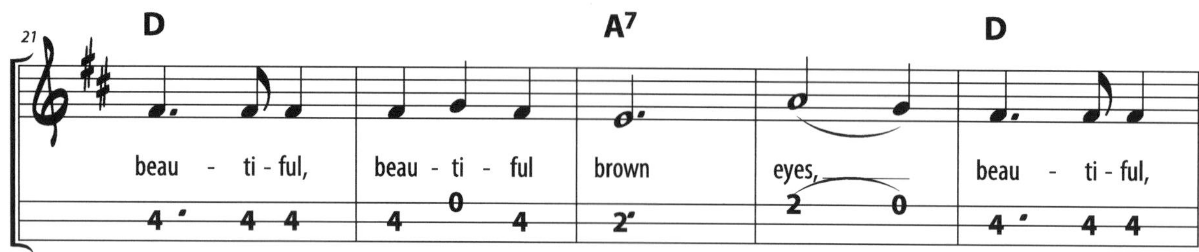

2 I staggered into the barroom,
I fell down on the floor.
And the very last words that I uttered,
"I'll never get drunk any more."
Beautiful, beautiful brown eyes ...

3 Seven long years I've been married,
I wish I was single again.
A woman don't know half her troubles,
until she has married a man.
Beautiful, beautiful brown eyes ...

Home on the Range

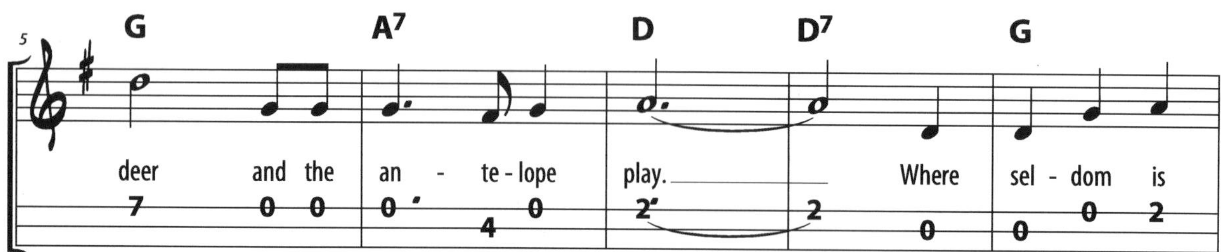

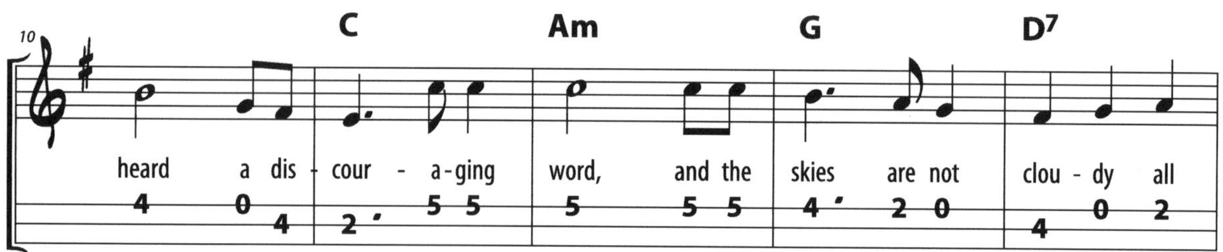

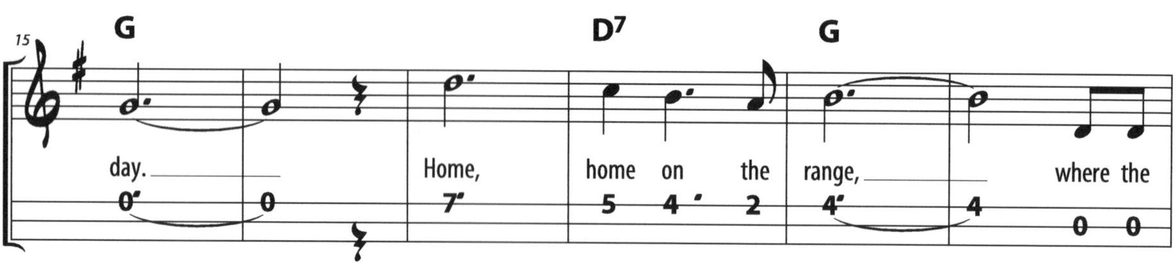

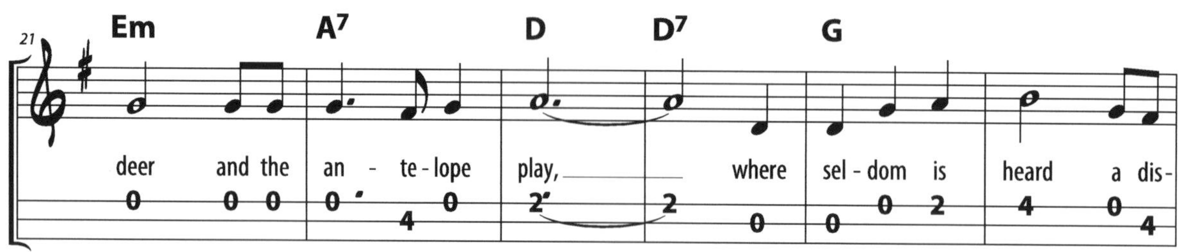

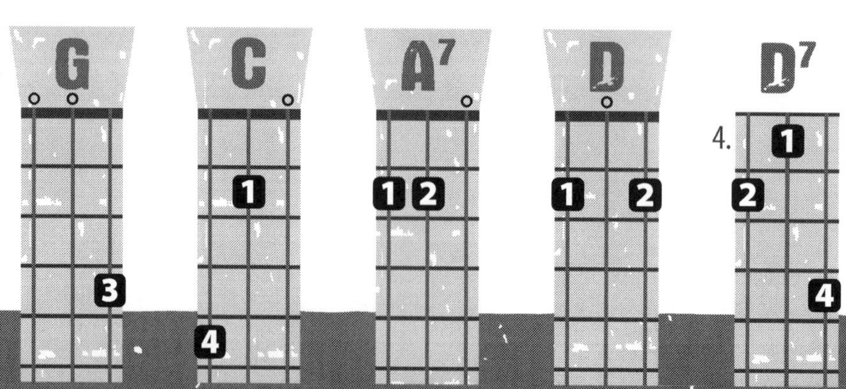

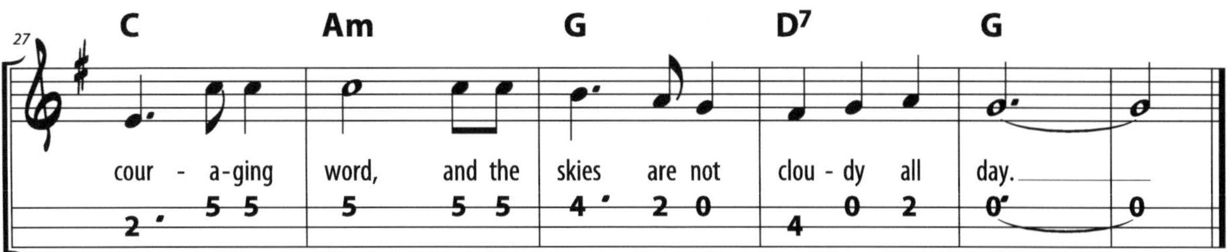

2 How often at night, when the heavens are bright
with the light from the glittering stars,
have I stood there amazed and I asked as I gazed,
if their glory exceeds that of ours.
Home, home ...

3 Where the air is so pure and the zephyrs so free
and the breezes so balmy and light,
that I would not exchange my home on the range
for all the cities so bright.
Home, home ...

STRUMMING PATTERN

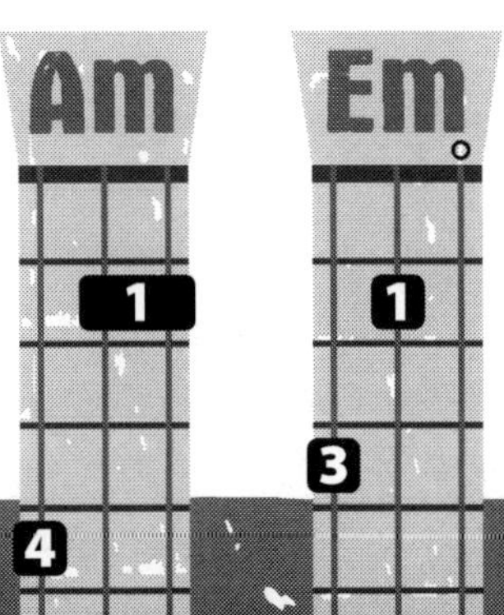

John Brown's Body

2 He's gone to be a soldier in the Army of the Lord. (3x)
His soul goes marching on.

CHORUS:

Glory, glory, hallelujah. (3x)
His soul goes marching on.

3 John Brown's knapsack is strapped upon his back. (3x)
His soul goes marching on.

4 John Brown died that the slaves might be free. (3x)
His soul goes marching on.

5 The stars above in Heaven now are looking kindly down. (3x)
His soul goes marching on.

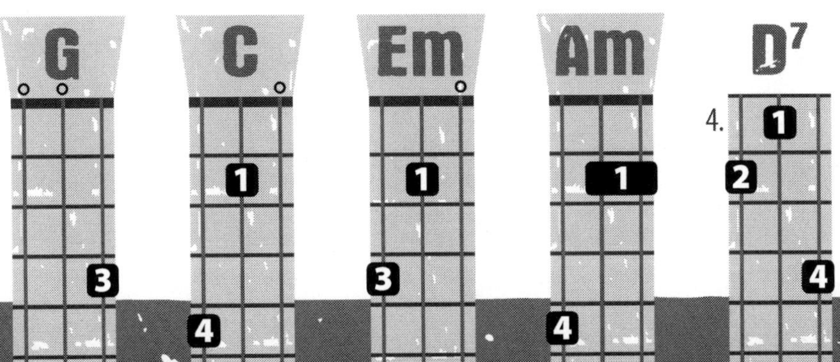

FOOTPRINTS IN THE SNOW

2 I dropped in to see her there was a big round moon,
her mother said she just stepped out but would be returning soon.
I found her little footprints and I traced them in the snow,
I found her when the snow was on the ground.
I traced her little footprints in the snow ...

3 Now she's up in heaven she's with the angel band,
I know I'm going to meet her in that promised land.
But every time the snow falls it brings back memories,
I found her when the snow was on the ground.
I traced her little footprints in the snow ...

STRUMMING PATTERN

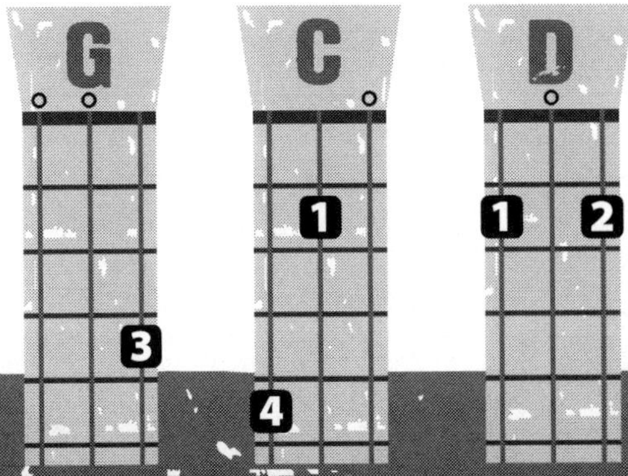

The Star Spangled Banner

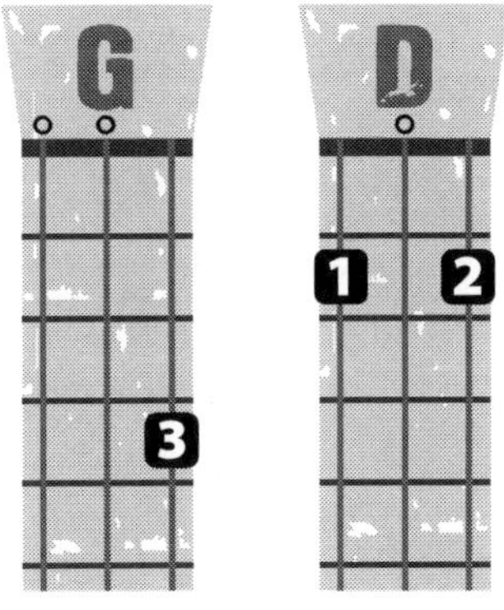

2 On the shore, dimly seen through the mists of the deep,
where the foe's haughty host in dread silence reposes,
what is that which the breeze, o'er the towering steep,
as it fitfully blows, half conceals, half discloses?
Now it catches the gleam of the morning's first beam,
in full glory reflected now shines in the stream:
'Tis the star-spangled banner! Oh long may it wave
o'er the land of the free and the home of the brave!

3 And where is that band who so vauntingly swore
that the havoc of war and the battle's confusion,
a home and a country should leave us no more!
Their blood has washed out their foul footsteps' pollution.
No refuge could save the hireling and slave
from the terror of flight, or the gloom of the grave:
And the star-spangled banner in triumph doth wave
o'er the land of the free and the home of the brave!

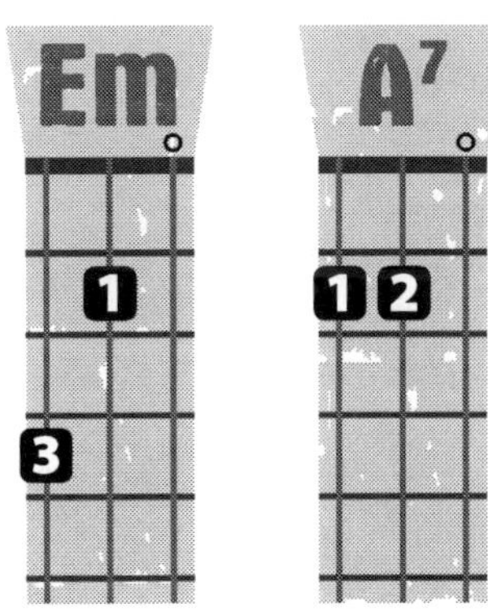

4 Oh! thus be it ever, when freemen shall stand
between their loved home and the war's desolation!
Blest with victory and peace, may the heav'n rescued land
praise the Power that hath made and preserved us a nation.
Then conquer we must, when our cause it is just,
and this be our motto: "In God is our trust."
And the star-spangled banner in triumph shall wave
O'er the land of the free and the home of the brave!

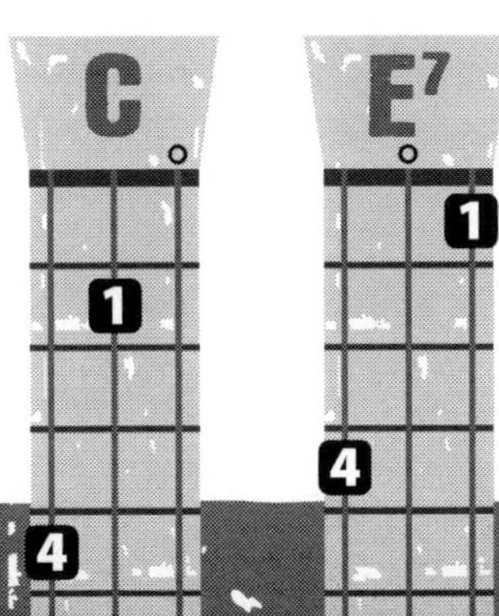

Beautiful Dreamer

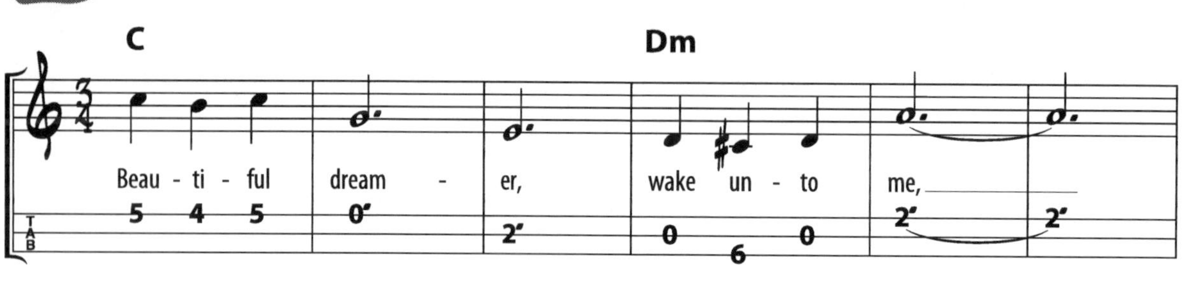

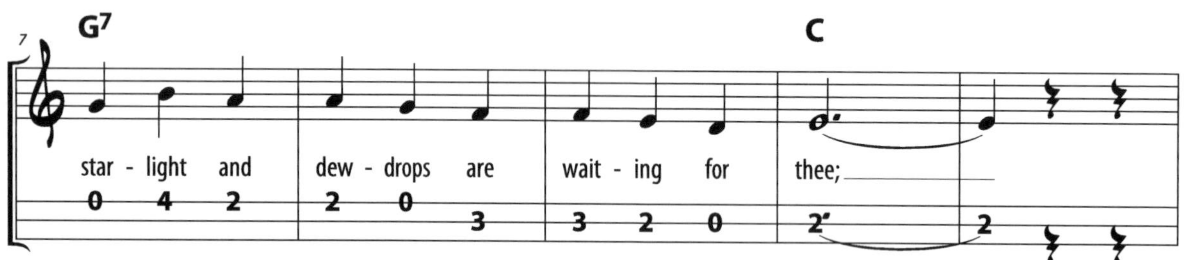

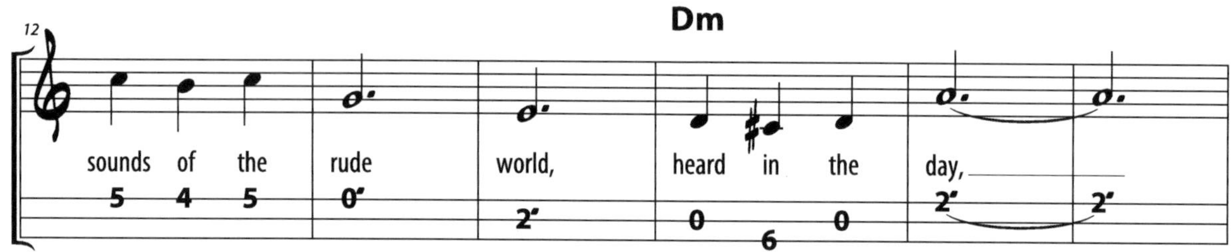

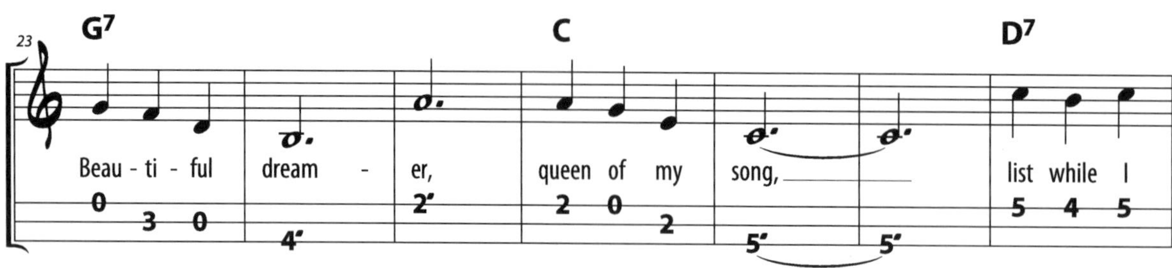

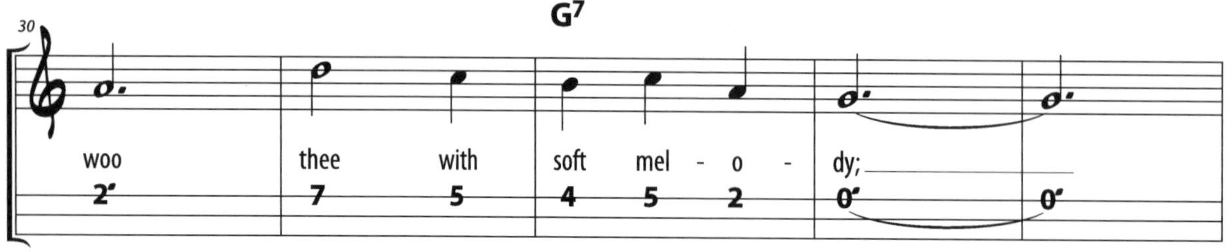

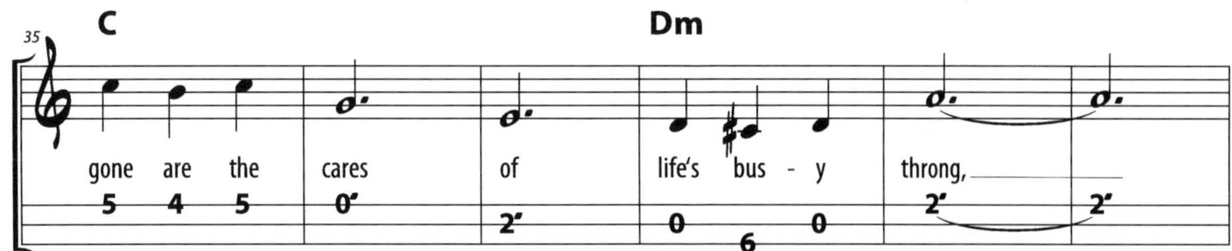

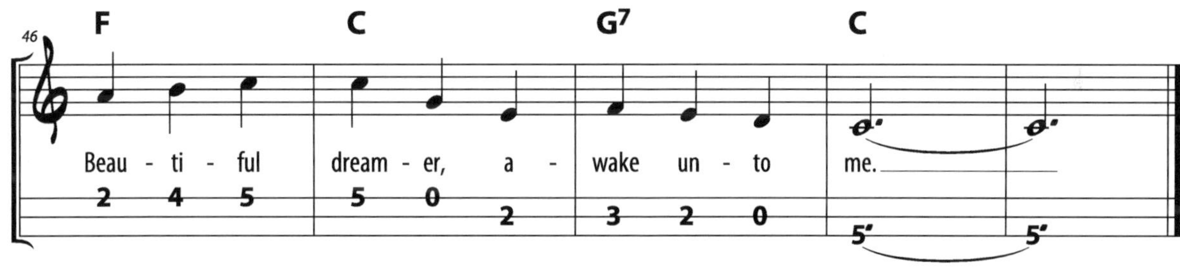

2 Beautiful dreamer, out on the sea,
mermaids are chanting the wild lorelei;
Over the streamlet vapors are borne,
waiting to fade at the bright coming morn.
Beautiful dreamer, beam on my heart,
e'en as the morn on the streamlet and sea;
Then will all clouds of sorrow depart,
beautiful dreamer, awake unto me!
Beautiful dreamer, awake unto me!

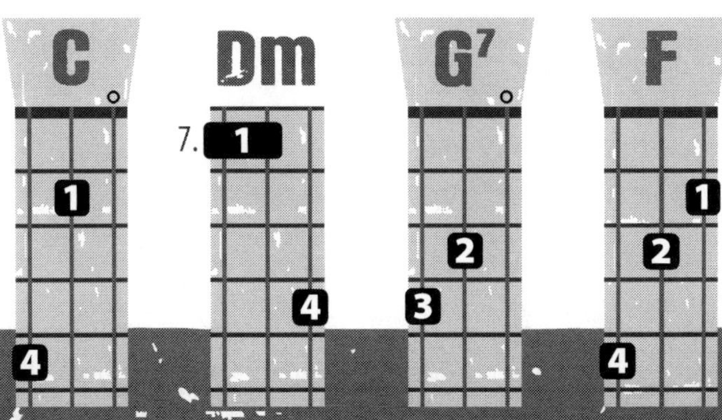

Bound for the Rio Grande

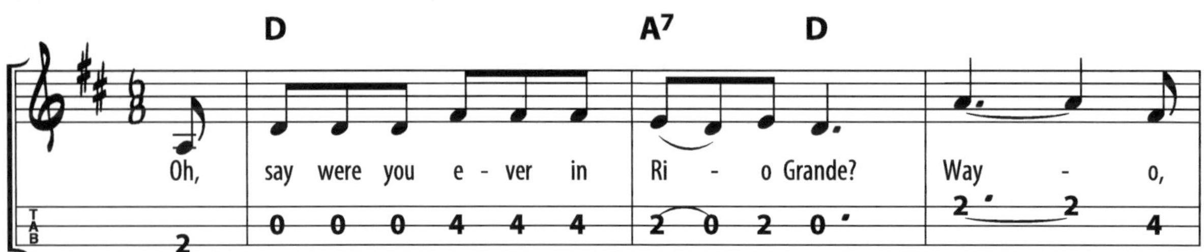

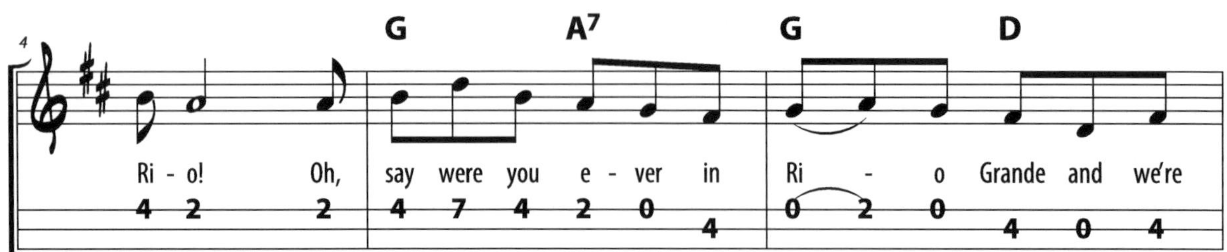

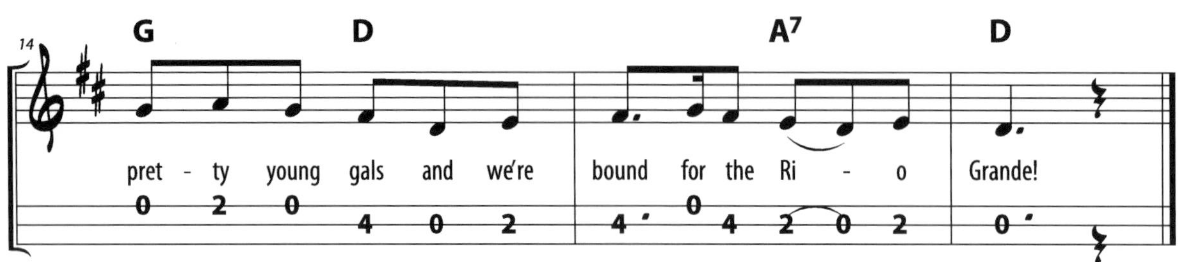

2 So it's pack up your sea-chest an' get underway,
the girls we are leavin' can have our half-pay.

3 Our ship went sailin' over the bar,
we've pointed her bow to the southern stars.

4 You Liverpool judies, we'll have you to know,
we're bound to the south'ard and glad for to go.

5 We're a Liverpool ship and a Liverpool crew,
you can stick to the coast but I'm damned if we do!

6 Goodbye to Ellen and Molly and Sue,
you park lane judies, it's goodbye to you.

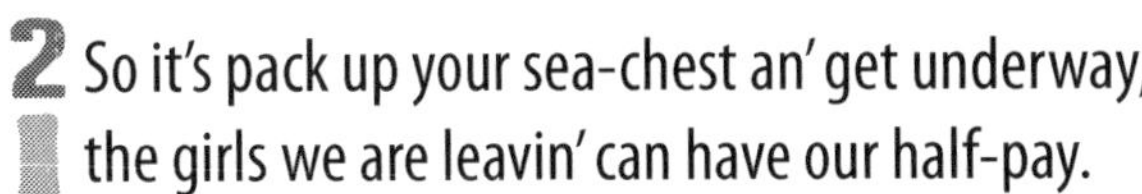

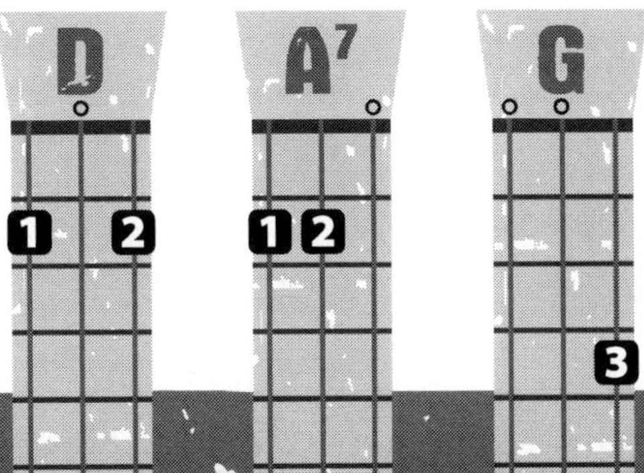

DANNY BOY

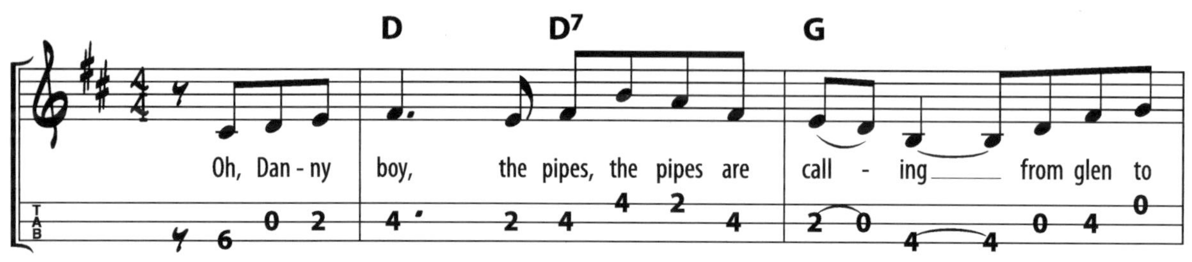
D D7 G
Oh, Dan - ny boy, the pipes, the pipes are call - ing from glen to

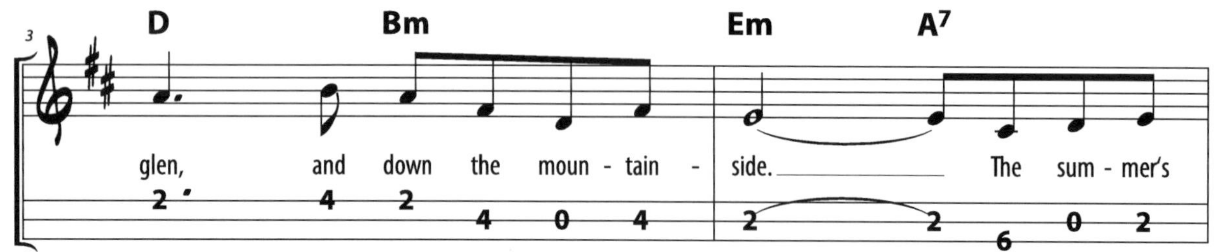
D Bm Em A7
glen, and down the moun - tain - side. The sum - mer's

D D7 G D A7
gone, and all the ro - ses fall - ing, 'tis you, 'tis you must go and I must

D G A7 D
bide. But come ye back when sum-mer's in the mead - ow, or when the

Bm G Em A7 D G
val - ley's hushed and white with snow. 'Tis I'll be there in sun-shine or in

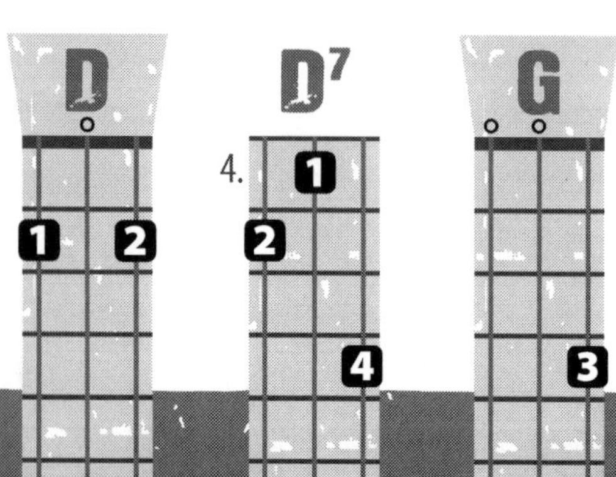
D
D7
G

2 But when you come, and all the flowers are dying,
and If I'm dead, as dead I well may be,
you come and find the place where I am lying,
and kneel and say an Ave there for me;

3 And I shall hear, though soft you tread above me,
and all my grave will warmer, sweeter be,
for you will bend and tell me that you love me,
and I shall sleep in peace until you come to me!

STRUMMING PATTERN

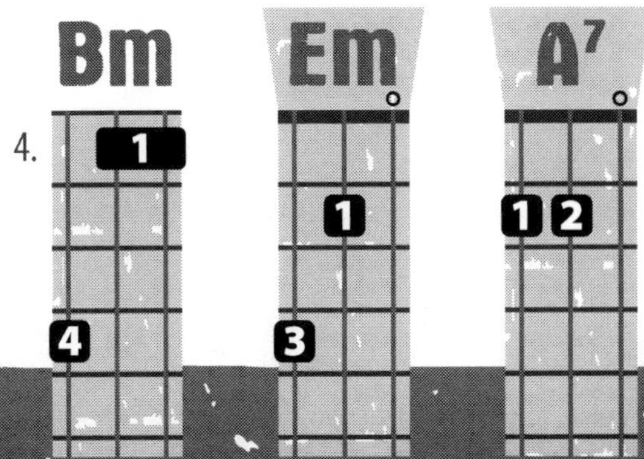

IT'S A LONG WAY TO TIPPERARY

26 G
long way ___ to Tip - per - ar - y, ___ to the sweet - est

31 C F B♭
girl I know! ___ Good - bye ___ Pic - ca - dil - ly, ___ fare - well,

39 A F B♭
Leices - ter Square, ___ it's a long, long way to Tip - per - ar -

45 F Dm G C F F
y, but my heart's ___ right there!" ___ "It's a there!" ___

2 Paddy wrote a letter
to his Irish Molly-O,
saying, "Should you not receive it,
write and let me know!"
"If I make mistakes in spelling,
Molly, dear," said he,
"Remember, it's the pen that's bad,
don't lay the blame on me!"

3 Molly wrote a neat reply
to Irish Paddy-O,
saying "Mike Maloney
wants to marry me, and so
leave the Strand and Piccadilly
or you'll be to blame,
for love has fairly drove me silly:
Hoping you're the same!"

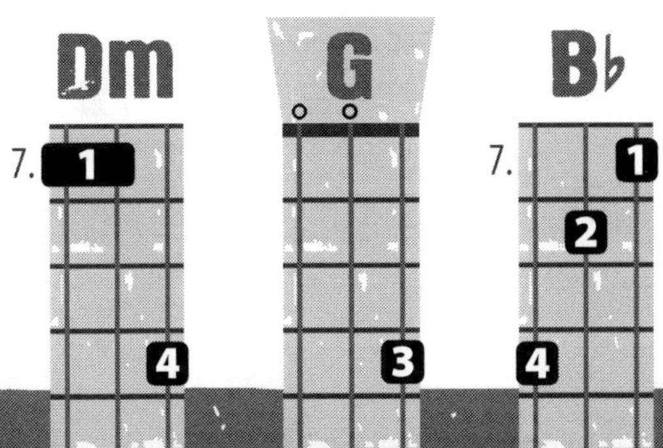

Angel Band

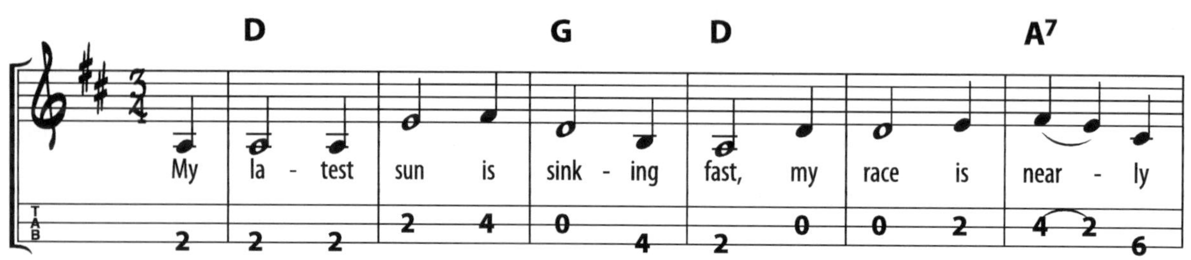
D G D A7
My la - test sun is sink - ing fast, my race is near - ly
T
A
B

7
D G D
run. My strong - est tri - als now are past, my

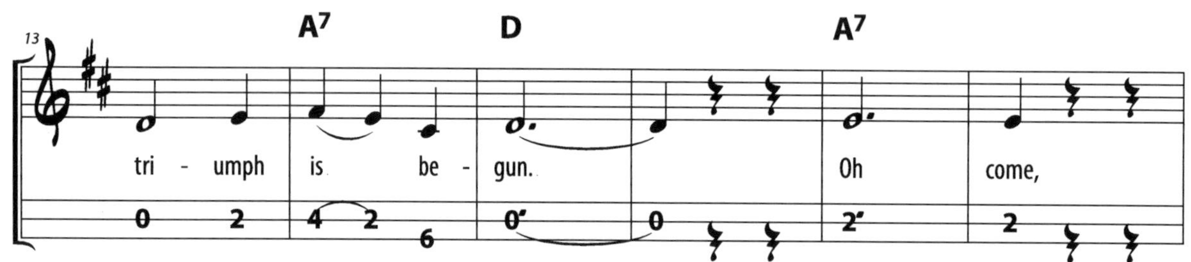
13
A7 D A7
tri - umph is be - gun. Oh come,

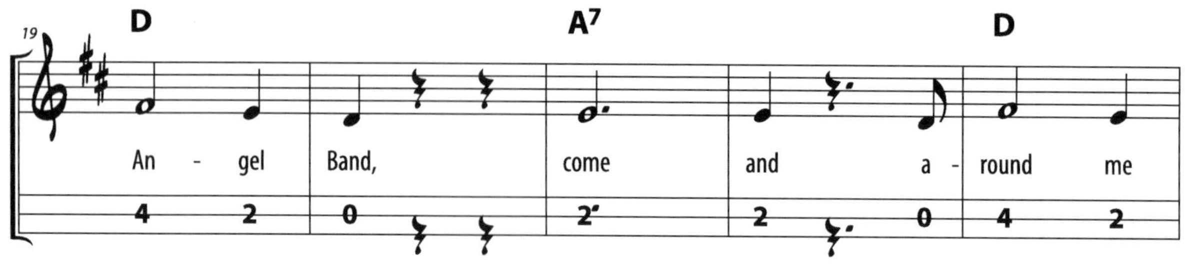
19
D A7 D
An - gel Band, come and a - round me

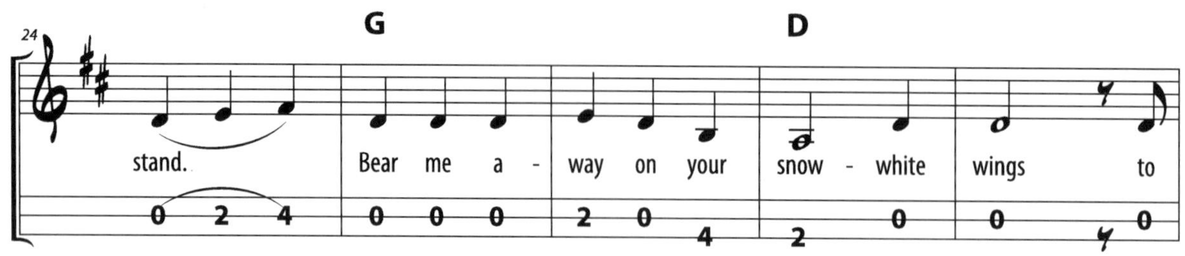
24
G D
stand. Bear me a - way on your snow - white wings to

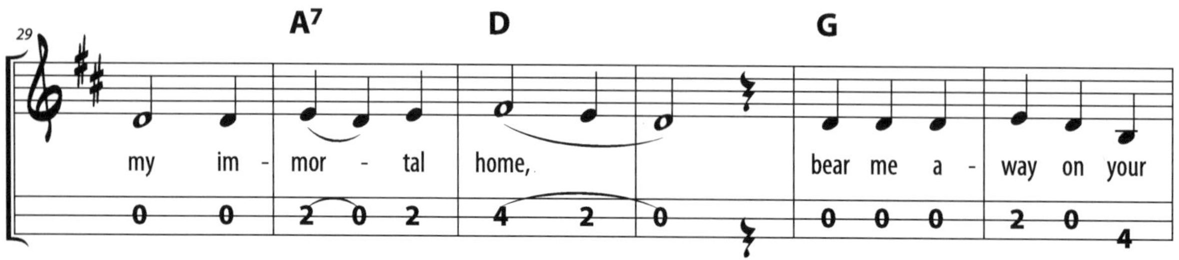
29
A7 D G
my im - mor - tal home, bear me a - way on your

2 I know I'm near the holy ranks of friends and kindred dear.
I brush the dew on Jordan's banks, the crossing must be near.
Oh come, Angel Band ...

3 I've almost gained my heavenly home, my spirit loudly sings.
The holy ones, behold they come, I hear the noise of wings.
Oh come, Angel Band ...

4 Oh bear my longing heart to him who bled and died for me.
Whose blood now cleanses from all sin and gives me victory.
Oh come, Angel Band ...

STRUMMING PATTERN

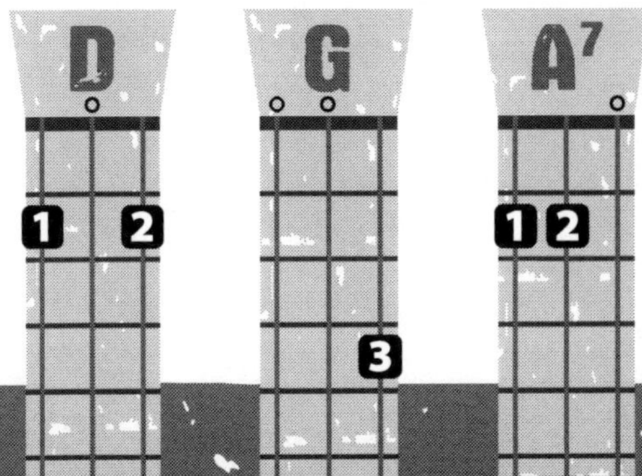

THE YELLOW ROSE OF TEXAS

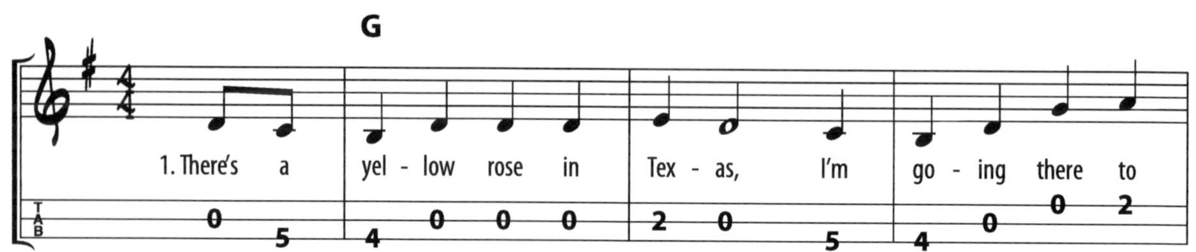

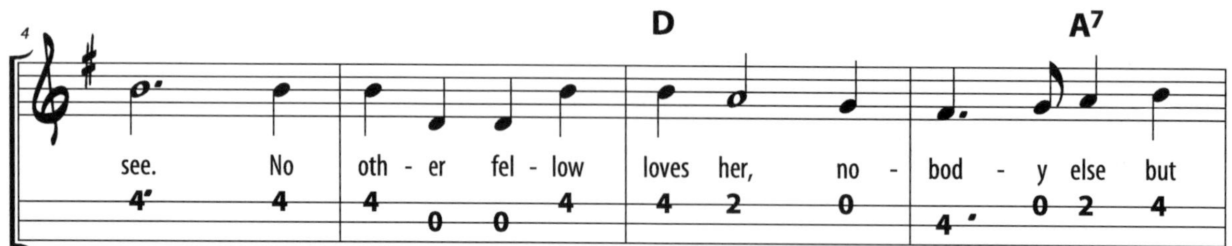

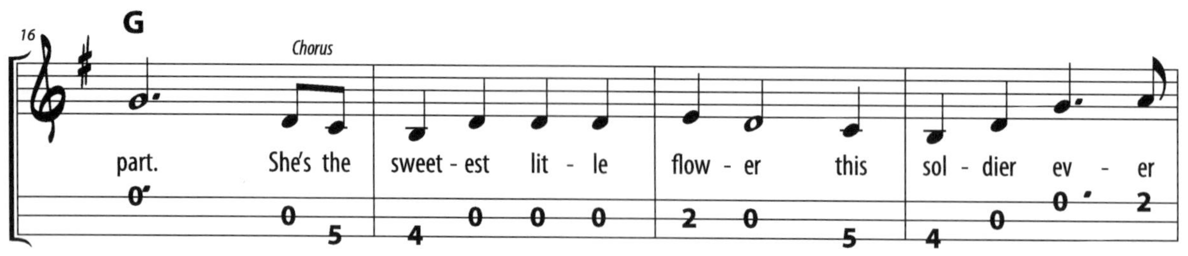

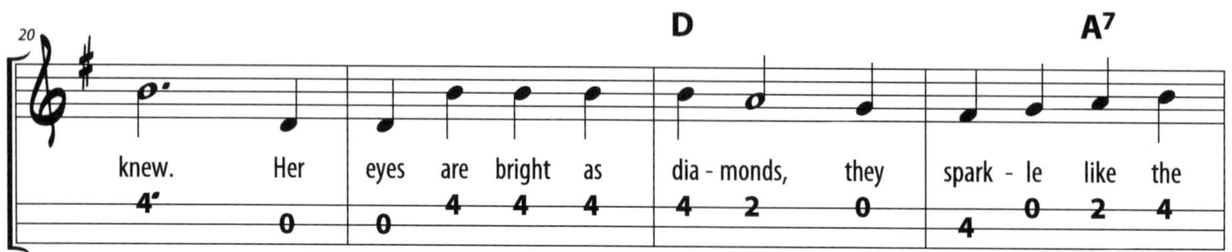

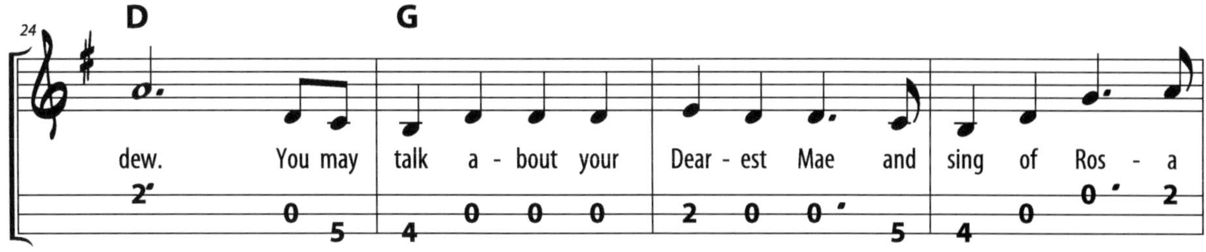

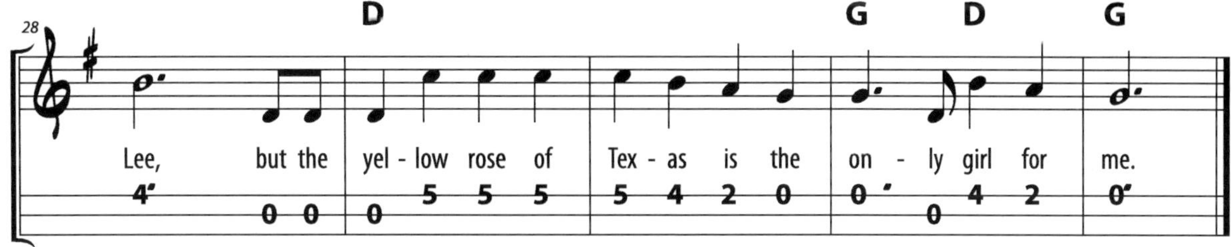

2 When the Rio Grande is flowing, the starry skies are bright,
she walks along the river in the quite summer night:
She thinks if I remember, when we parted long ago,
I promised to come back again, and not to leave her so.

3 Oh now I'm going to find her, for my heart is full of woe,
and we'll sing the songs togeather, that we sung so long ago
we'll play the bango gaily, and we'll sing the songs of yore,
and the Yellow Rose of Texas shall be mine forevermore.

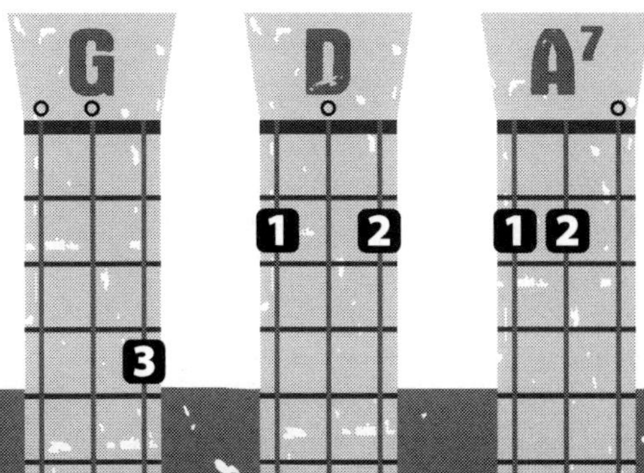

WAYFARING STRANGER

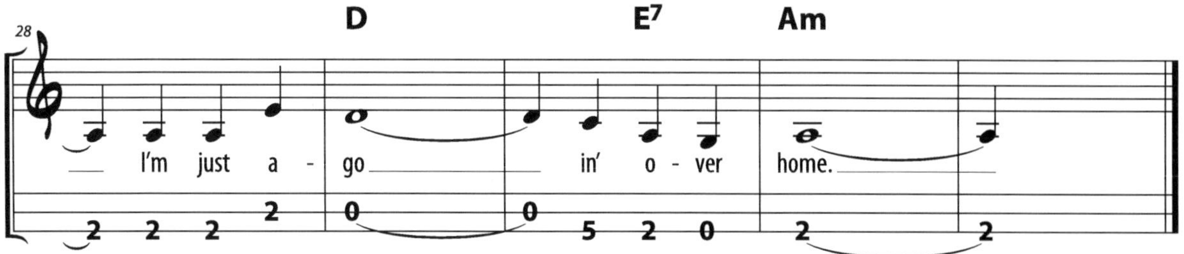

2 I know dark clouds will gather 'round me,
I know my way is rough and steep.
Yet golden fields lie just before me,
where God's redeemed shall ever sleep.
I am going there to see my father/mother,
she/he said he'd/she'd meet me when I come,
I am only going over Jordan,
I am only going over home.

3 I want to wear a crown of glory,
when I get home to that good land.
I want to shout salvation's story,
in concert with the blood-washed band.
I am going there to meet my Saviour,
to sing his praise forever more,
I am just a-going over Jordan,
Im just a-going over home.

STRUMMING PATTERN

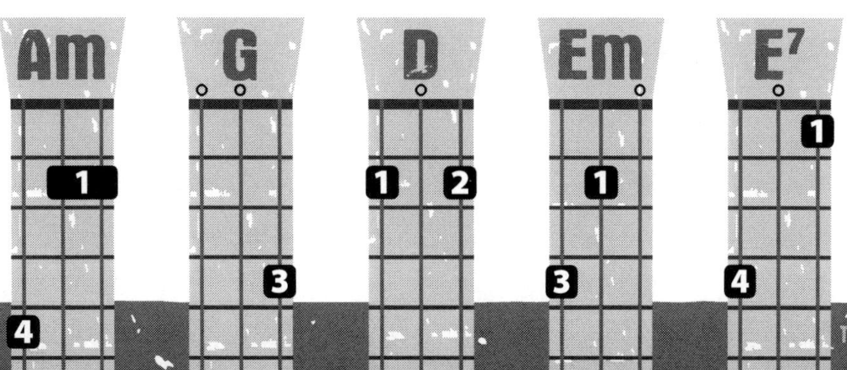

Camptown Races

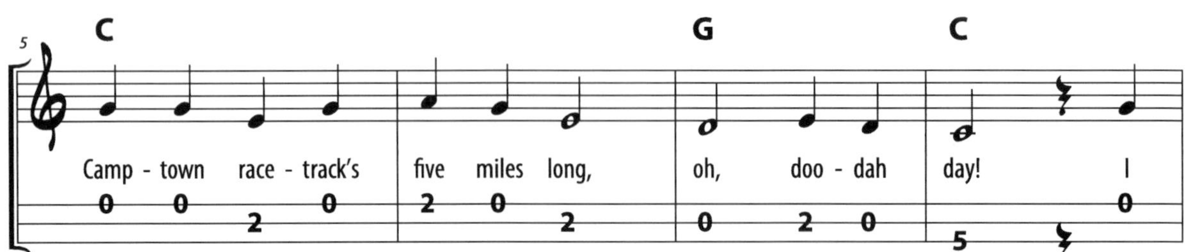

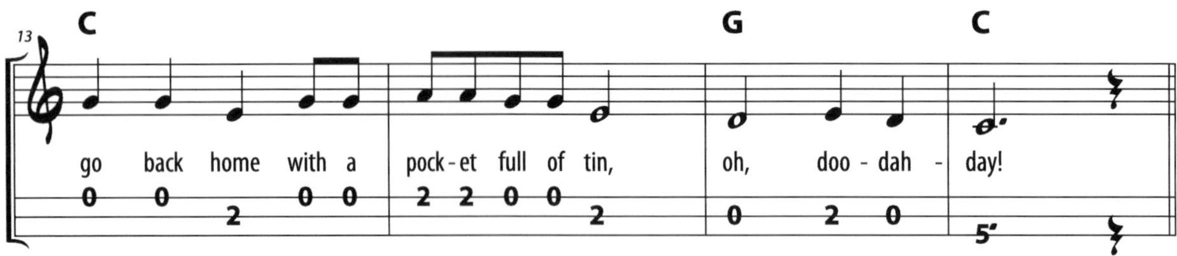

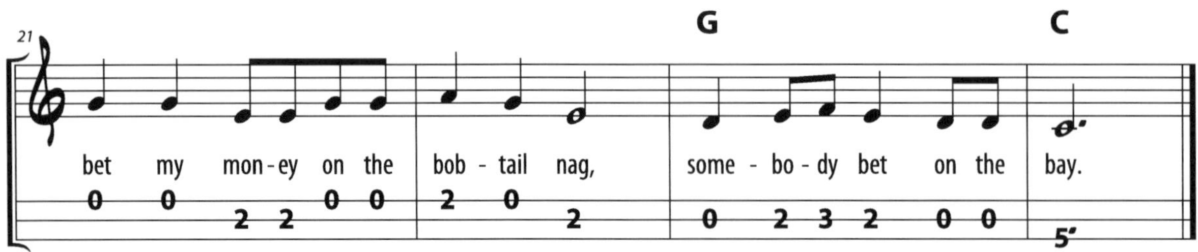

2 De long tail filly and de big black hoss, doo-dah, doo-dah!
Dey fly de track and dey both cut across, oh, doo-dah-day!
De blind hoss sticken in a big mud hole, doo-dah, doo-dah!
Can't touch bottom wid a ten foot pole, oh, doo-dah-day!

CHORUS

3 Old muley cow come on to de track, doo-dah, doo-dah!
De bob-tail fling her ober his back, oh, doo-dah-day!
Den fly along like a rail-road car, doo-dah, doo-dah!
Runnin' a race wid a shootin' star, oh, doo-dah-day!

CHORUS

4 See dem flyin' on a ten mile heat, doo-dah, doo-dah!
Round de race track, den repeat, oh, doo-dah-day!
I win my money on de bob-tail nag, doo-dah, doo-dah!
I keep my money in an old tow-bag, oh, doo-dah-day!

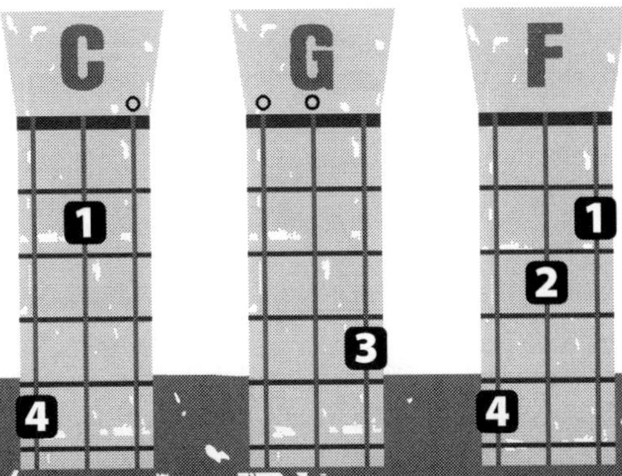

MY BONNIE LIES OVER THE OCEAN

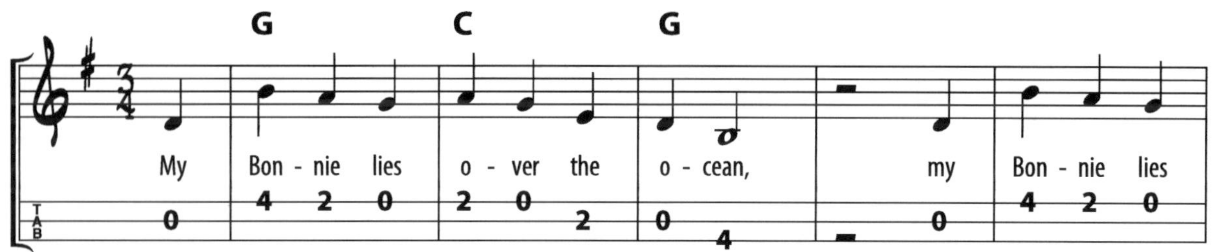

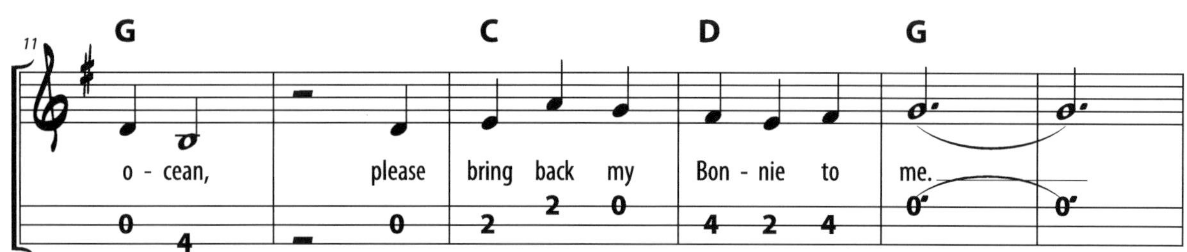

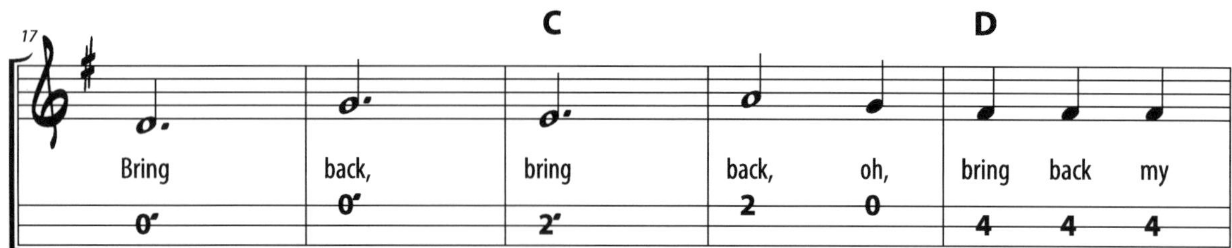

2 Last night as I lay on my pillow,
last night as I lay on my bed.
Last night as I lay on my pillow,
I dreamed that my Bonnie was dead.
Bring back, bring back,
bring back my Bonnie to me, to me.
Bring back, bring back,
bring back my Bonnie to me.

3 Oh blow ye the winds o'er the ocean,
and blow ye the winds o'er the sea.
Oh blow ye the winds o'er the ocean,
and bring back my Bonnie to me.
Bring back, bring back,
bring back my Bonnie to me, to me.
Bring back, bring back,
bring back my Bonnie to me.

4 The winds have blown over the ocean,
the winds have blown over the sea.
The winds have blown over the ocean,
and brought back my Bonnie to me.
Bring back, bring back,
bring back my Bonnie to me, to me.
Bring back, bring back,
bring back my Bonnie to me.

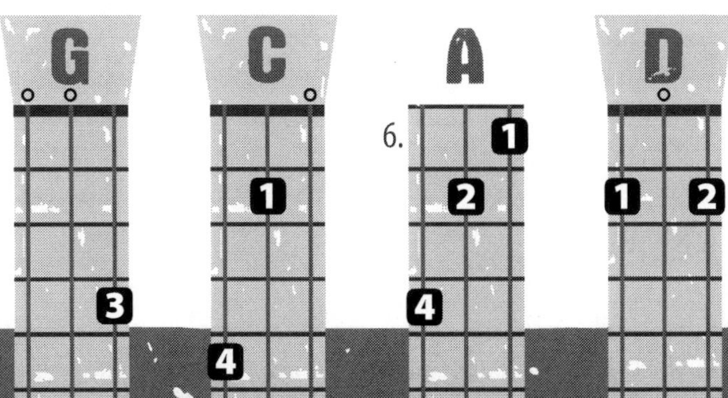

GOD REST YE MERRY, GENTLEMEN

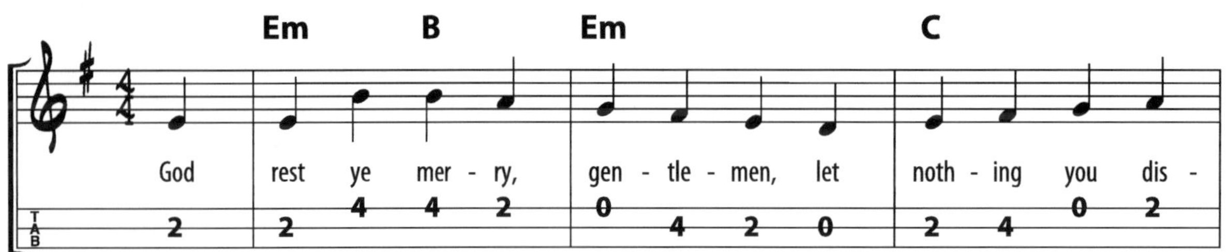

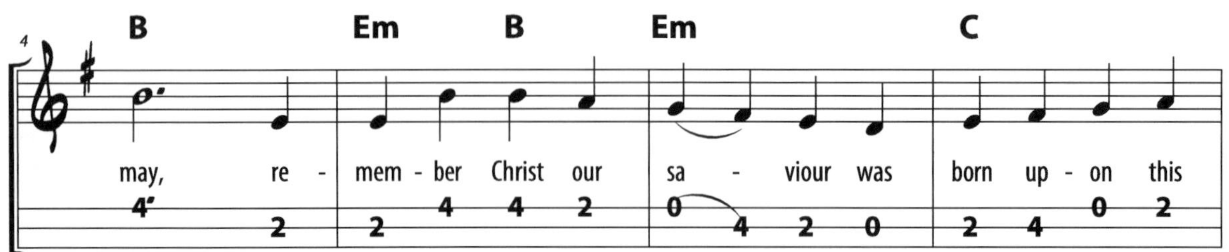

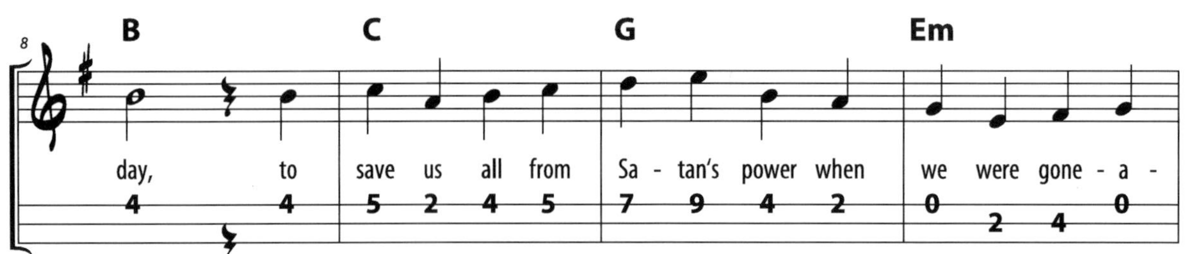

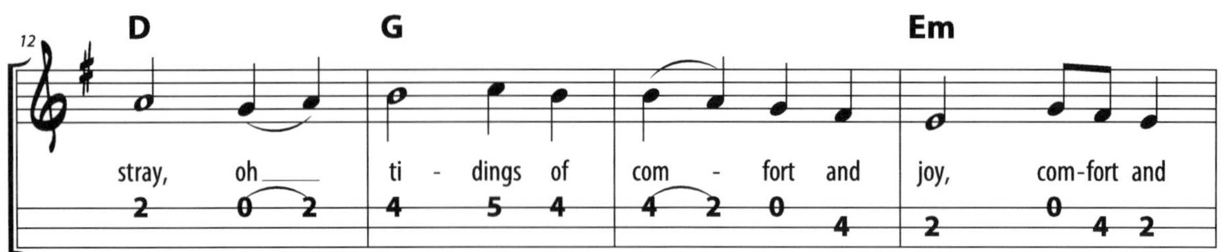

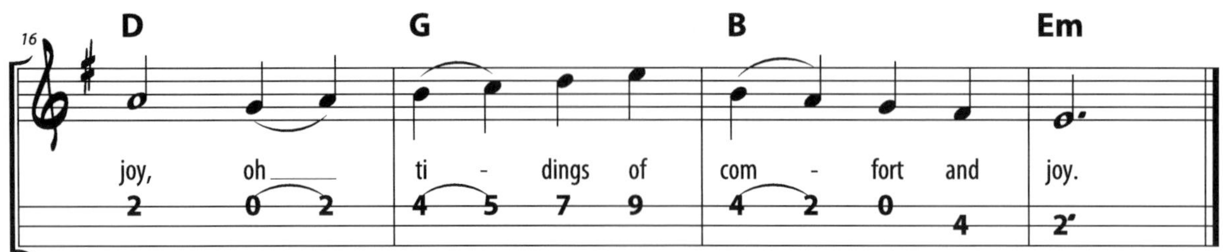

2 In Bethlehem, in Israel,
this blessed Babe was born,
and laid within a manger
upon this blessed morn,
the which His Mother Mary
did nothing take in scorn:
O tidings ...

3 From God our heavenly Father
a blessed angel came,
and unto certain shepherds
brought tidings of the same,
how that in Bethlehem was born
the Son of God by name:
O tidings ...

4 The shepherds at those tidings
rejoicèd much in mind,
and left their flocks a-feeding
in tempest, storm and wind,
and went to Bethlehem straightway,
this blessèd Babe to find:
O tidings ...

5 But when to Bethlehem they came,
whereat this Infant lay,
they found Him in a manger,
where oxen feed on hay;
His mother Mary kneeling,
unto the Lord did pray:
O tidings ...

6 Now to the Lord sing praises,
all you within this place,
and with true love and brotherhood
each other now embrace;
This holy tide of Christmas
all others doth deface:
O tidings ...

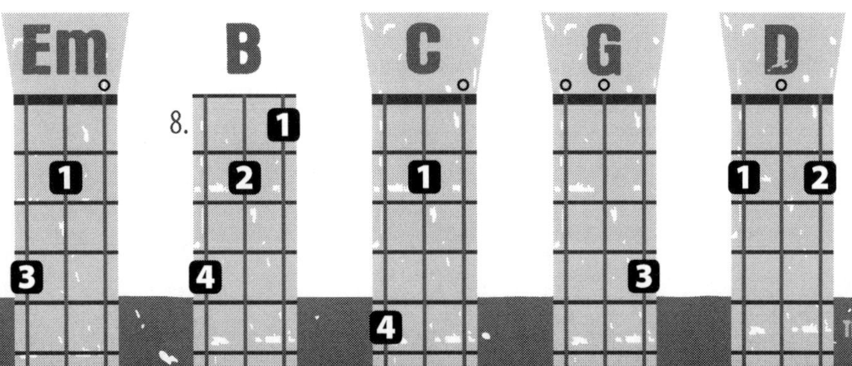

A BEAUTIFUL LIFE

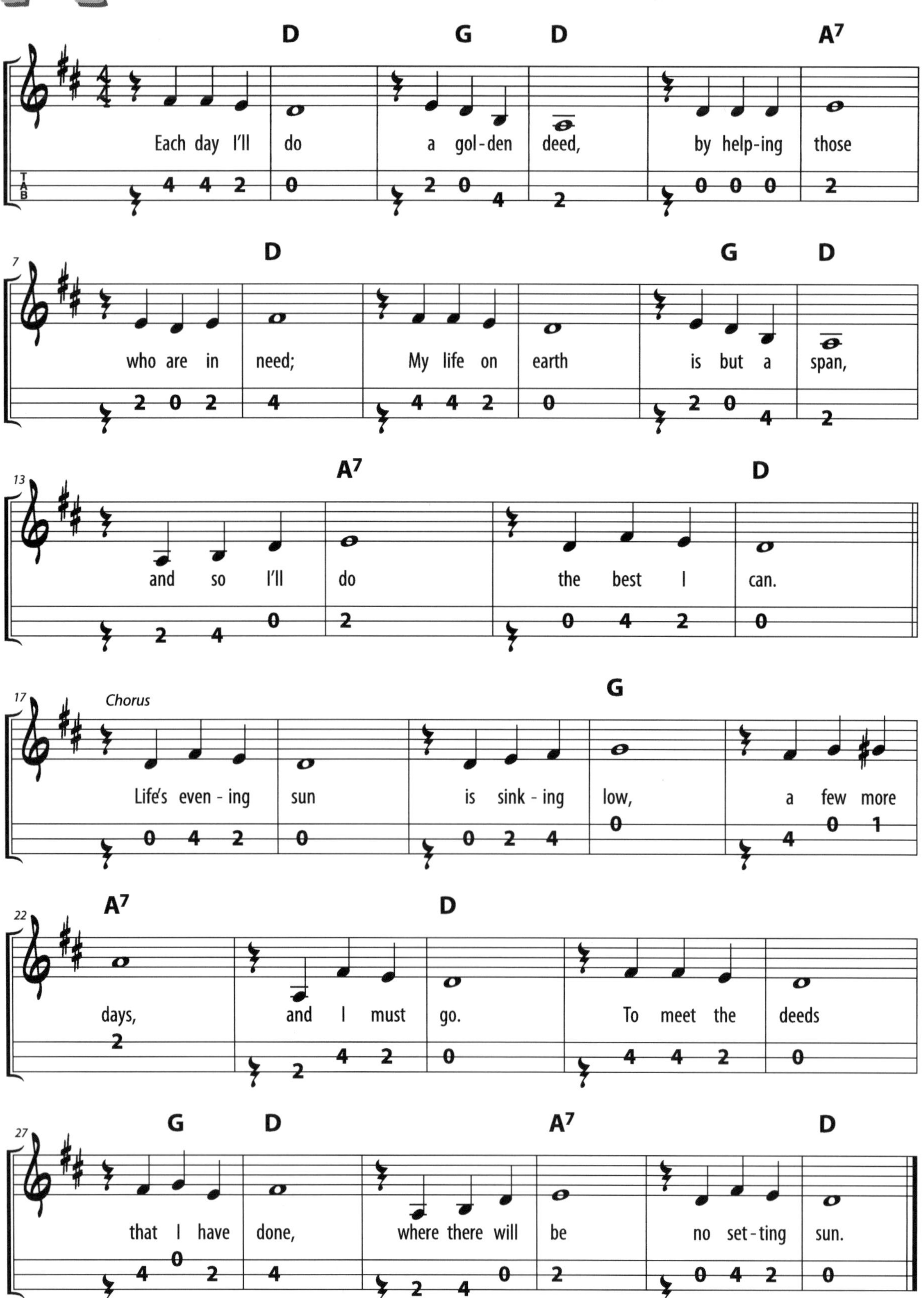

2 To be a child of God each day,
my light must shine along the way;
I'll sing His praise while ages roll,
and strive to help some troubled soul.
Life's evening sun is sinking low ...

3 The only life that will endure,
is one that's kind and good and pure;
And so for God I'll take my stand,
each day I'll lend a helping hand.
Life's evening sun is sinking low ...

4 I'll help someone in time of need,
and journey on with rapid speed;
I'll help the sick and poor and weak,
And words of kindness to them speak.
Life's evening sun is sinking low ...

5 While going down life's weary road,
I'll try to lift some trav'ler's load;
I'll try to turn the night to day,
make flowers bloom along the way.
Life's evening sun is sinking low ...

D G A7

1 2
3
1 2

BANKS OF THE OHIO

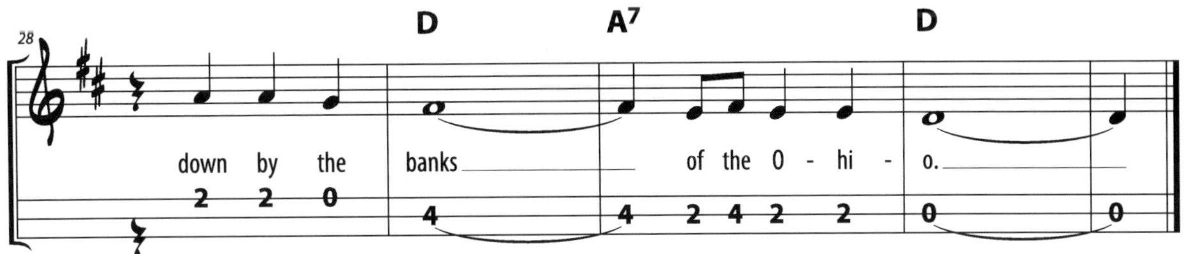

2 I held a knife against her breast
as into my arms she pressed,
"Willie, oh Willie, don't murder me,
I'm not prepared for eternity."

3 I started home 'twist twelve and one,
crying "My God! What have I done?
Killed the only woman I loved,
because she would not be my bride."

STRUMMING PATTERN

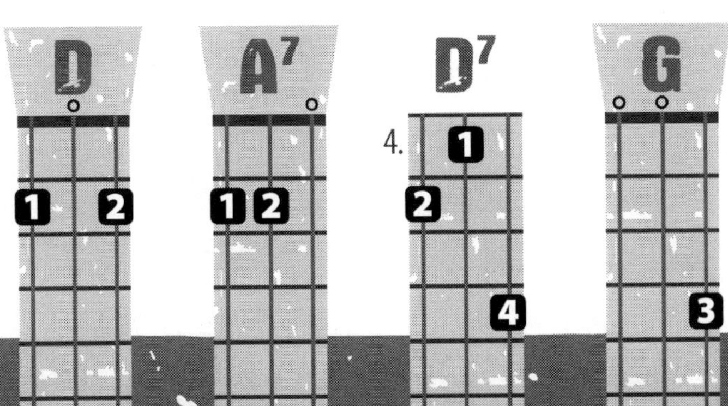

CARRY ME BACK TO OLD VIRGINNY

2 Carry me back to old Virginny,
there let me live till I wither and decay.
Long by the old dismal swamp have I wandered,
there's where this old life of mine will pass away.
Father and mother have long since gone before me,
soon we will meet on that bright and golden shore.
There we'll be happy and free from all sorrow,
there's where we'll meet and we'll never part no more.

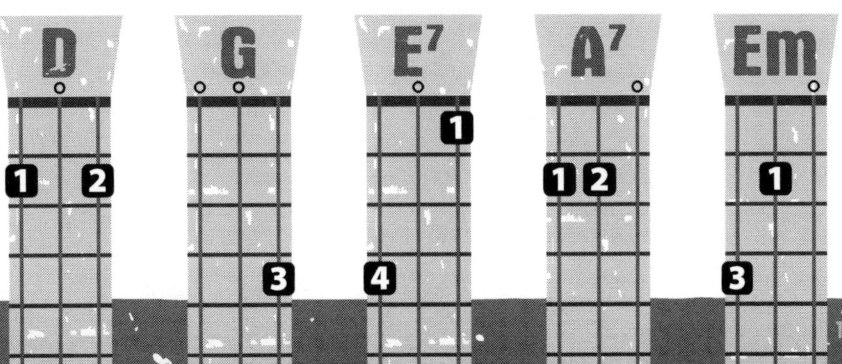

BILLY BOY

C G7
Oh, where have you been, Bil - ly Boy, Bil - ly
2 3 0 0 0 5 2 3 0 0 2

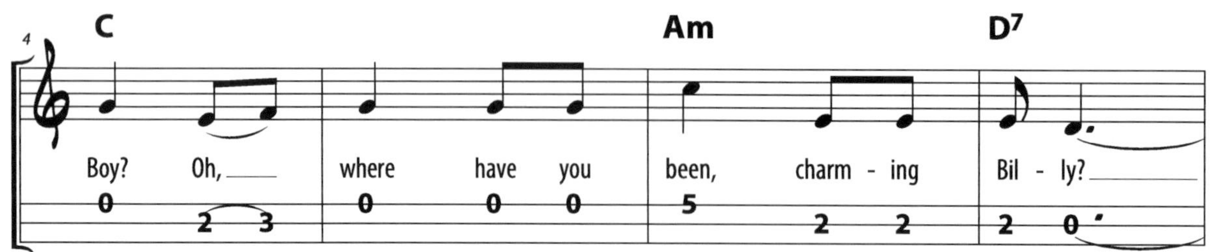
4
C Am D7
Boy? Oh, where have you been, charm - ing Bil - ly?
0 2 3 0 0 0 5 2 2 2 0

8
G7 C
I have been to seek a wife, she's the dar - ling of my
0 0 2 3 3 3 3 3 0 3 2 0 2 3

12
F C G7 C
life, she's a young thing and can - not leave her moth - er.
0 5 2 0 2 3 0 3 0 4 0 5 5

2 Did she bid you to come in, Billy Boy, Billy Boy?
Did she bid you to come in, charming Billy?
Yes, she bade me to come in, there's a dimple in her chin.
She's a young thing and cannot leave her mother.

3 Can she make a cherry pie, BIlly Boy, Billy Boy?
Can she make a cherry pie, charming Billy?
She can make a cherry pie, quick as a cat can wink an eye,
she's a young thing and cannot leave her mother.

4 Did she set for you a chair, Billy Boy, Billy Boy?
Did she set for you a chair, charming Billy?
Yes, she sat for me a chair, she has ringlets in her hair.
She's a young thing and cannot leave her mother.

5 How old is she now, Billy Boy, Billy Boy?
How old is she now, charming Billy?
Three times six and four times seven, twenty-eight and eleven,
she's a young thing and cannot leave her mother.

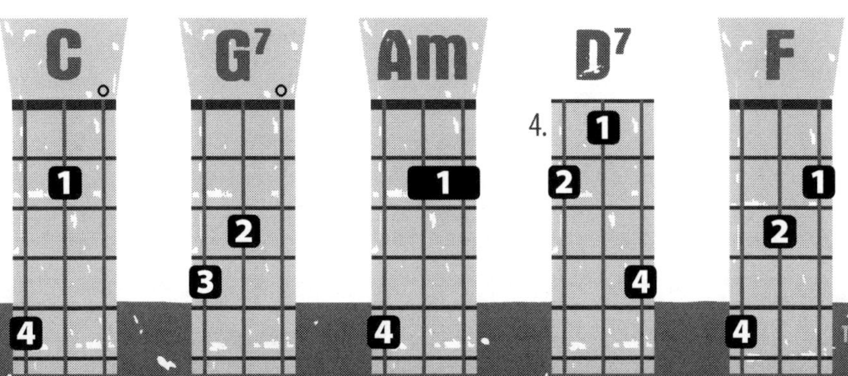

ENGINE 143

D
G
A - long came the F. F. V., the swift - est on the
0 0 0 2 4 4 4 2 0 2 0 0

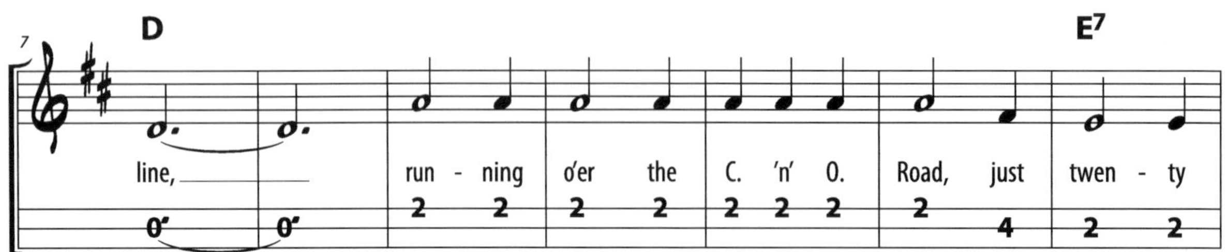
7
D
E7
line,
run - ning o'er the C. 'n' O. Road, just twen - ty
0 0 2 2 2 2 2 2 2 2 4 2 2

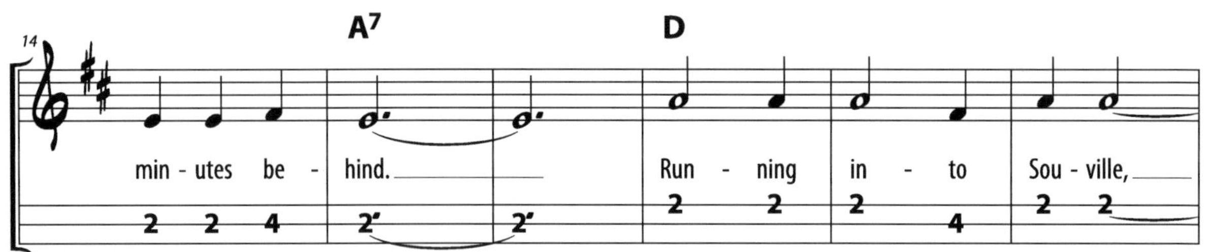
14
A7
D
min - utes be - hind.
Run - ning in - to Sou - ville,
2 2 4 2 2 2 2 2 4 2 2

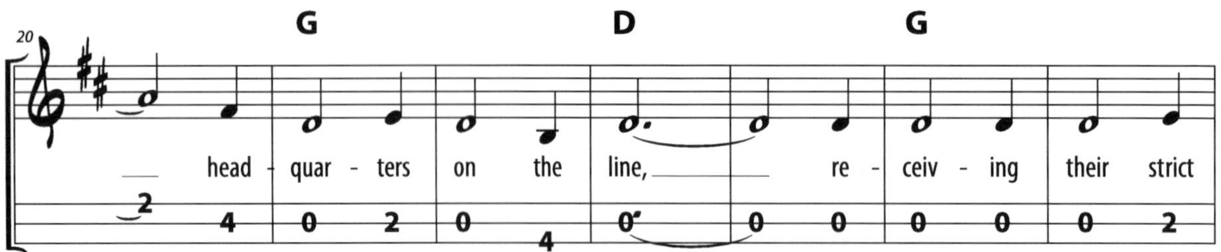
20
G
D
G
head - quar - ters on the line, re - ceiv - ing their strict
2 4 0 2 0 4 0 0 0 0 0 0 2

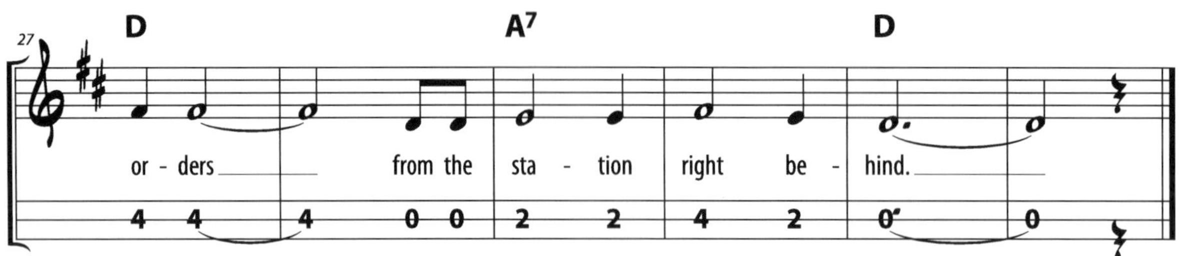
27
D
A7
D
or - ders from the sta - tion right be - hind.
4 4 4 0 0 2 2 4 2 0 0

2 Georgie's mother came to him, a bucket on her arm,
saying to her darling son, be careful how you run.
Many a man that's lost his life trying to make lost time,
And if you run your engine right, you'll get there right on time.

3 Up the tracks she darted against a rock she crashed,
upside down the engine turned and Georgie's head was smashed.
His head against the firebox door and the flames were rolling high,
I'm glad I was born for an engineer on the C. 'n' O. Road to die.

4 The doctor said to Georgie, my darling boy be still,
your life may yet be saved, if it is God's precious will.
Oh no, said George, that will not do, I want to die so free,
I want to die for the engine I love: One Hundred and Forty-Three.

5 The doctor said to Georgie, your life cannot be saved,
murdered on a railway and laid in a lonesome grave.
His face was covered up with blood, his eyes they could not see,
and the very last words poor Georgie said were, Nearer, my God, to Thee.

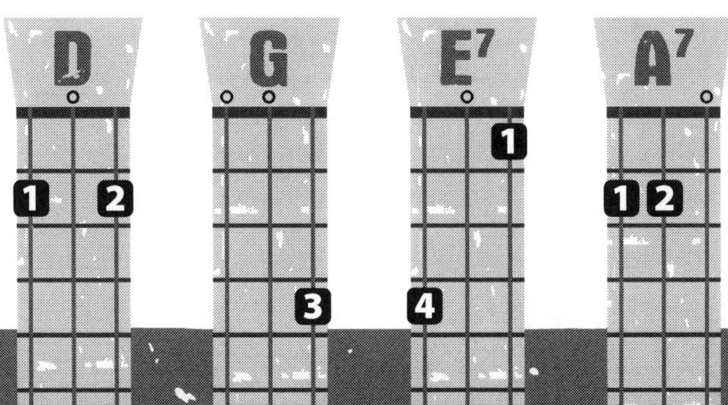

CLEMENTINE

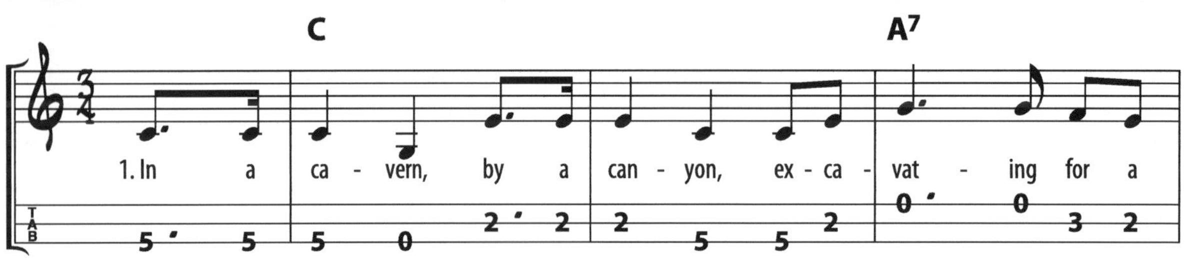

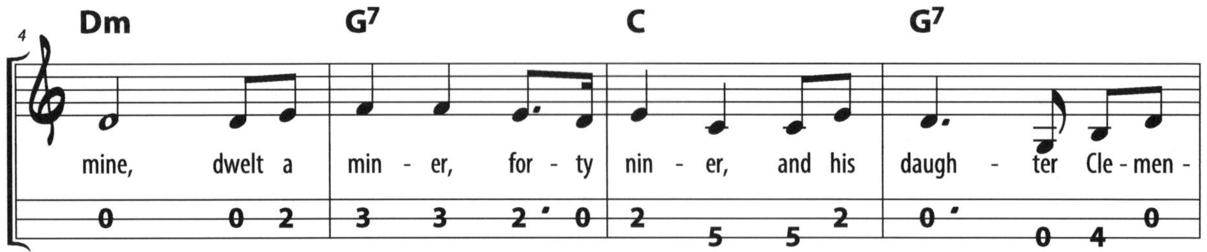

STRUMMING PATTERN

2 Light she was, and like a fairy,
and her shoes were number nine,
herring boxes without topses,
sandals were for Clementine.

3 Drove she ducklings to the water
every morning just at nine,
struck her foot agains a splinter,
fell into the foaming brine.

4 Rosy lips above the water,
blowing bubbles mighty fine,
but, alas, I was no swimmer,
so I lost my Clementine.

5 How I missed her! How I missed her!
How I missed my Clementine!
But I kissed her little sister,
and forgot my Clementine.

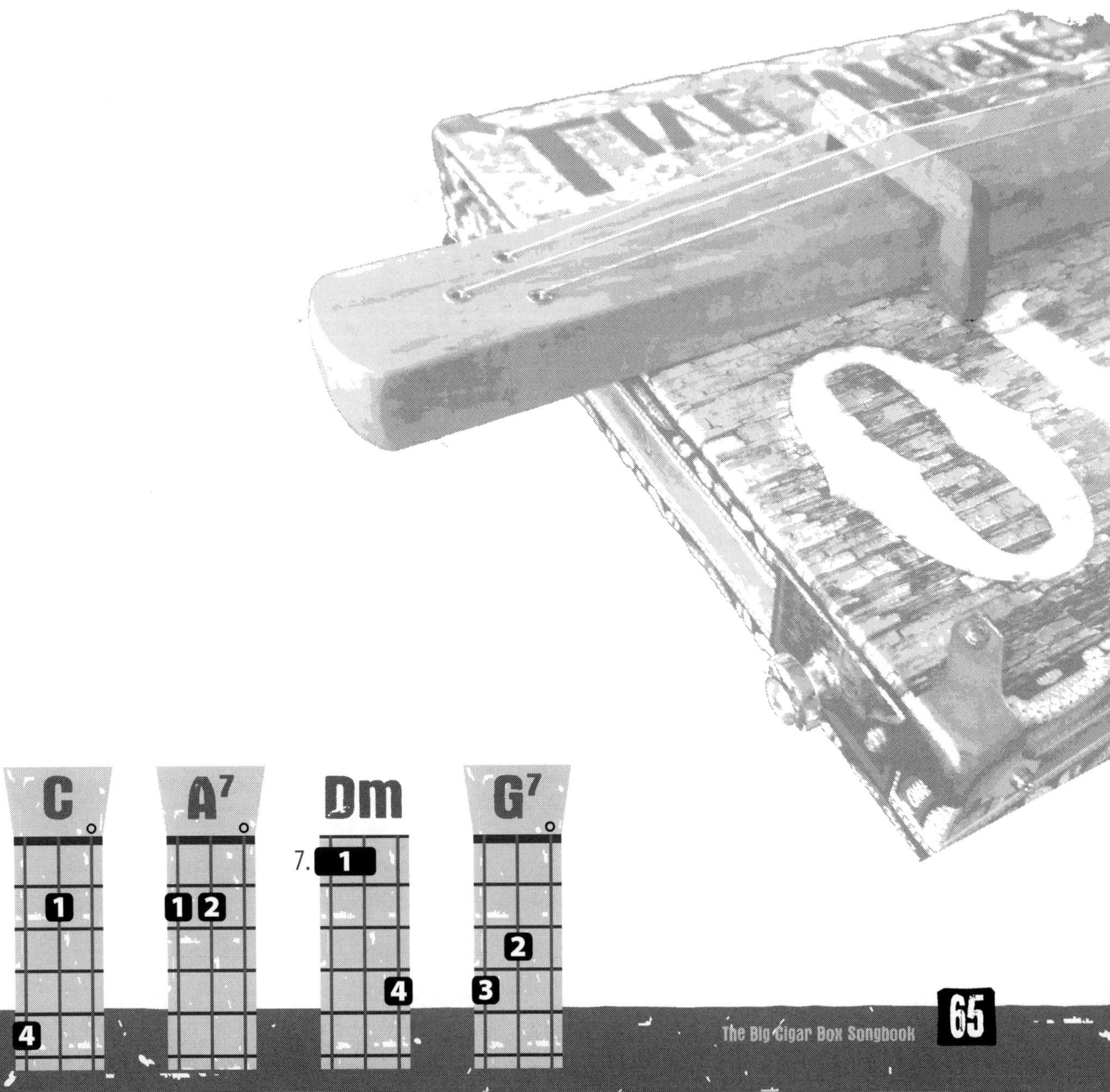

CINDY

D
A7
You ought to see my Cin - dy, she lives a - way down south, and

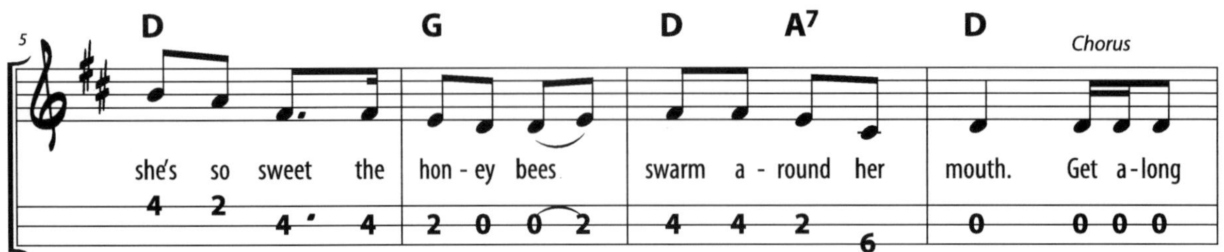
5
D
G
D
A7
D
Chorus
she's so sweet the hon - ey bees swarm a - round her mouth. Get a - long

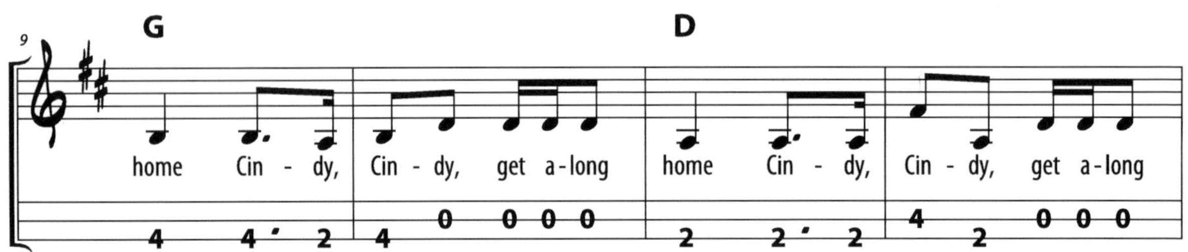
9
G
D
home Cin - dy, Cin - dy, get a - long home Cin - dy, Cin - dy, get a - long

13
G
D
A7
D
home Cin - dy, Cin - dy, I'll mar - ry you some - day.

STRUMMING PATTERN
You ought to see my

2 The first I seen my Cindy she was standing in the door,
her shoes and stocking in her hand her feet all over the floor.

3 She took me to her parlor she cooled me with her fan,
she said I was the prettiest thing in the shape of mortal man.

4 She kissed me and she hugged me she called me suger plum,
she throwed her arms around me I thought my time had come.

5 Oh Cindy is a pretty girl Cindy is a peach,
she threw her arms around my neck and hung on like a leech.

6 And if I was a sugar tree standing in the town,
each time my Cindy passed I'd shake some sugar down.

7 And if had a needle and thread fine as I could sew,
I'd sew that gal to my coat tails and down the road I'd go.

8 I wish I was an apple a-hanging on a tree,
every time that Cindy passed she'd take a bite of me.

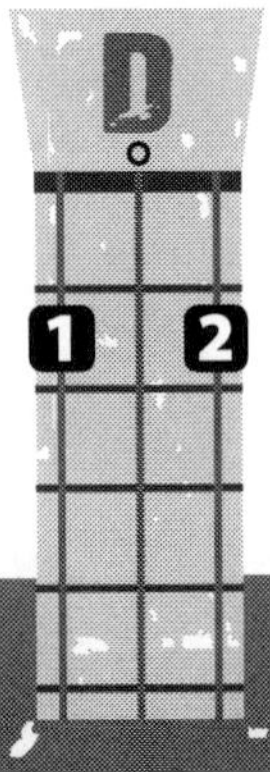

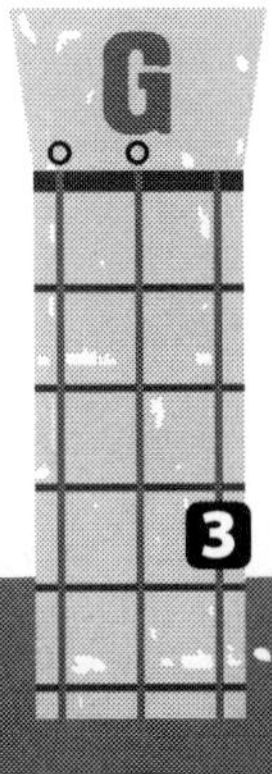

D A7 G

KUM BA YAH

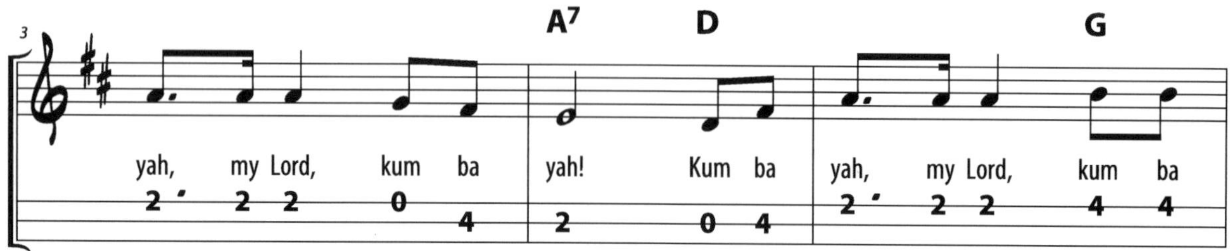

2 Someone's crying, Lord, kum ba yah!

3 Someone's singing, Lord, kum ba yah!

4 Someone's praying, Lord, kum ba yah!

STRUMMING PATTERN

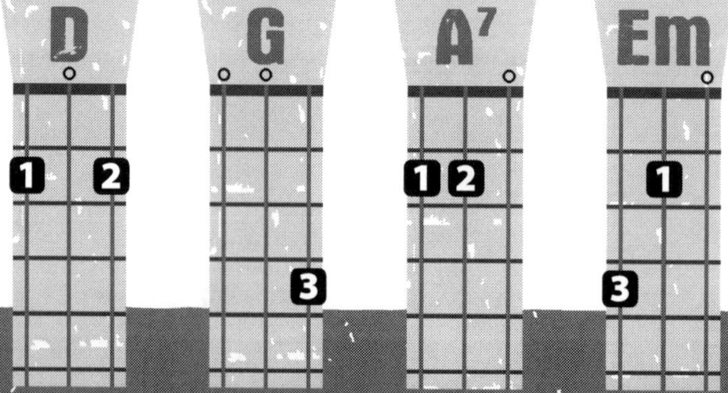

Michael, Row the Boat Ashore

2 Michael boat a gospelboat, Halleluja ...

3 Brother lend a helping hand, Halleluja ...

4 Sister help to trim the sail, Halleluja ...

5 Boasting talk will sink your soul, Halleluja ...

6 Jordan-stream is deep and wide, Halleluja ...

7 Jesus stand on the other side, Halleluja ...

Strumming Pattern

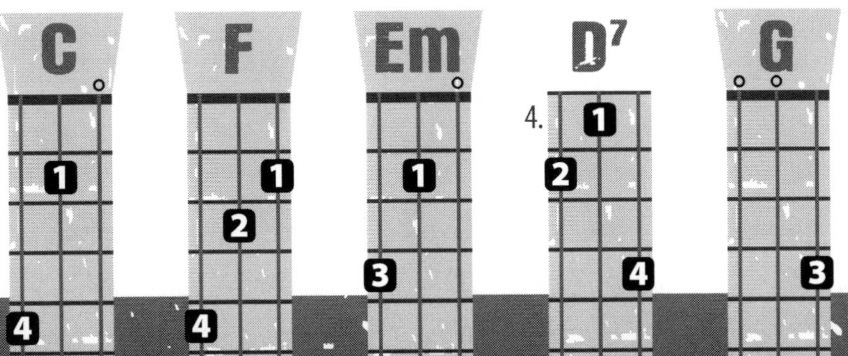

ON TOP OF OLD SMOKEY

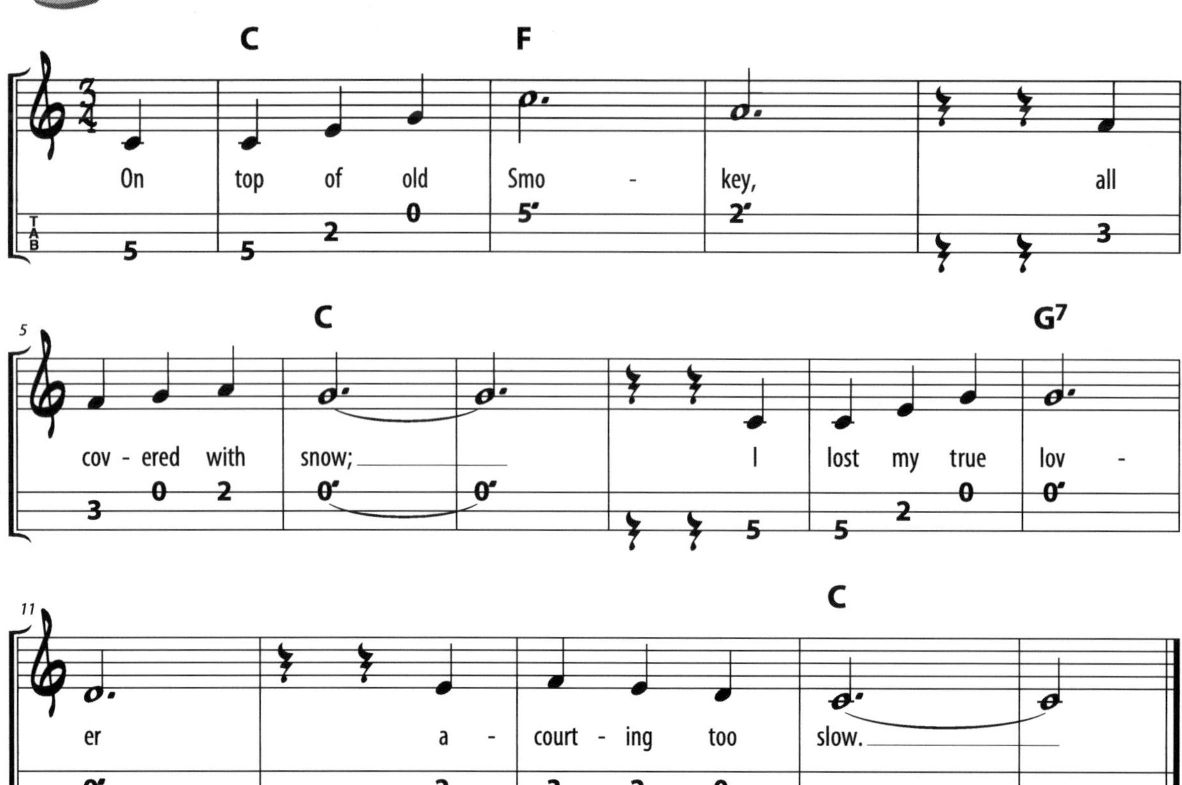

STRUMMING PATTERN

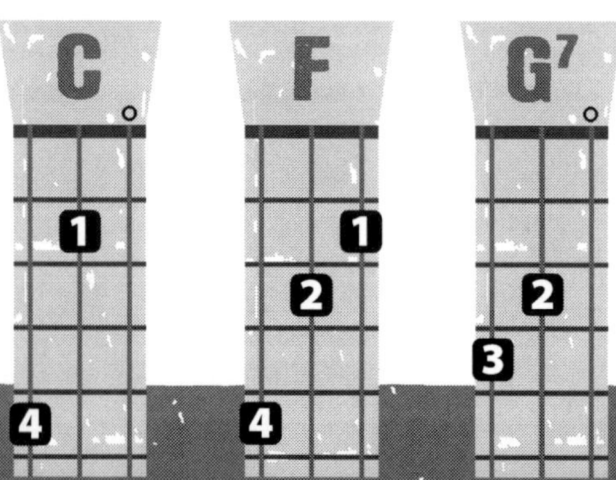

SAILOR ON THE DEEP BLUE SEA

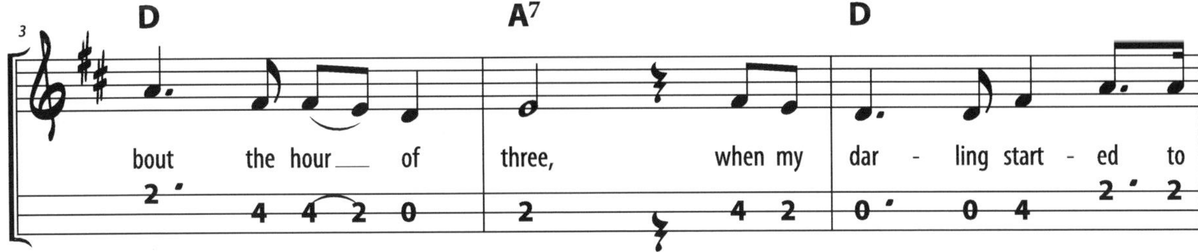

2 Oh, he promised to write me a letter,
he said he'd write to me;
But I've not heard from my darling
who is sailing on the deep blue sea.

3 Oh, my mother's dead and buried,
my pa's forsaken me,
and I have no one for to love me
but the sailor on the deep blue sea.

4 Oh captain, can you tell me
where can my sailor be;
Oh yes, my little maiden,
he is drownded in the deep blue sea.

5 Farewell to friends and relations,
it's the last you'll see of me;
For I'm going to end my troubles
by drowning in the deep blue sea.

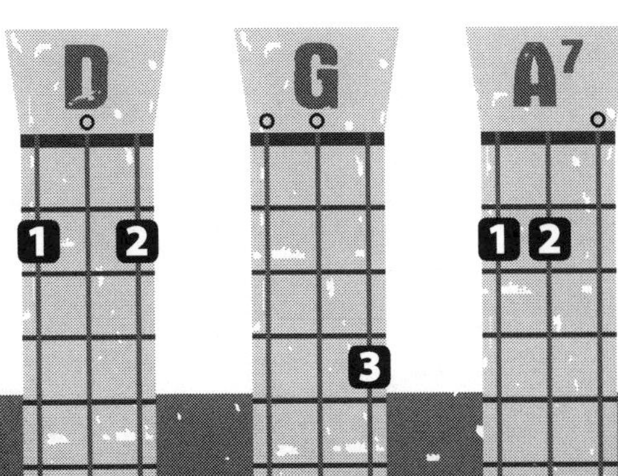

STRUMMING PATTERN

THE WILD ROVER

2 I went to an alehouse I used to frequent,
and I told the landlady me money was spent.
I asked her for credit, she answered me "nay,
such a custom as yours I could have any day".

3 I pulled from me pocket a handful of gold,
and on the round table it glittered and rolled.
She said "I have whiskeys and wines of the best,
and the words that I told you were only in jest".

4 I'll have none of your whiskeys nor fine Spanish wines,
for your words show you clearly as no friend of mine.
There's others most willing to open a door,
To a man coming home from a far distant shore.

5 I'll go home to me parents, confess what I've done,
and I'll ask them to pardon their prodigal son.
And if they forgive me as oft times before,
I never will play the wild rover no more.

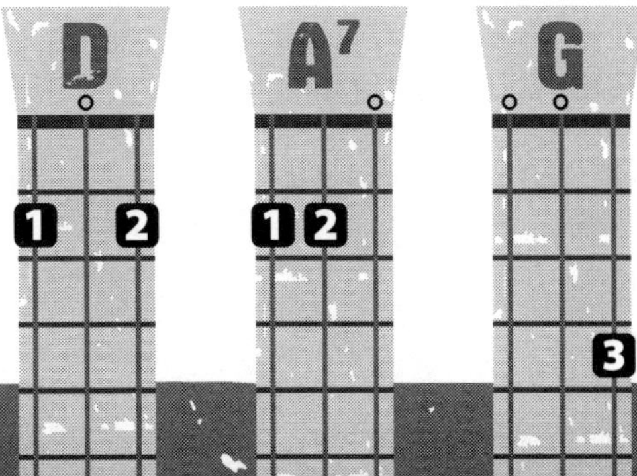

Whiskey in the Jar

2 I counted out his money, and it made a pretty penny.
I put it in my pocket and I took it home to Jenny.
She said and she swore, that she never would deceive me,
but the devil take the women, for they never can be easy.

3 I went into my chamber, all for to take a slumber,
I dreamt of gold and jewels and for sure it was no wonder.
But Jenny took my charges and she filled them up with water,
Then sent for captain Farrel to be ready for the slaughter.

4 It was early in the morning, as I rose up for travel,
The guards were all around me and likewise captain Farrel.
I first produced my pistol, for she stole away my rapier,
But I couldn't shoot the water so a prisoner I was taken.

5 If anyone can aid me, it's my brother in the army,
If I can find his station down in Cork or in Killarney.
And if he'll come and save me, we'll go roving near Kilkenny,
And I swear he'll treat me better than me darling sportling Jenny.

6 Now some men take delight in the drinking and the roving,
But others take delight in the gambling and the smoking.
But I take delight in the juice of the barley,
And courting pretty fair maids in the morning bright and early.

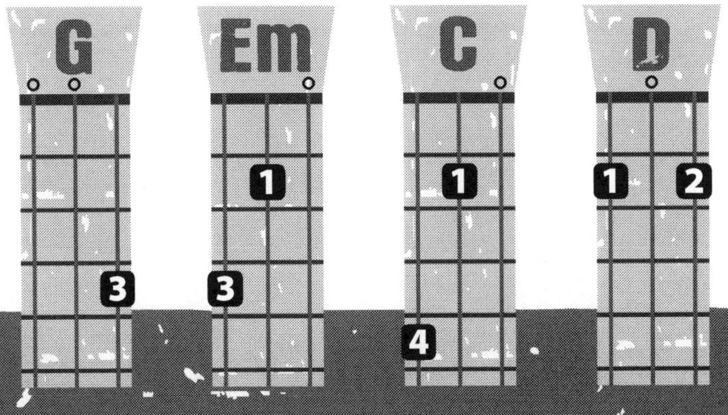

G Em C D

She Moved Through the Fair

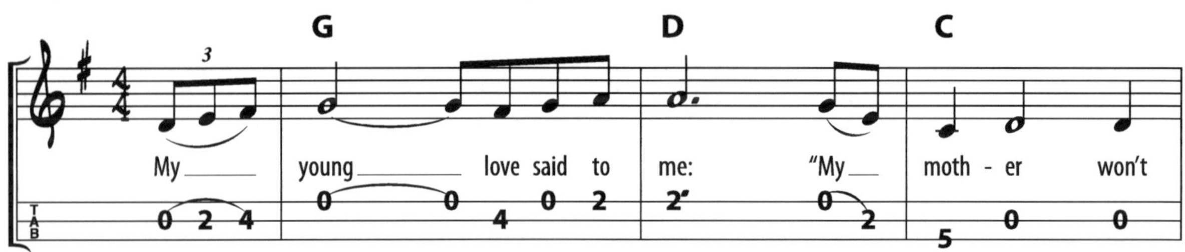

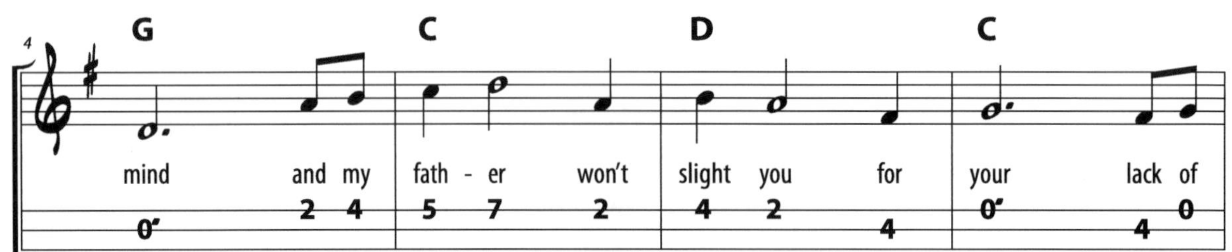

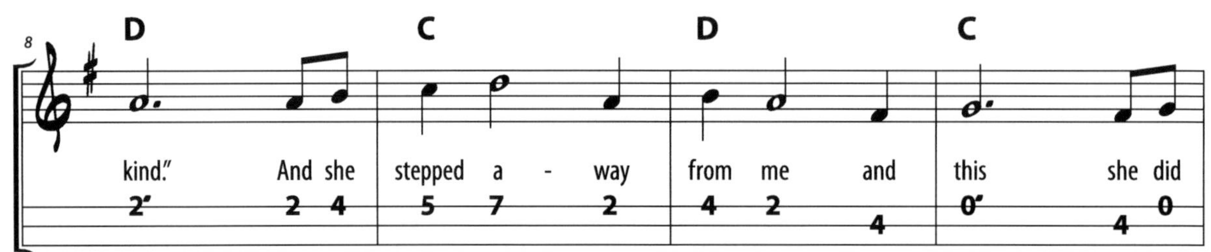

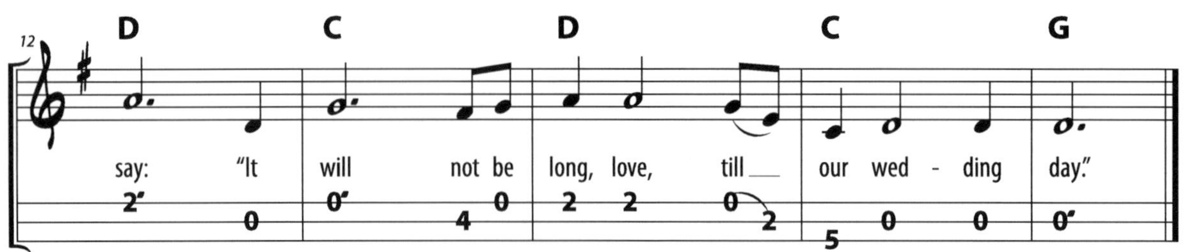

2 She stepped away from me
and she moved through the fair
and fondly I watched her,
move here and move there.
And then she made her way homeward,
with one star awake,
as the swan in the evening
moved over the lake.

3 The people were saying,
no two e'er were wed,
but one had a sorrow
that never was said.
And I smiled as she passed
with her goods and her gear,
and that was the last
that I saw of my dear

4 Last night she came to me,
my dead love came in.
so softly she came
that her feet made no din.
as she laid her hand on me,
and this she did say:
It will not be long, love,
'til our wedding day.

STRUMMING PATTERN

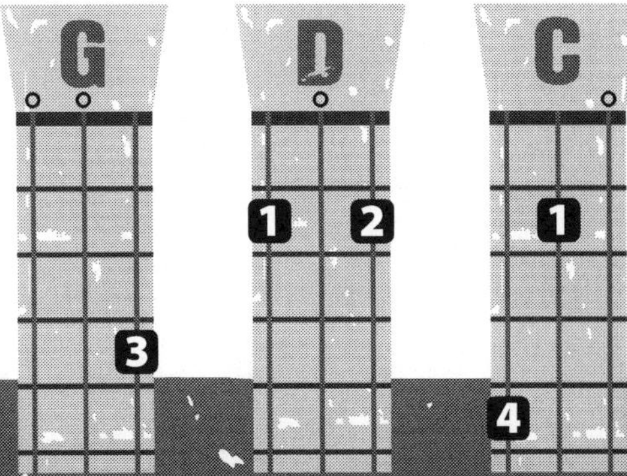

SWEET BY AND BY

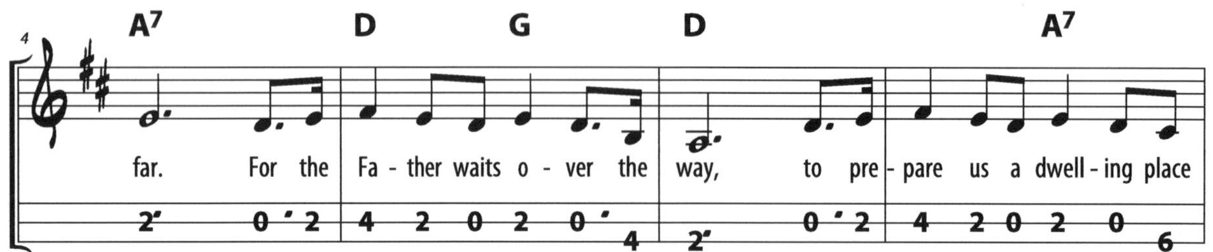

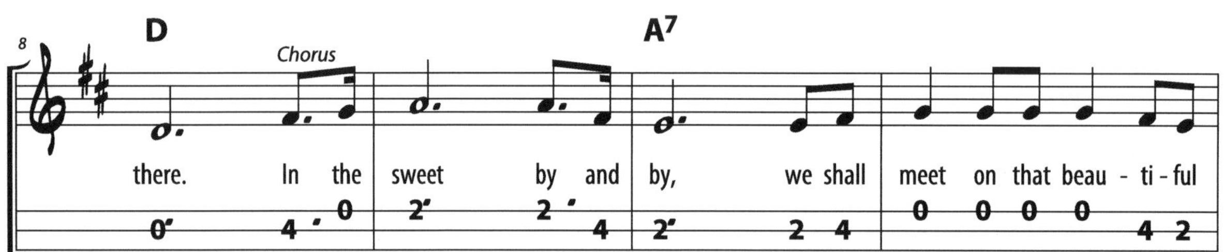

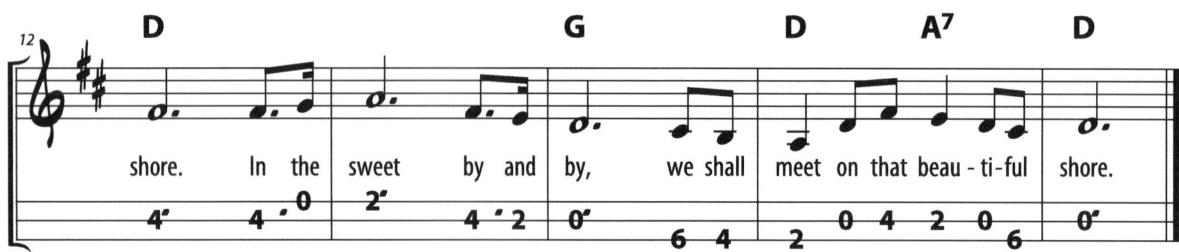

2 We shall sing on that beautiful shore,
the melodious songs of the blessed.
And our spirits shall sorrow no more,
not a sigh for the blessing of rest.
In the sweet by and by ...

3 To our bountiful Father above,
we will offer our tribute of praise.
For the glorious gift of His love,
and the blessings that hallow our days.
In the sweet by and by ...

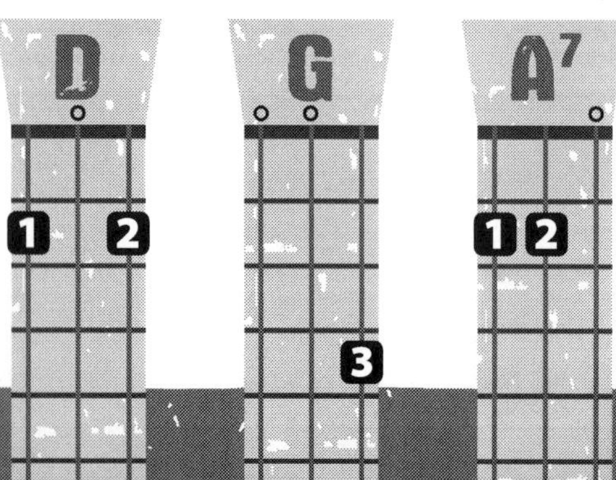

TOM DOOLEY

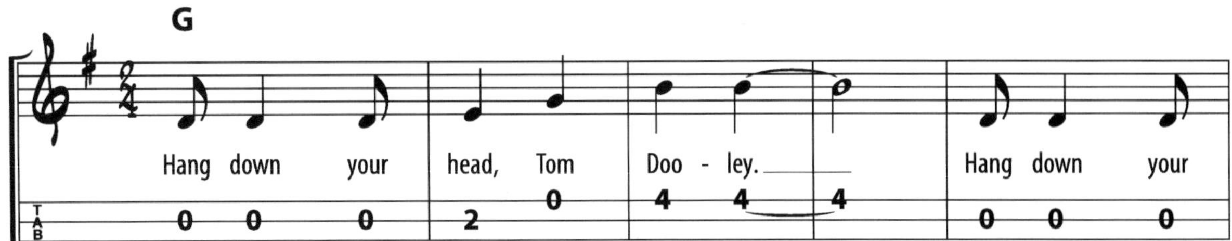

2 This time tomorrow,
reckon where I'll be?
If it hadn't been for Grayson,
I'd a-been in Tennessee.

3 This time tomorrow,
reckon where I'll be?
Down in some lonesome valley,
hangin' from a white oak tree.

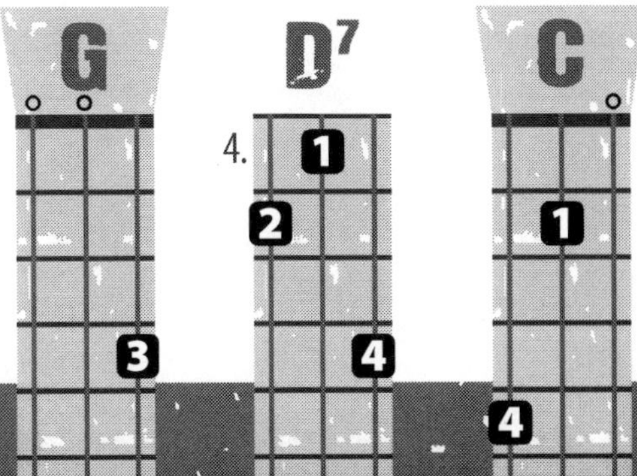

All the Good Times Are Past and Gone

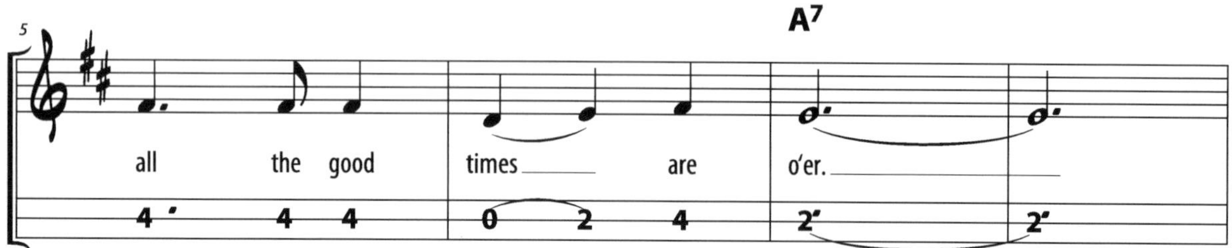

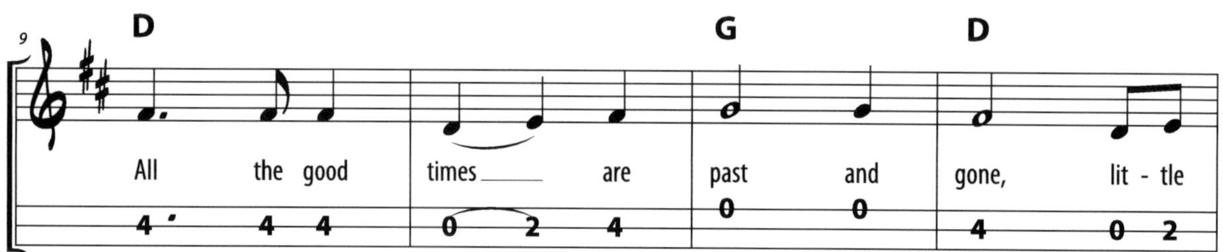

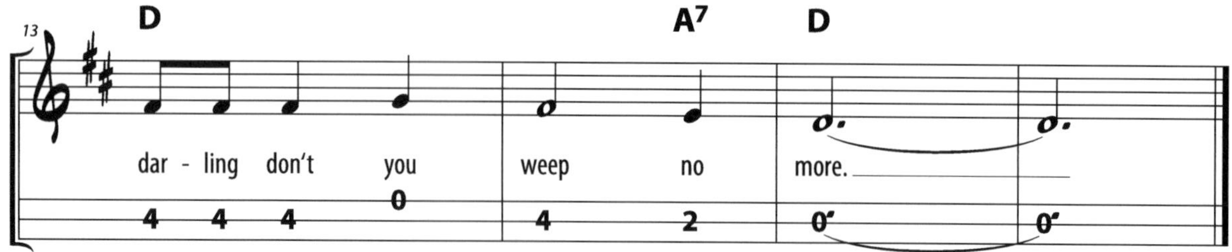

2 See that east-bound passenger train,
coming around the bend.
It's taking away my own true love,
to never return again.

3 I wish dear Lord I'd never been born,
or died when I was young.
I never would've seen those two brown eyes,
or heard your lying tongue.

4 See that lonesome turtle dove,
flying from pine to pine.
He's mourning for his own true love,
just like I mourn for mine.

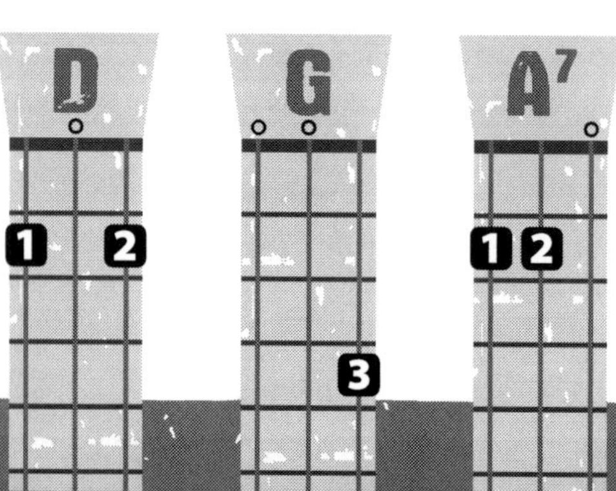

AMAZING GRACE

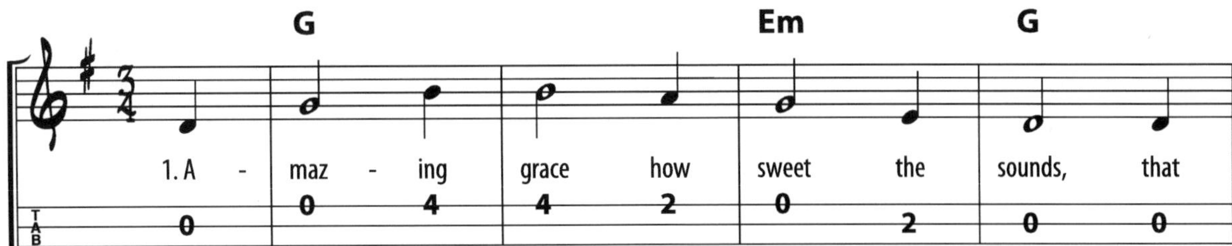

2 'Twas grace that taught my heart to fear,
and grace my fear relived.
How precious did that grace appear,
the hour I first believed.

3 When we've been there ten thousand years,
bright shining as the sun.
We've no less days to sing God's praise,
than when we first begun.

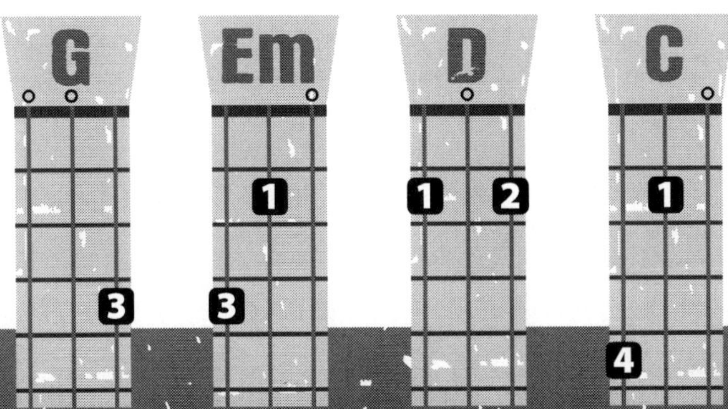

Shenandoah

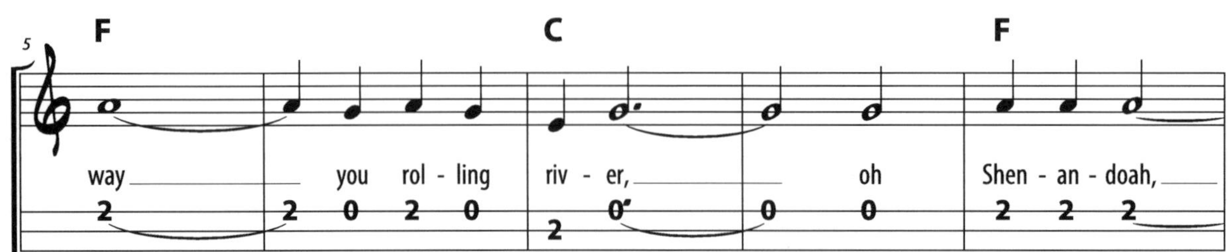

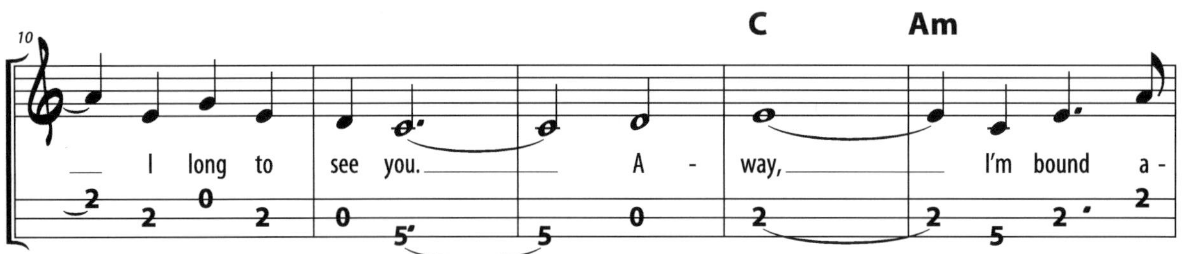

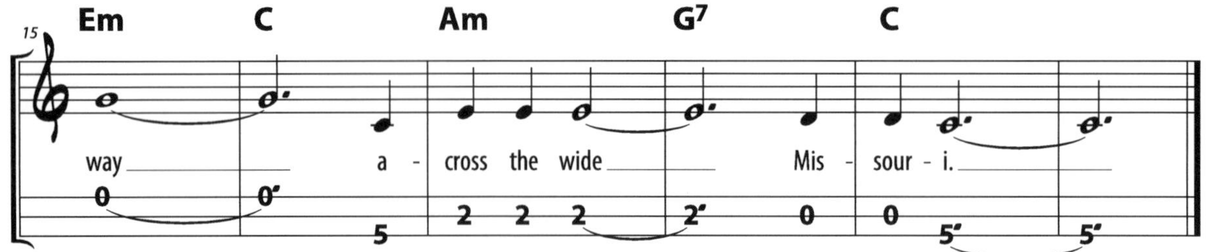

2 Oh Shenandoah,
I love your daughter,
away, you rolling river.
For her I'd cross,
your roaming waters,
away, I'm bound away,
'cross the wide Missouri.

3 'Tis seven years,
since last I've seen you,
away, you rolling river.
'Tis seven years,
since last I've seen you,
away, we're bound away,
'cross the wide Missouri.

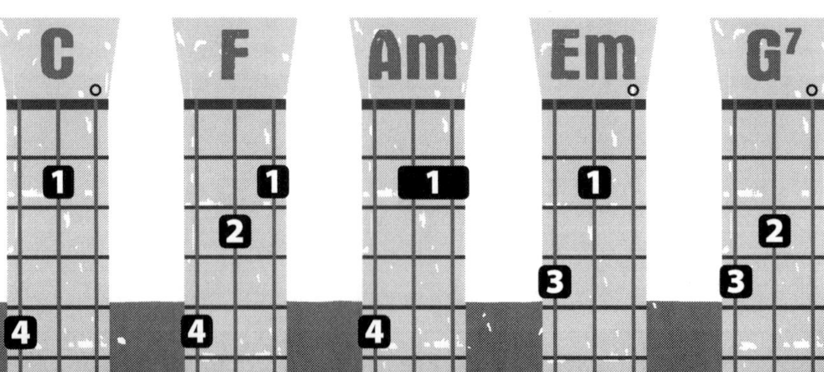

SHADY GROVE

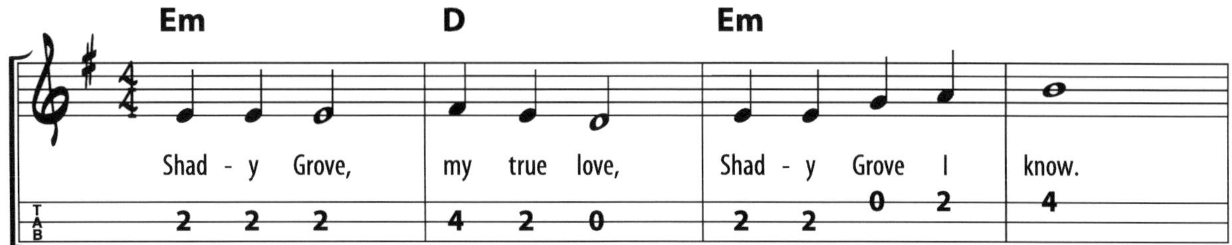

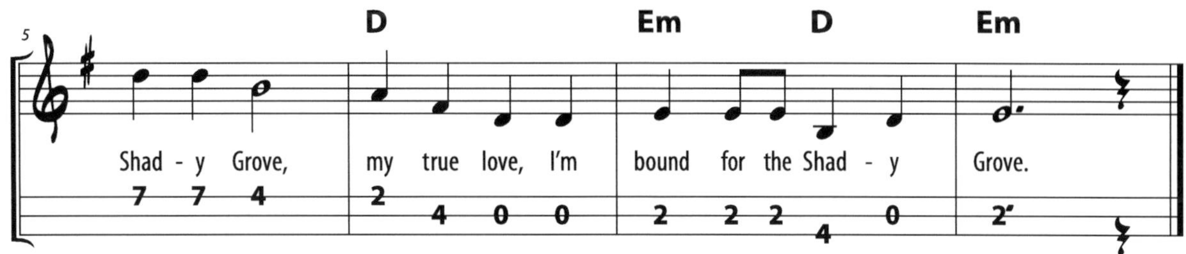

2 Peaches in the summertime,
apples in the fall.
If I can't have my Shady Grove,
I'll have no one at all.

3 Cheeks as red as a blooming rose,
eyes of the deepest brown.
She is the darling of my heart,
prettiest girl in town.

4 The first time I saw Shady Grove,
she was standing at the door.
Shoes and stockings in her hand,
little bare feet on the floor.

STRUMMING PATTERN

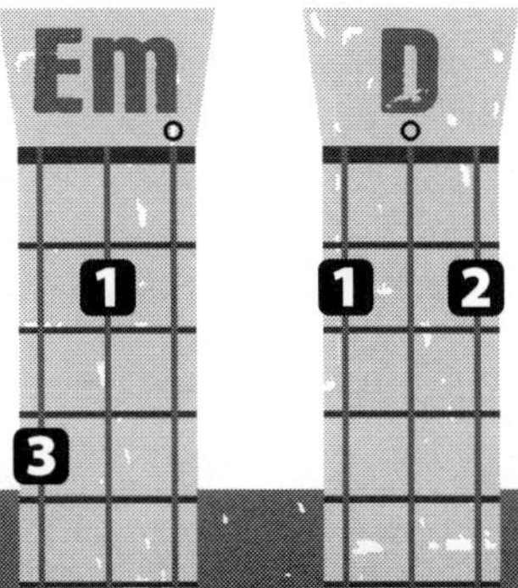

Waltzing Matilda

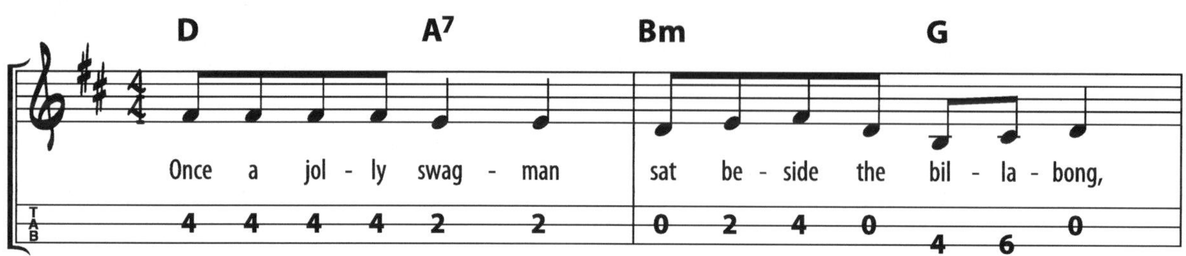

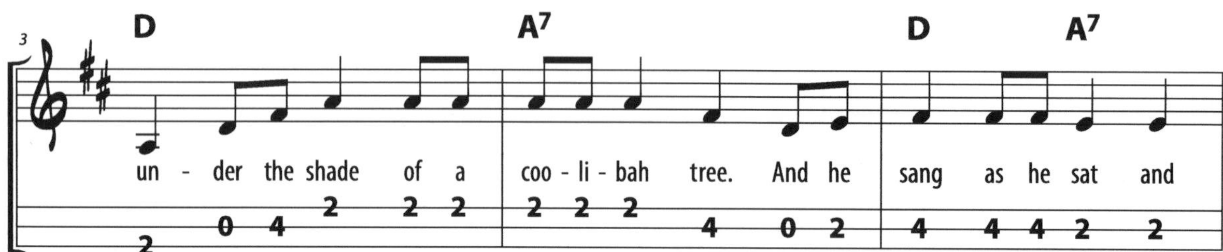

2 Down came a jumbuck to drink at that billabong.
Up jumped the swagman and grabbed him with glee.
And he sang as he shoved that jumbuck in his tucker bag:
"You'll come a-waltzing Matilda with me."
Waltzing Matilda, waltzing Matilda,
"You'll come a-waltzing Matilda with me",
and he sang as he shoved that jumbuck in his tucker bag:
"You'll come a-waltzing Matilda with me."

3 Up rode the squatter, mounted on his thoroughbred.
Down came the troopers, one, two, and three.
"Whose is that jumbuck you've got in your tucker bag?
You'll come a-waltzing Matilda with me."
Waltzing Matilda, waltzing Matilda,
"You'll come a-waltzing Matilda with me",
"Whose is that jumbuck you've got in your tucker bag?
You'll come a-waltzing Matilda with me."

4 Up jumped the swagman and sprang into the billabong.
"You'll never take me alive!" said he,
and his ghost may be heard as you pass by that billabong:
"Who'll come a-waltzing Matilda with me?"
Waltzing Matilda, waltzing Matilda,
"You'll come a-waltzing Matilda with me",
and his ghost may be heard as you pass by that billabong:
"Who'll come a-waltzing Matilda, with me?"

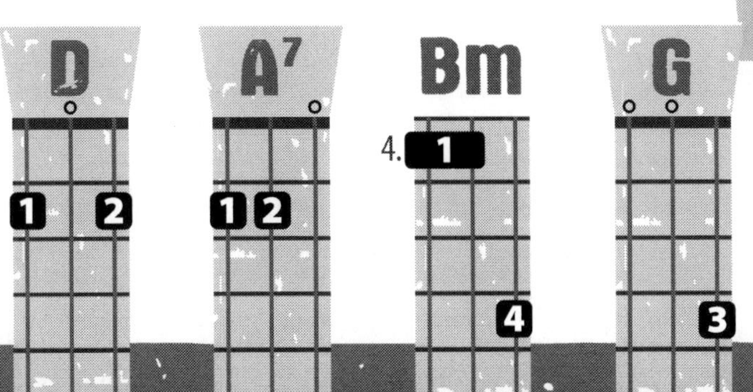

DON'T THIS ROAD LOOK ROUGH AND ROCKY

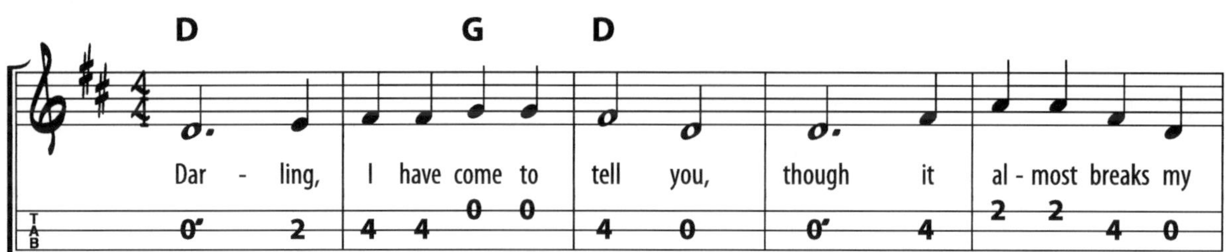

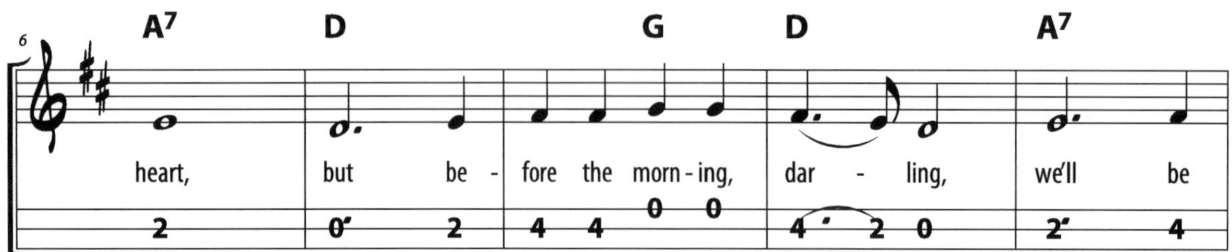

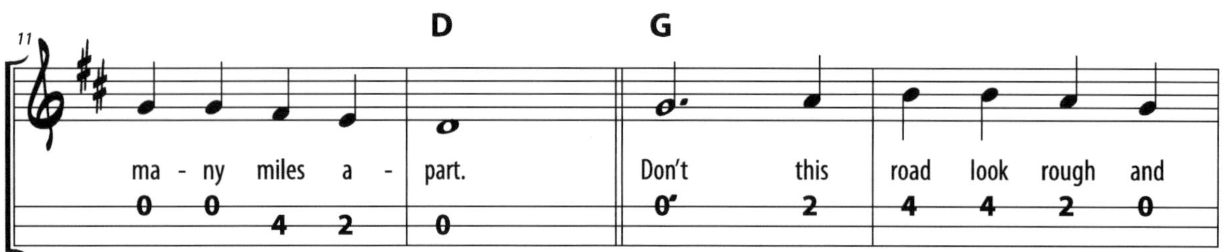

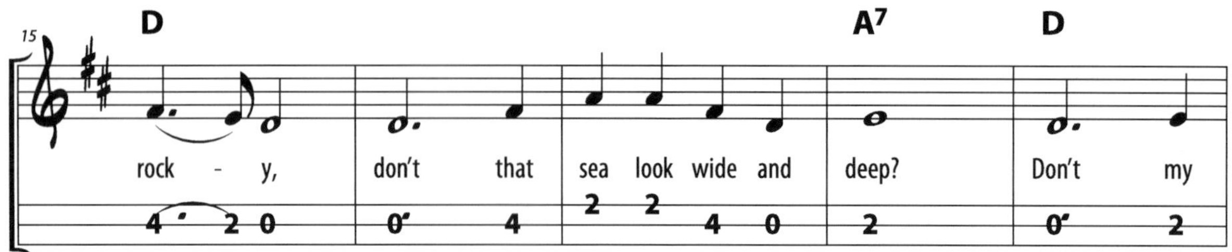

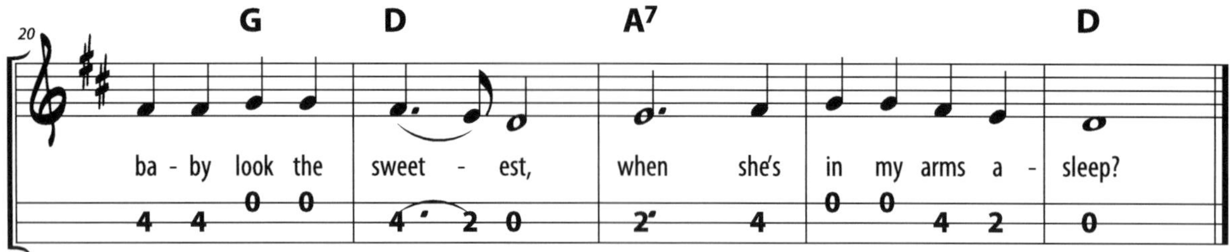

2 Can't you hear the night birds crying,
far across the deep blue sea?
While of others you are thinking,
won't you sometimes think of me?
Don't this road look rough and rocky ...

3 One more kiss before I leave you,
one more kiss before we part.
You have caused me lots of trouble,
darling you have broke my heart.
Don't this road look rough and rocky ...

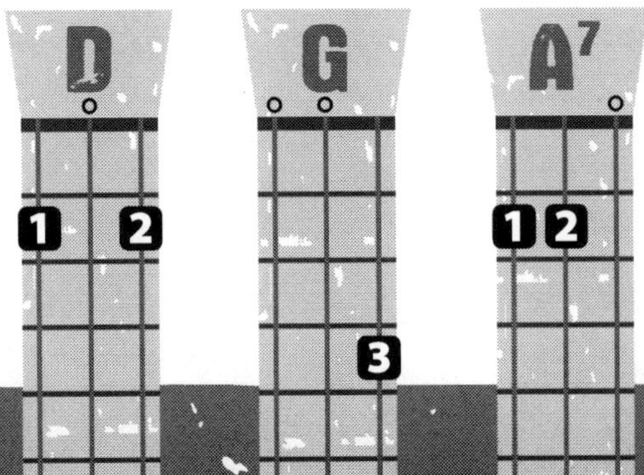

Banks of Allan Water

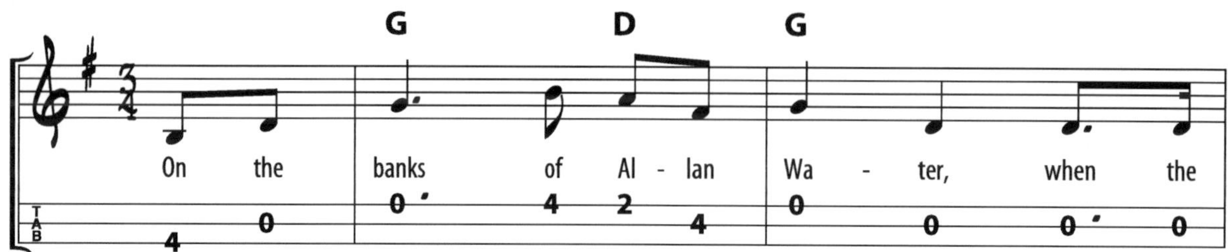

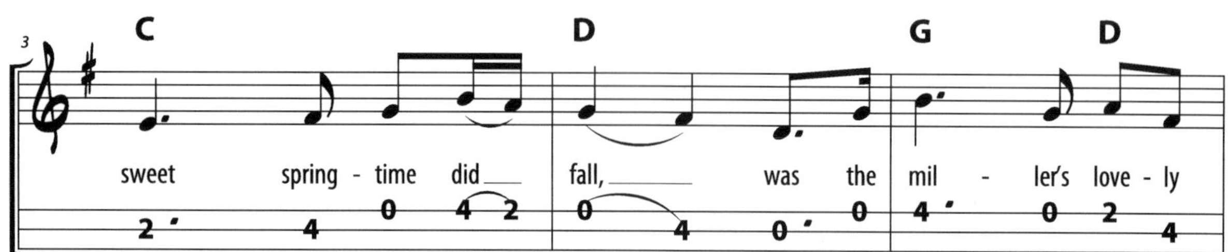

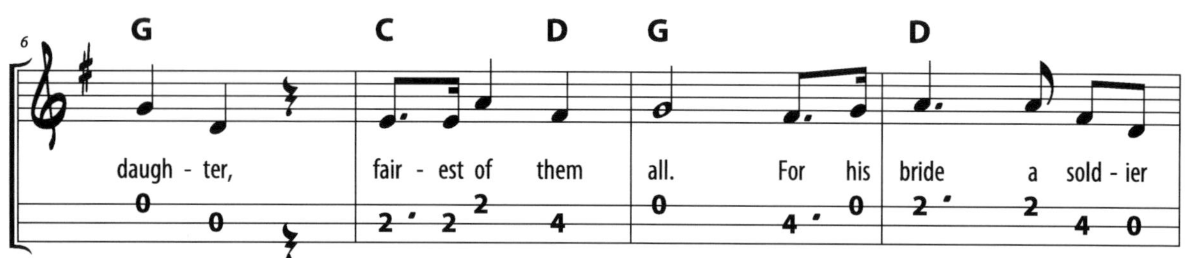

2 On the banks of Allan Water,
when brown autumn spread his store.
There I saw the miller's daughter,
but she smiled no more.
For the summer, grief had brought her
and the soldier false was he,
on the banks of Allan Water,
none so sad as she.

3 On the banks of Allan Water,
when the winter snow fell fast.
Still was seen the miller's daughter
chilling blew the blast.
But the miller's lovely daughter,
both from cold and care was free.
On the banks of Allan Water
there a corpse lay she.

COTTON-EYED JOE

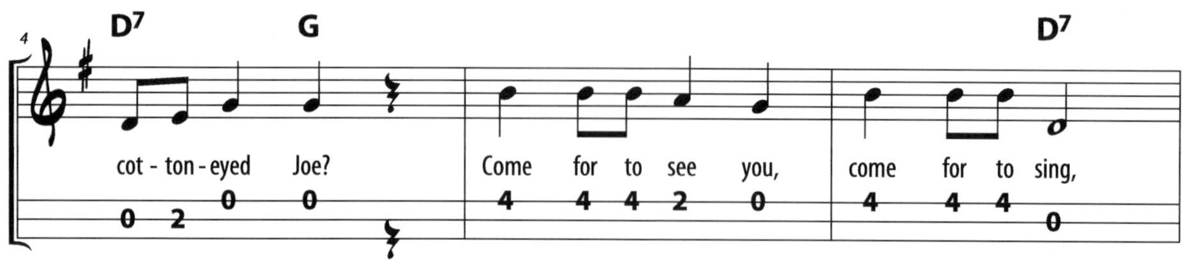

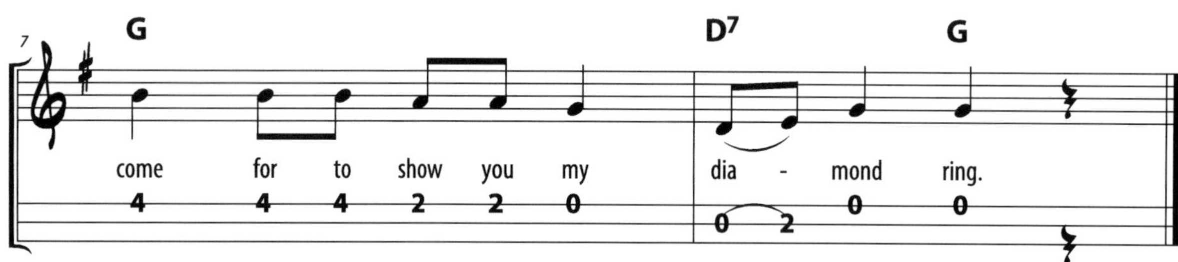

2 Do you remember a long time ago,
there was a man called cotton-eyed Joe?
Could have been married a long time ago,
hadn't it been for cotton-eyed Joe.

3 Old bull fiddle and a shoe-string bow,
wouldn't play nothin' like cotton-eyed Joe.
Play it fast or play it slow,
can't play nothin' like cotton-eyed Joe.

STRUMMING PATTERN

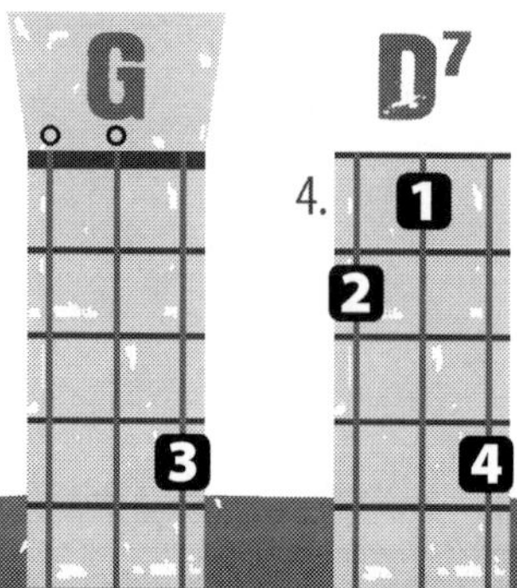

Cumberland Gap

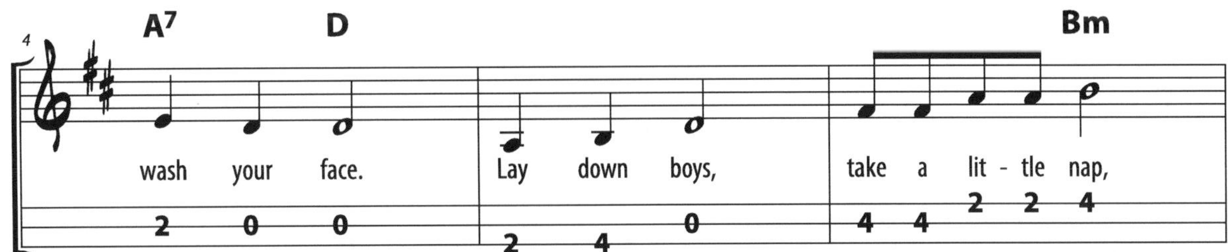

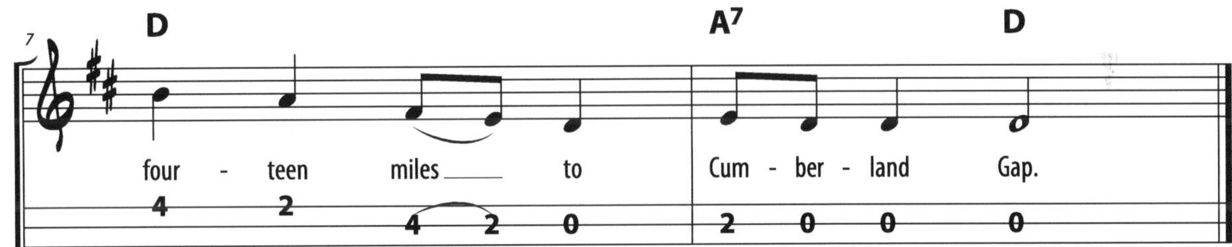

2 Me and my wife and my wife's pap,
we all live down in Cumberland Gap.
Me and my wife and my wife's pap,
we all live down in Cumberland Gap.

3 Cumberland Gap with its cliffs and rocks,
home of the panther, bear and fox.
Cumberland Gap with its cliffs and rocks,
home of the panther, bear and fox.

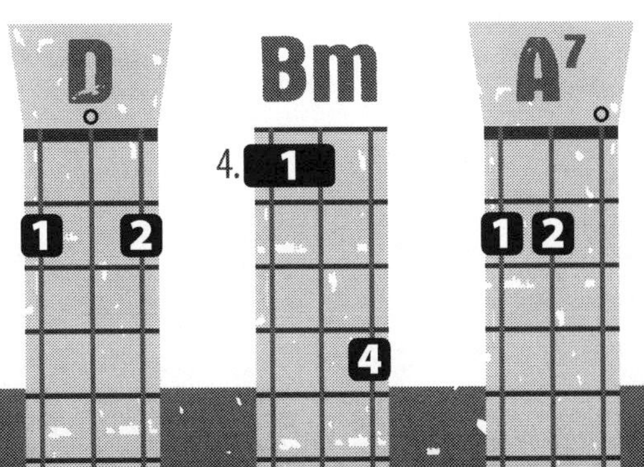

Erie Canal

D A7
We were for - ty miles from Al - ba - ny, for - get it I nev - er
D A7 D G D A7
shall. What a ter - ri - ble storm we had one night on the E - ri - e Ca -
D
nal. Oh, the E - r - ie was a - ris - ing and the
A7 D A7 D G
gin was a - get - ting low. And I scarce - ly think we'll get a drink till we
D A7 D A7 D
get to Buff - a - lo - o - o, till we get to Buff - a - lo.

2 We were loaded down with barley,
we were chock-full up on rye.
The captain he looked down at me
with his gol-durned wicked eye.
Oh, the Erie was a-rising ...

3 Two days out from Syracuse
the vessel struck a shoal;
We like to all be foundered
on a chunk o' Lackawanna coal.
Oh, the Erie was a-rising ...

4 We hollered to the captain
on the towpath, treadin' dirt.
He jumped on board and stopped the leak
with his old red flannel shirt.
Oh, the Erie was a-rising ...

5 The cook she was a grand old gal,
stood six foot in her socks.
Had a foot just like an elephant,
and her breath would open locks.
Oh, the Erie was a-rising ...

6 The wind began to whistle,
the waves began to roll.
We had to reef our royals
on that ragin' canal.
Oh, the Erie was a-rising ...

7 The cook came to our rescue,
she had a ragged dress;
We hissed her upon the pole
as a signal of distress.
Oh, the Erie was a-rising ...

8 When we got to Syracuse
off-mule, he was dead;
The nigh mule got blind staggers,
and we cracked him on the head.
Oh, the Erie was a-rising ...

9 The captain, he got married,
the cook, she went to jail.
And I'm the only son-of-a-gun
that's left to tell the tale.
Oh, the Erie was a-rising ...

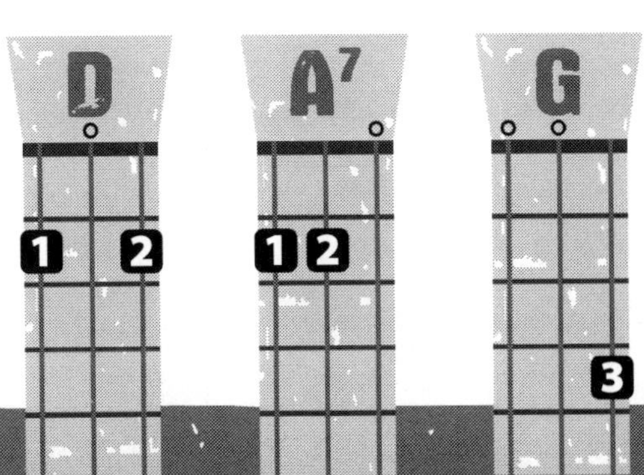

Banks of Sacramento

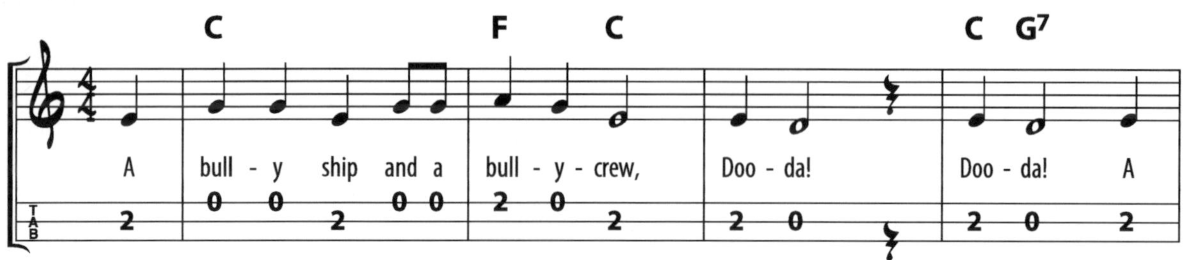

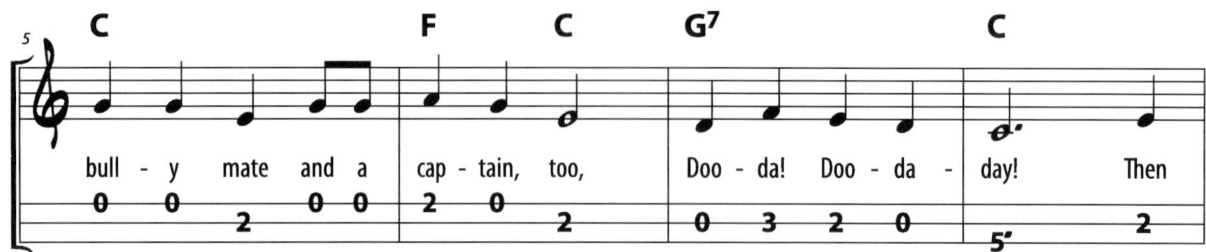

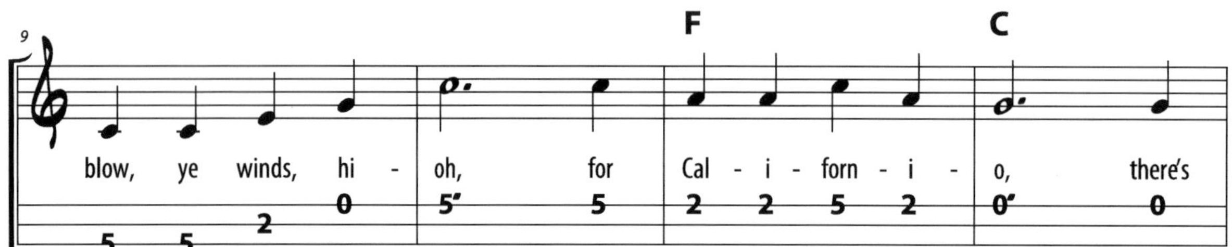

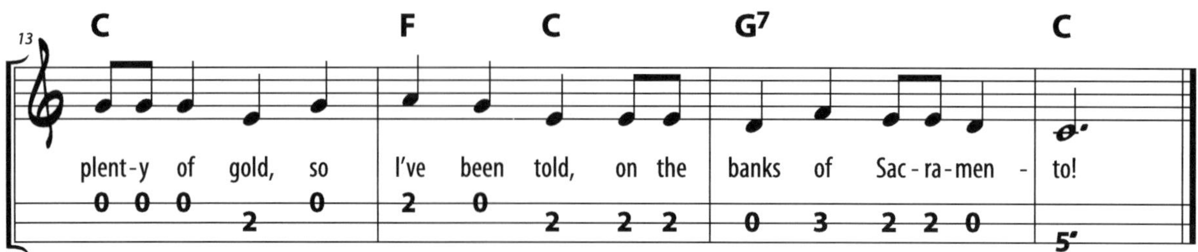

2 Oh, heave, my lads, oh heave and sing,
oh, heave and make those oak sticks sing.

3 Our money gone, we shipped to go,
around Cape Horn, through ice and snow.

4 Oh, around the Horn with a mainskys'l set
around Cape Horn and we're all wringin' wet.

5 Around Cape Horn in the month of May,
with storm winds blowing every day.

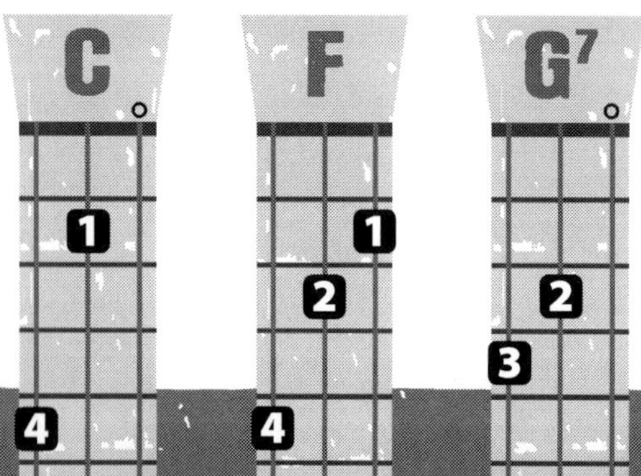

COLORADO TRAIL

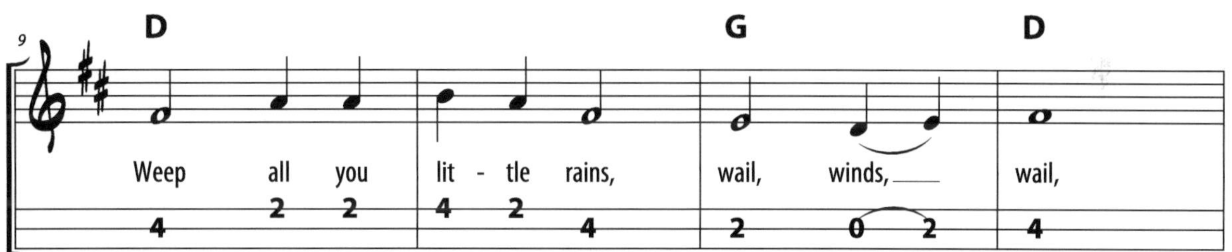

STRUMMING PATTERN

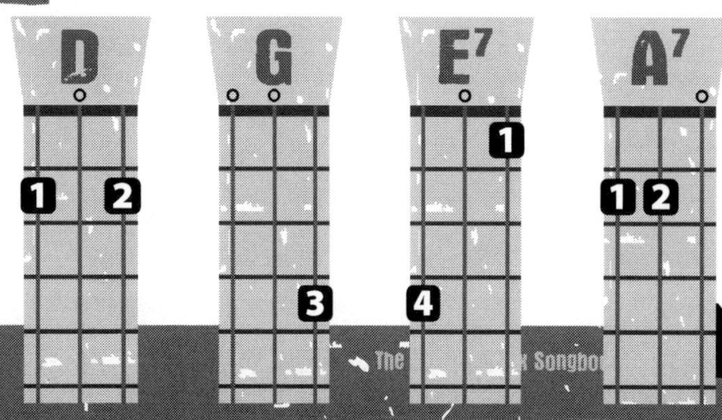

Auld Lang Syne

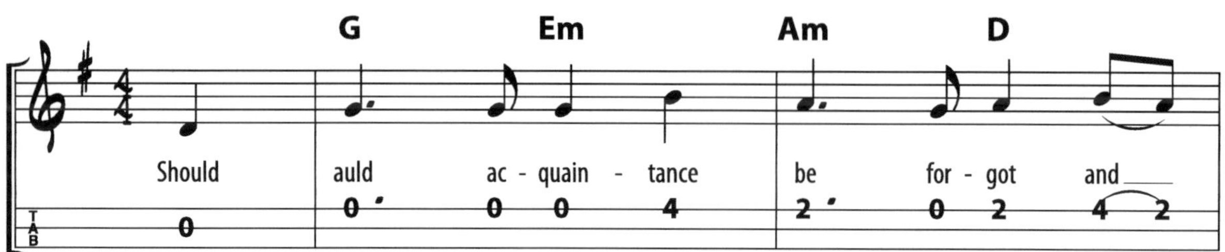

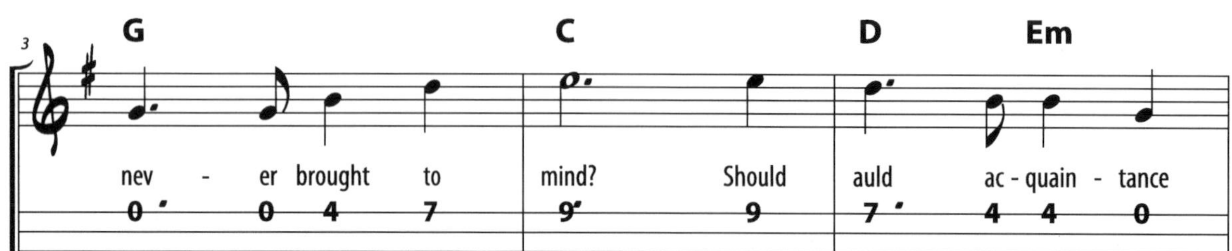

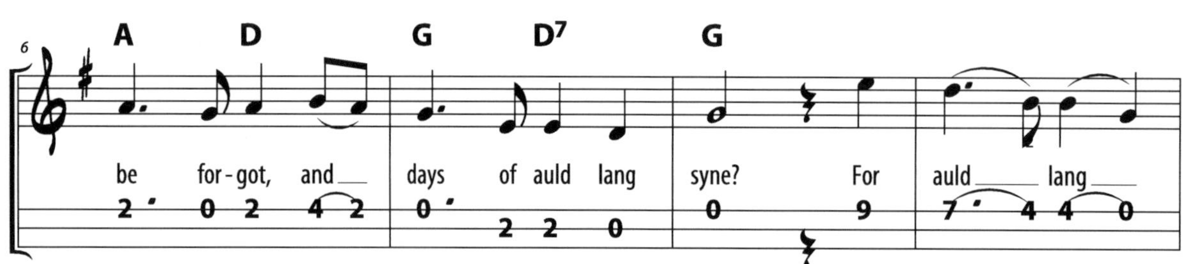

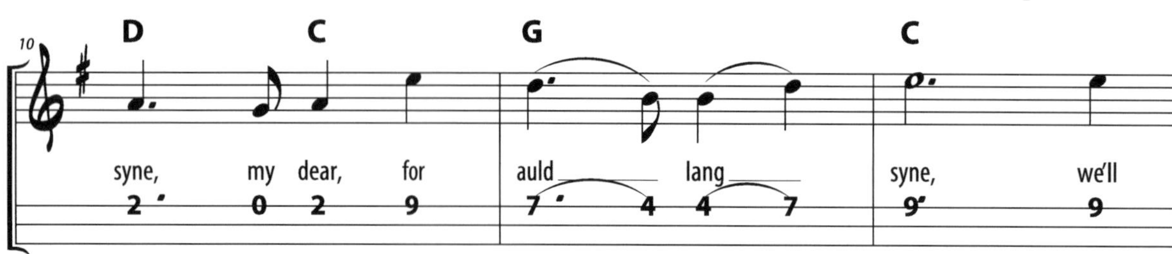

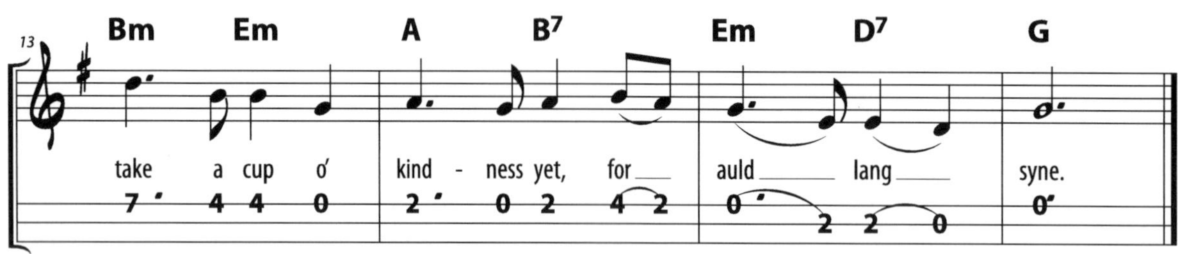

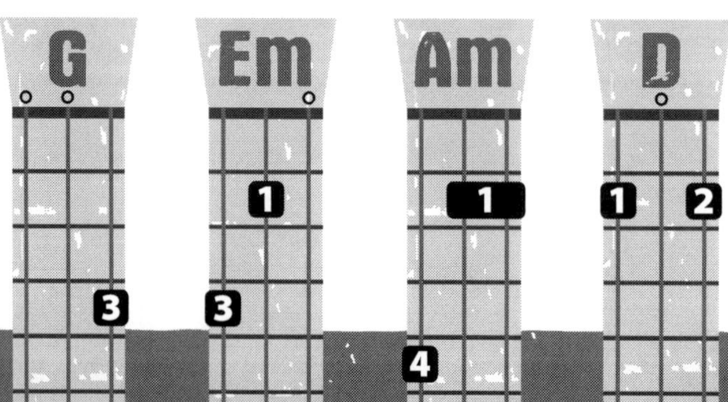

CHORUS:

For auld lang syne, my dear,
for auld lang syne,
we'll take a cup o' kindness yet,
for auld lang syne.

2 And surely ye'll be your pint-stoup!
and surely I'll be mine!
And we'll tak' a cup o' kindness yet,
for auld lang syne.

3 We twa hae run about the braes,
and pou'd the gowans fine;
But we've wander'd mony a weary fit,
sin' auld lang syne.

4 We twa hae paidl'd in the burn,
frae morning sun till dine;
But seas between us braid hae roar'd
sin' auld lang syne.

5 And there's a hand, my trusty fiere!
and gie's a hand o' thine!
And we'll tak' a right gude-willie waught,
for auld lang syne.

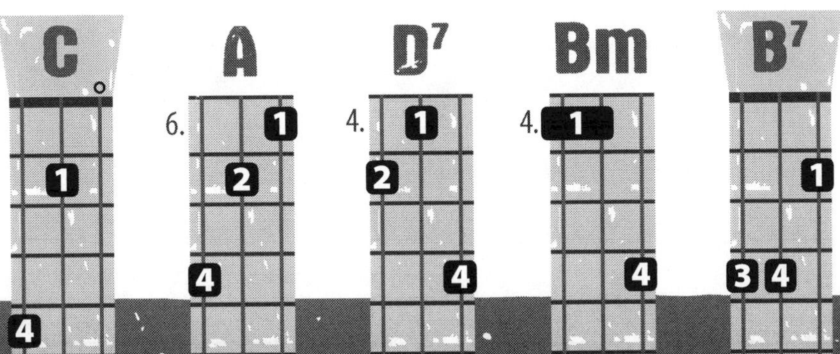

Billy the Kid

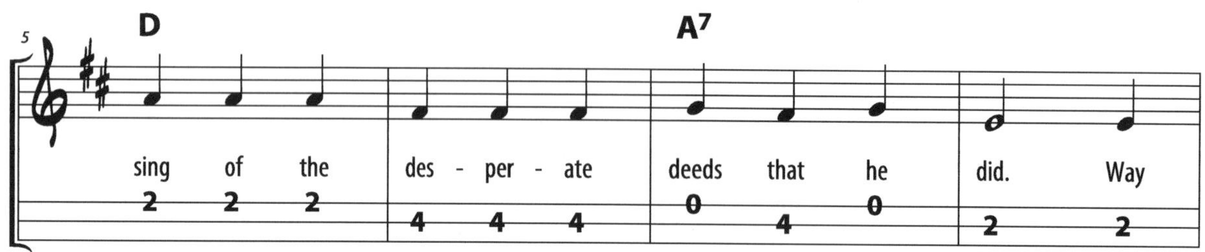

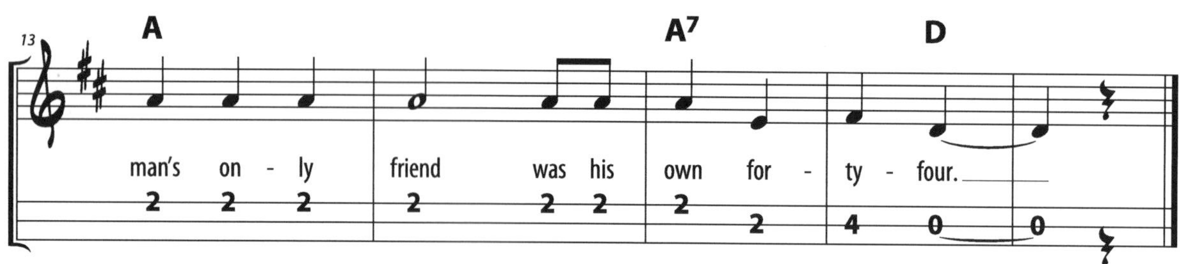

Strumming Pattern

2 When Billy the Kid was a very young lad,
in old Silver City he went to the bed.
Way out in the west with a knife in his hand,
at the age of twelve years he killed his first man.

3 Fair Mexico maidens play guitars and sing,
songs about Billy their boy bandit king.
Now here is young manhood that reached its sad end,
de'd notches on his pistol for twenty-one men.

4 Now 'twas on the same night that poor Billy died,
he said to his friends: "I'm not satisfied.
It's twenty-one men that I've put bullets through,
and sherriff Pat Garrett's gonna make twenty-two".

5 Now this is how Billy the Kid met his fate,
the bright moon was shining and the hour was late.
Shot down by Pat Garrett who once was his friend,
the poor outlaw's life had reached its sad end.

6 There's many a fine boy with a face fine and fair,
who starts out in life with a chance to be square.
But just like poor Billy he wanders astray,
then he loses his life in the very same way.

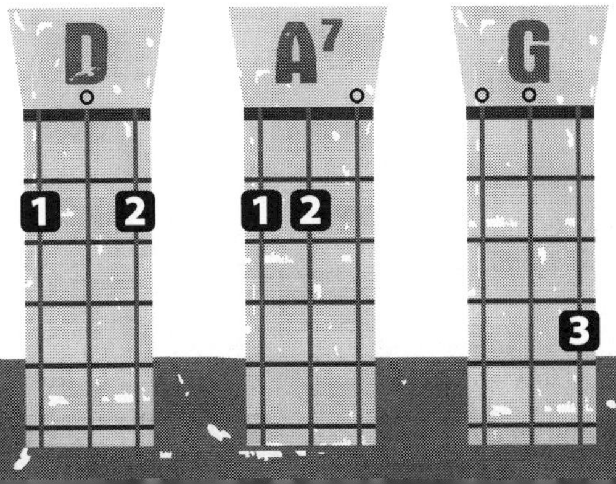

D A7 G

DOWN IN THE VALLEY

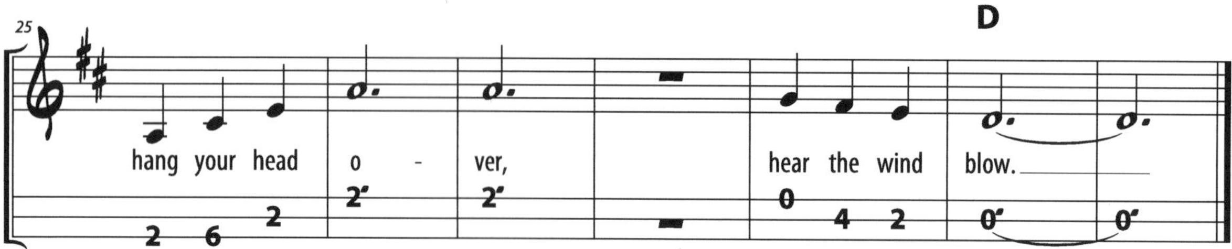

2 Roses love sunshine, violets love dew,
angels in Heaven know I love you,
know I love you, dear, know I love you,
angels in Heaven know I love you.

3 If you don't love me, love whom you please,
throw your arms round me, give my heart ease,
give my heart ease, dear, give my heart ease,
throw your arms round me, give my heart ease.

4 Build me a castle, forty feet high;
So I can see her as she rides by,
as she rides by, dear, as she rides by,
so I can see her as she rides by.

5 Write me a letter, send it by mail;
Send it in care of the Birmingham jail,
Birmingham jail, dear, Birmingham jail,
send it in care of the Birmingham jail.

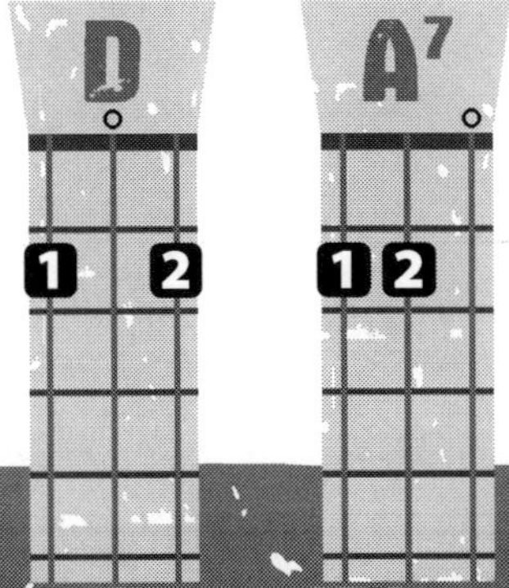

BUFFALO GALS

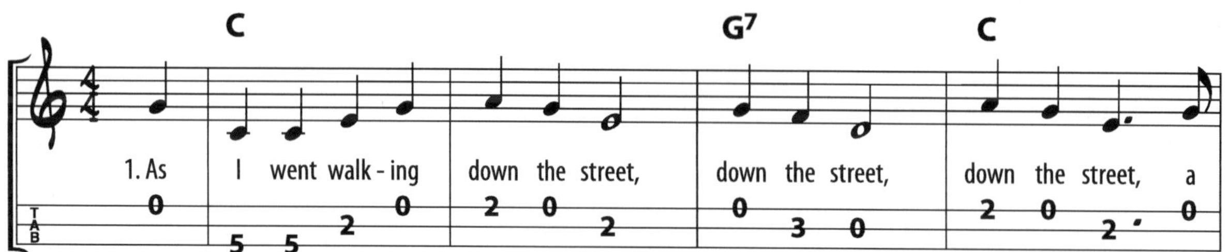

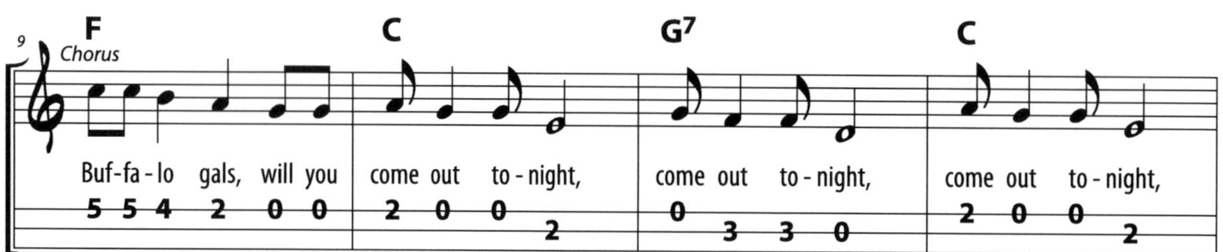

2 I asked her would she have some talk,
have some talk, have some talk.
Her feet covered the whole sidewalk
as she stood close by me.

3 I asked her would she have a dance,
have a dance, have a dance.
I thought I might get a chance
to shake a foot with her.

4 I'd like to make that gal my wife,
gal my wife, gal my wife.
I'd be happy all my life.
If I had her by me.

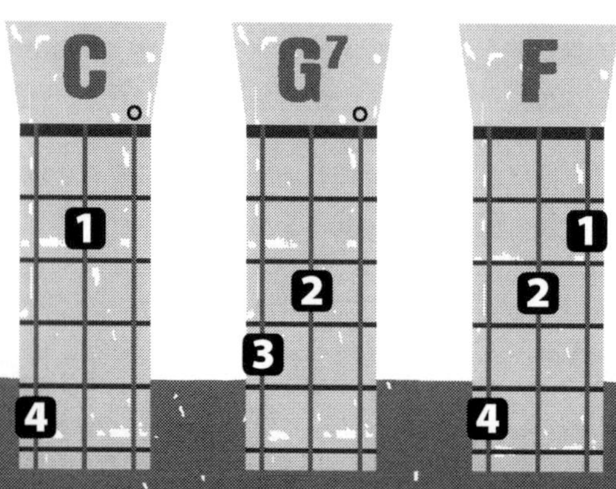

AWAY IN A MANGER

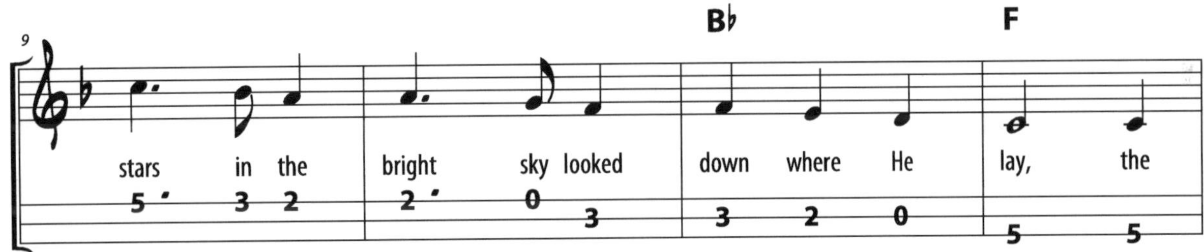

2 The cattle are lowing
the poor Baby wakes.
But little Lord Jesus
no crying He makes.

I love Thee, Lord Jesus,
look down from the sky
and stay by my side,
'til morning is nigh.

3 Be near me, Lord Jesus,
I ask Thee to stay.
Close by me forever
and love me I pray.
Bless all the dear children
in Thy tender care
and take us to heaven
to live with Thee there.

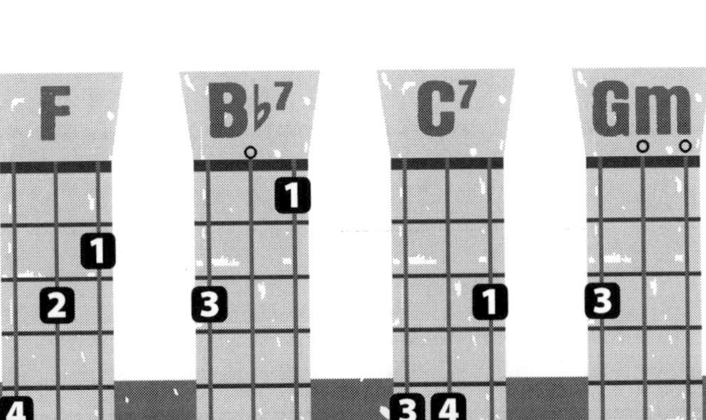

DARLING COREY

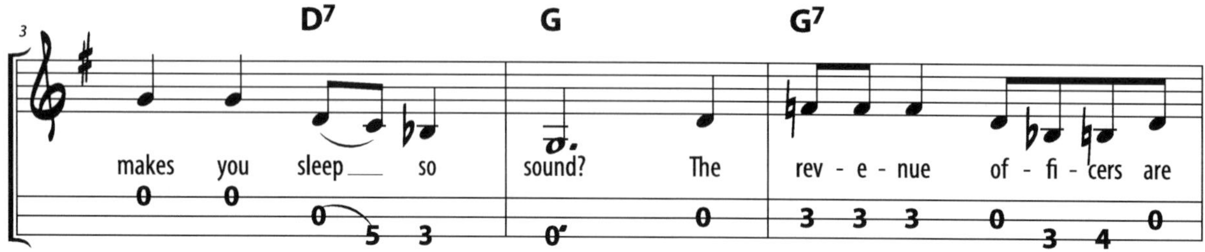

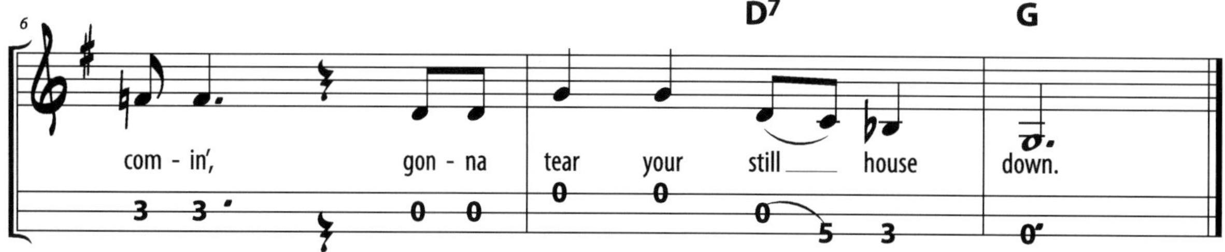

CHORUS

Dig a hole, dig a hole in the meadow,
dig a hole in the cold, cold ground.
Dig a hole, dig a hole in the meadow,
gonna lay darling Corey down.

2 Oh the first time I saw darling Corey,
she was standing in the door.
She had her shoes and her stockings in her hand
and her little bare feet on the floor.
Dig a hole, dig a hole in the meadow ...

3 Oh the next time I saw darling Corey,
she was standing by the banks of the sea.
She had a .44 strapped around her body
and a banjo on her knee.
Dig a hole, dig a hole in the meadow ...

4 Oh the last time I saw darling Corey,
she had a wine glass in her hand.
She was drinking that sweet liquor
with a low-down gamblin' man.
Dig a hole, dig a hole in the meadow ...

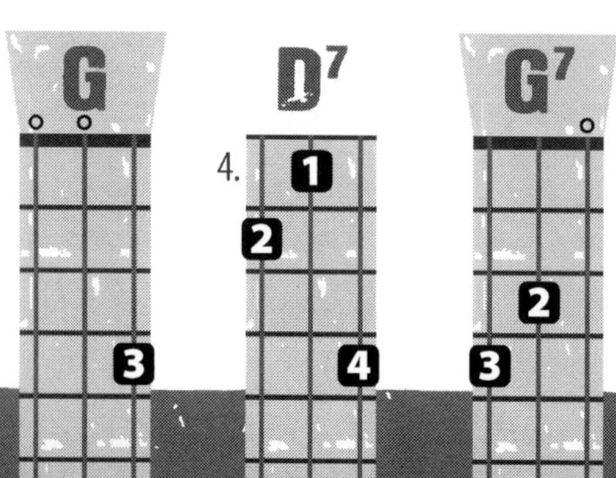

Good Night, Ladies

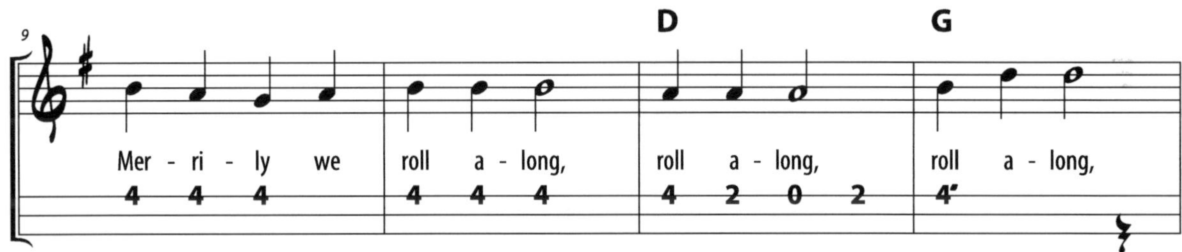

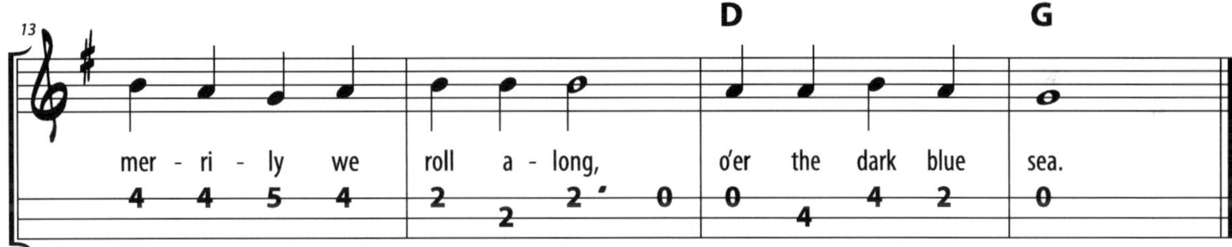

2 Farewell, ladies! (3x)
We're going to leave you now.
Merrily we roll along,
roll along, roll along,
merrily we roll along,|
o'er the deep blue sea.

3 Sweet dreams, ladies! (3x)
We're going to leave you now.
Merrily we roll along,
roll along, roll along,
merrily we roll along,|
o'er the deep blue sea.

G D C

Jesse James

G C G
Jes - se James was a lad who killed ma-ny a man, he
0 0 4 4 2 0 0 2 0 0 2 0 0

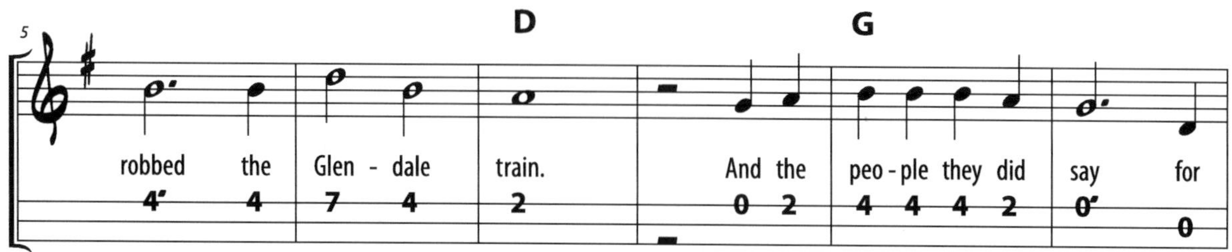
5
D G
robbed the Glen - dale train. And the peo - ple they did say for
4 4 7 4 2 0 2 4 4 4 2 0 0

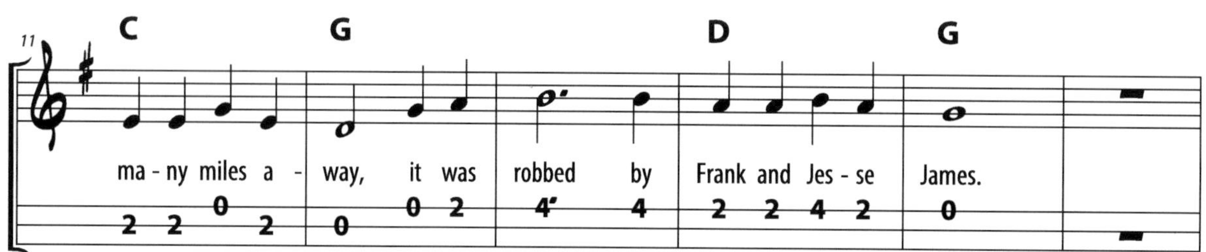
11
C G D G
ma - ny miles a - way, it was robbed by Frank and Jes - se James.
2 2 0 2 0 0 2 4 4 2 2 4 2 0

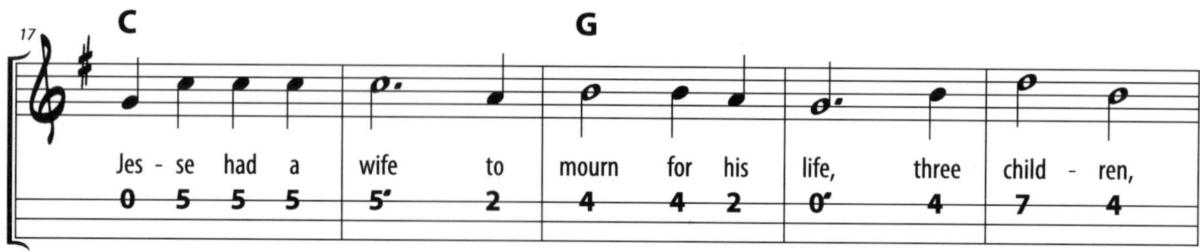
17
C G
Jes - se had a wife to mourn for his life, three child - ren,
0 5 5 5 5 2 4 4 2 0 4 7 4

22
D G
they were brave. But that dirt - y lit - tle cow - ard who
7 4 2 0 2 4 4 4 2 0 0 0

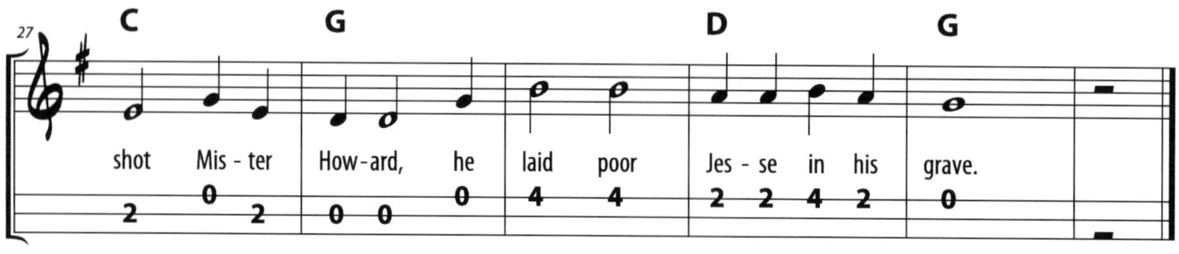
27
C G D G
shot Mis - ter How - ard, he laid poor Jes - se in his grave.
2 0 2 0 0 0 4 4 2 2 4 2 0

2 Well it was Robert Ford, that dirty little coward,
I wonder how he feels.
For he ate of Jesse's bread and he slept in Jesse's bed,
and he laid poor Jesse in his grave.
Jesse had a wife ...

3 Jesse was a man, a friend to the poor,
he'd never rob a mother or a child.
There never was a man with the law in his hand,
that could take Jesse James alive.
Jesse had a wife ...

4 People held their breath when they heard of Jesse's death,
and wondered how he ever came to fall,
Robert Ford, it was a fact, he shot Jesse in the back,
while Jesse hung a picture on the wall.
Jesse had a wife ...

STRUMMING PATTERN

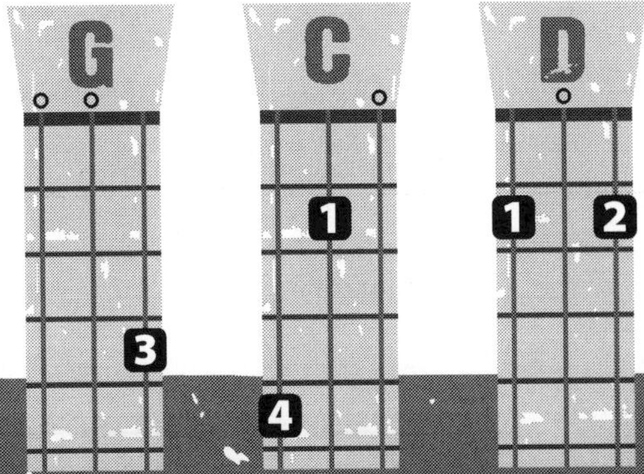

HOME! SWEET HOME!

2 An exile from home, spendor dazzles in vain,
oh, give me my lowly thatched cottage again;
The birds singing gaily, that come at my call;
Give me them, with that peace of mind, dearer than all.

3 To thee, I'll return, overburdened with care,
the heart's dearest solace will smile on me there.
No more from that cottage again will I roam,
be it ever so humble, there's no place like home.

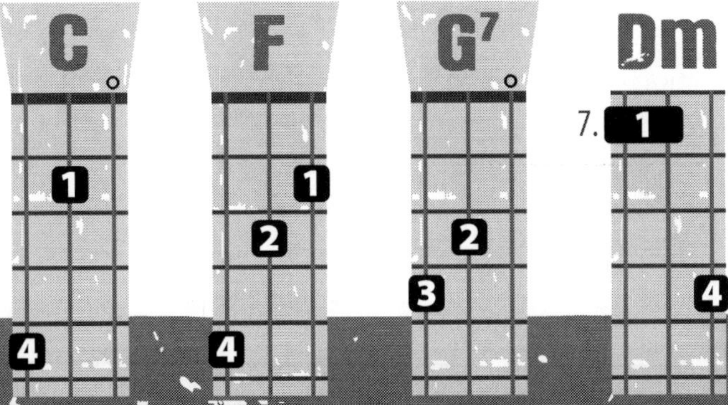

HARD TIMES COME AGAIN NO MORE

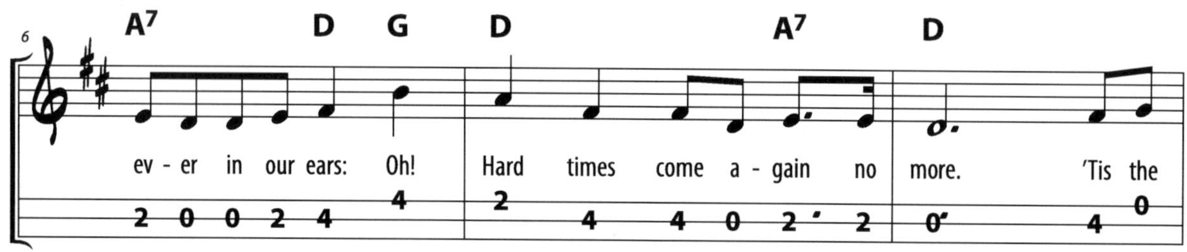

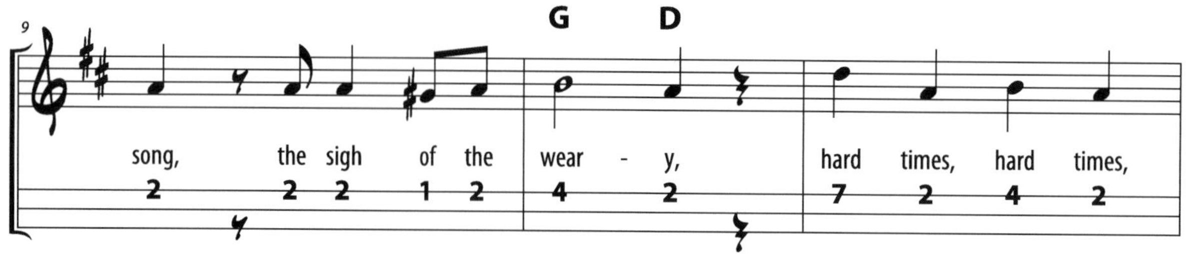

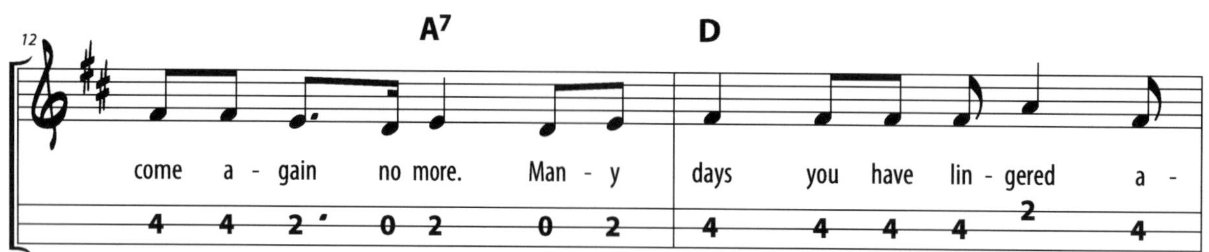

2 While we seek mirth and beauty and music light and gay,
there are frail forms fainting at the door;
Though their voices are silent, their pleading looks will say
Oh! Hard times come again no more.
'Tis the song, the sigh of the weary ...

3 There's a pale drooping maiden who toils her life away,
with a worn heart whose better days are o'er:
Though her voice would be merry, ,tis sighing all the day,
Oh! Hard times come again no more.
'Tis the song, the sigh of the weary ...

4 'Tis a sigh that is wafted across the troubled wave,
'tis a wail that is heard upon the shore,
'tis a dirge that is murmured around the lowly grave
Oh! Hard times come again no more.
'Tis the song, the sigh of the weary ...

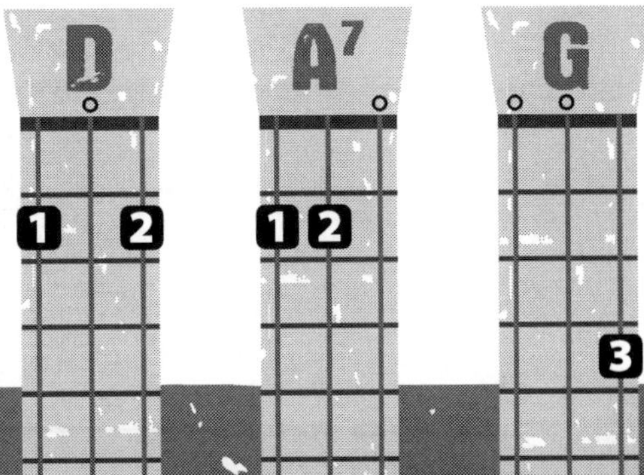

JINGLE BELLS

2 A day or two ago I thought I'd take a ride,
and soon Miss Fannie Bright was seated by my side.
The horse was lean and lank, misfortune seemed his lot,
he got into a drifted bank and we got upsot.

3 A day or two ago, the story I must tell.
I went out on the snow, and on my back I fell;
A gent was riding by in a one-horse open sleigh,
he laughed as there I sprawling lie, But quickly drove away.

4 Now the ground is white, go it while you're young,
take the girls tonight and sing this sleighing song.
Just get a bobtailed bay, two-forty for his speed,
then hitch him to an open sleigh, and crack! You'll take the lead.

D G A7 Em E7

LITTLE BROWN JUG

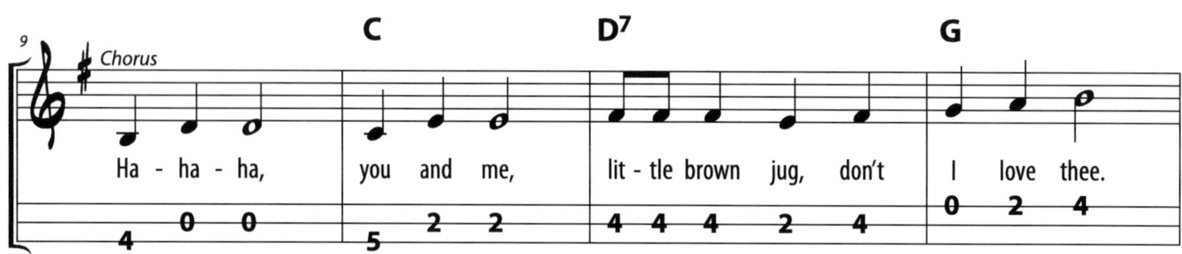

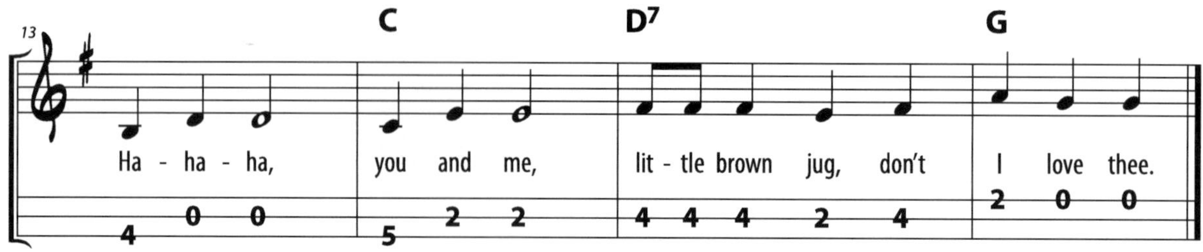

2 When I go toiling on the farm
I take the little jug under my arm;
Place it under a shady tree,
little brown jug, 'tis you and me.

3 'Tis you that makes me friends and foes,
'tis you that makes me wear old clothes;
But, seeing you're so near my nose,
tip her up and down she goes.

4 If all the folks in Adam's race
were gathered together in one place,
I'd let them go without a tear
before I'd part from you, my dear.

5 If I'd a cow that gave such milk,
I'd dress her in the finest silk;
Feed her up on oats and hay,
and milk her twenty times a day.

6 I bought a cow from Farmer Jones,
and she was nothing but skin and bones;
I fed her up as fine as silk,
she jumped the fence and strained her milk.

7 And when I die don't bury me at all,
just pickle my bones in alcohol;
Put a bottle o' booze at my head and feet
and then I know that I will keep.

8 The rose is red, my nose is too,
the violet's blue and so are you;
And yet, I guess, before I stop,
we'd better take another drop.

Strumming Pattern

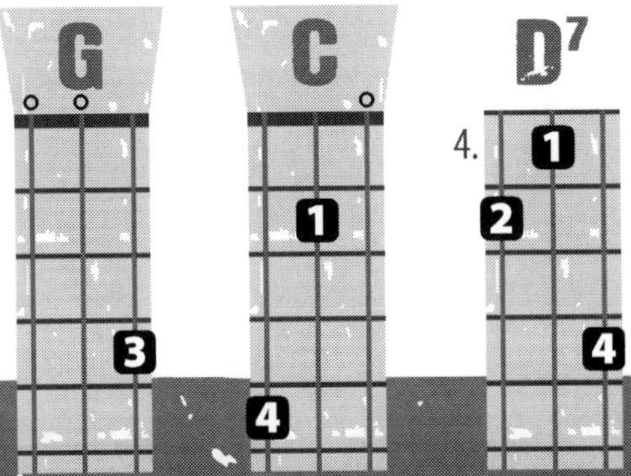

NINE POUND HAMMER

2 I'm going on the mountain just to see my baby,
and I ain't coming back, no, I ain't coming back.
Roll on buddy ...

3 There ain't one hammer down in this tunnel,
that can ring like mine, that can ring like mine.
Roll on buddy ...

4 Rings like silver, shines like gold,
rings like silver, shines like gold.
Roll on buddy ...

5 This old hammer it killed John Henry,
ain't gonna kill me, ain't gonna kill me.
Roll on buddy ...

6 It's a long way to Harlan, it's a long way to Hazard,
just to get a little brew, just to get a little brew.
Roll on buddy ...

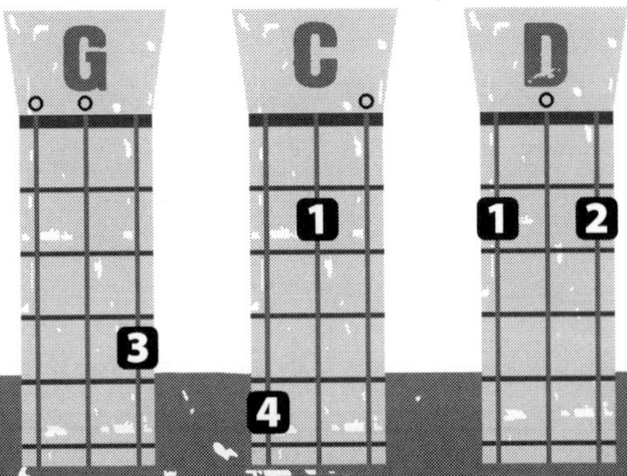

Reilly's Daughter

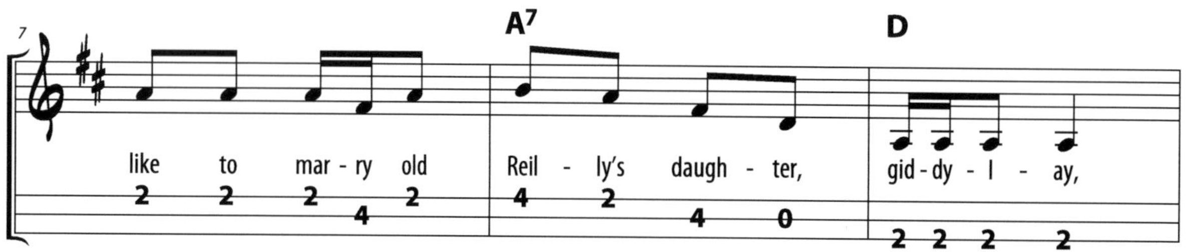

2 Reilly played on the big bass drum.
Reilly had a mind for murder and slaughter.
Reilly had a bright red glittering eye
and he kept that eye on his lovely daughter.
Giddy i-ae, Giddy i-ae ...

3 Her hair was black and her eyes were blue.
The colonel and the major and the captain sought her.
The sergeant and the private and the drummer boy too.
But they never had a chance with Reilly's daughter.
Giddy i-ae, Giddy i-ae ...

4 I got me a ring and a parson, too.
Got me a scratch in a married quarter.
Settled me down to a peaceful life,
happy as a king with Reilly's daughter.
Giddy i-ae, Giddy i-ae ...

5 Suddenly a footstep on the stairs
who should it be but Reilly out for slaughter.
With two pistols in his hands
looking for the man who had married his daughter.
Giddy i-ae, Giddy i-ae ...

6 I caught O'Reilly by the hair,
rammed his head in a pail of water.
Fired his pistols into the air,
a damned sight quicker than I married his daughter.
Giddy i-ae, Giddy i-ae ...

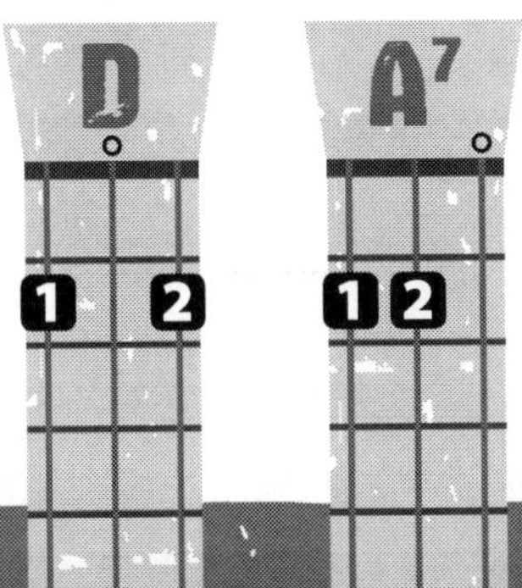

Scarborough Fair

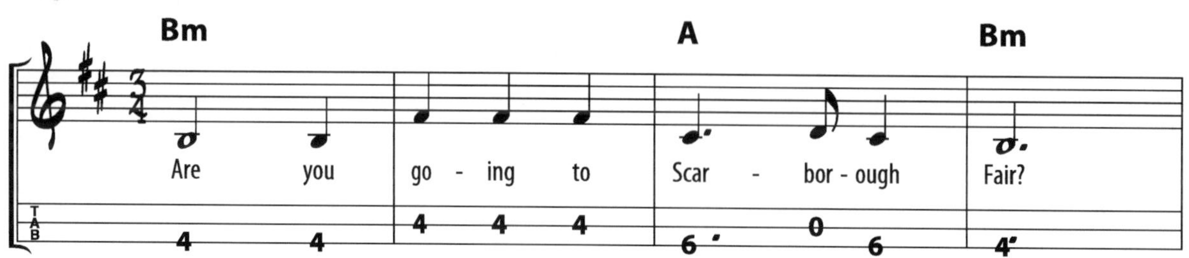

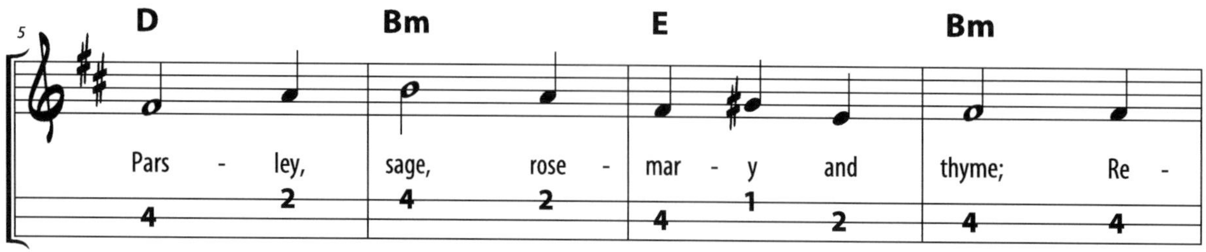

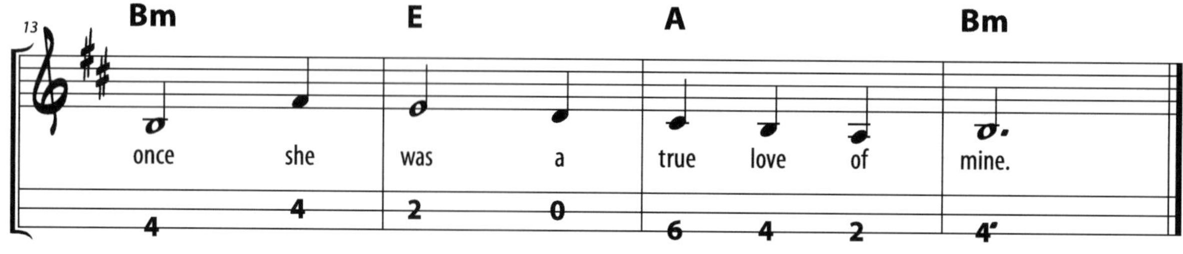

Strumming Pattern

2 Tell her to make me a cambric shirt,
parsley, sage, rosemary, and thyme;
Without a seam or needlework,
then she shall be a true love of mine.

3 Tell her to wash it in yonder well,
parsley, sage, rosemary, and thyme;
where never spring water or rain ever fell,
and she shall be a true love of mine.

4 Tell her to dry it on yonder thorn,
parsley, sage, rosemary, and thyme;
Which never bore blossom since Adam was born,
then she shall be a true love of mine.

5 Now he has asked me questions three,
parsley, sage, rosemary, and thyme;
I hope he'll answer as many for me
before he shall be a true love of mine.

6 Tell him to buy me an acre of land,
parsley, sage, rosemary, and thyme;
Between the salt water and the sea sand,
then he shall be a true love of mine.

7 Tell him to plough it with a ram's horn,
parsley, sage, rosemary, and thyme;
And sow it all over with one pepper corn,
and he shall be a true love of mine.

8 Tell him to sheer't with a sickle of leather,
parsley, sage, rosemary, and thyme;
And bind it up with a peacock feather.
And he shall be a true love of mine.

9 Tell him to thrash it on yonder wall,
parsley, sage, rosemary, and thyme,
and never let one corn of it fall,
then he shall be a true love of mine.

10 When he has done and finished his work.
Parsley, sage, rosemary, and thyme:
Oh, tell him to come and he'll have his shirt,
and he shall be a true love of mine.

Bm 4. 1 4

A 6. 1 2 4

D 1 2

E 1 2 4

G 3

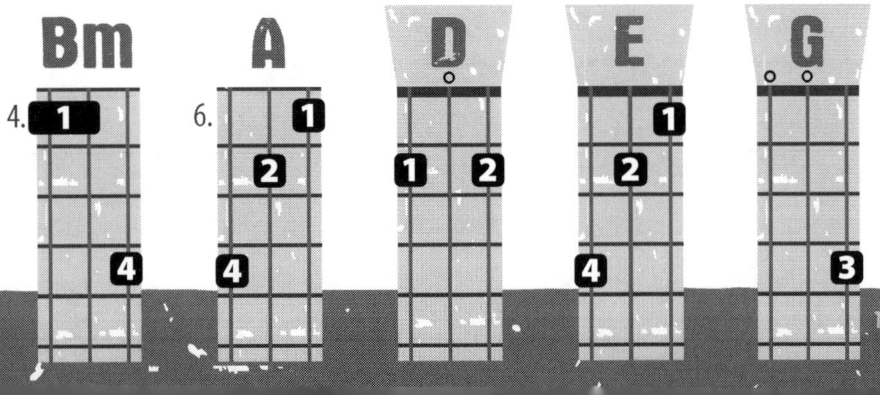

Shortnin' Bread

2 Put on the skillet, slip on the lid,
mama's gonna bake a little shortnin' bread.
This ain't all she's gonna do.
Mama's gonna make a little coffee, too.
Mama's little baby loves ...

3 When those children, sick in bed,
heard that talk about shortnin' bread.
Popped up well, to dance and sing,
skipped around and cut the pigeon wing.

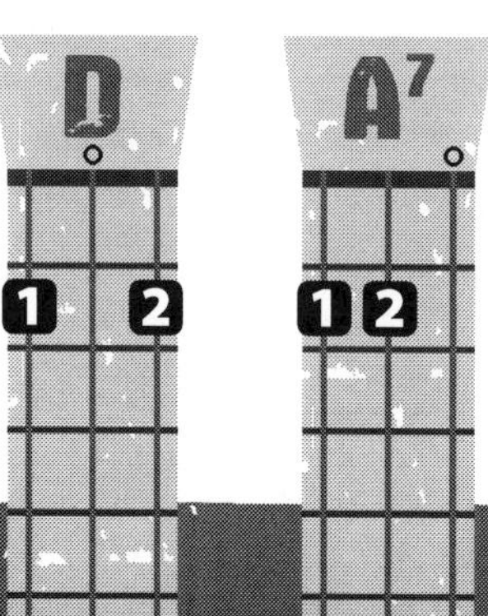

GREENSLEEVES

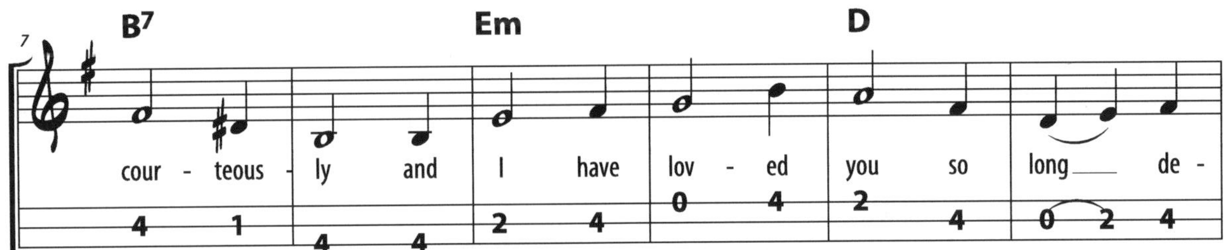

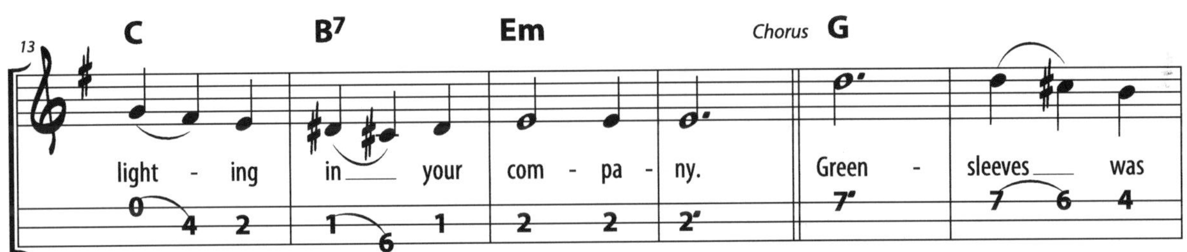

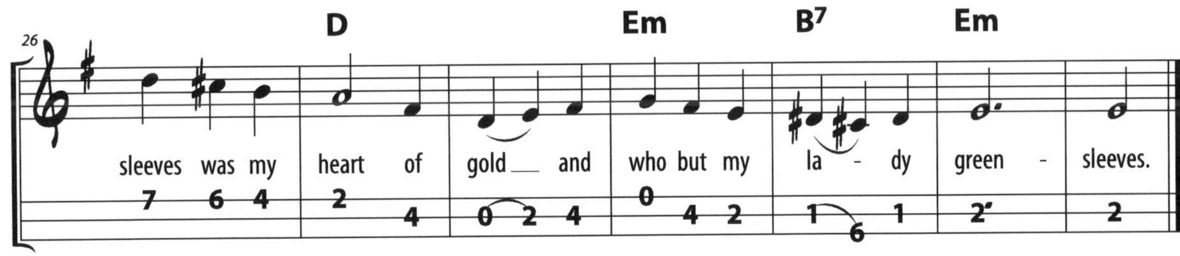

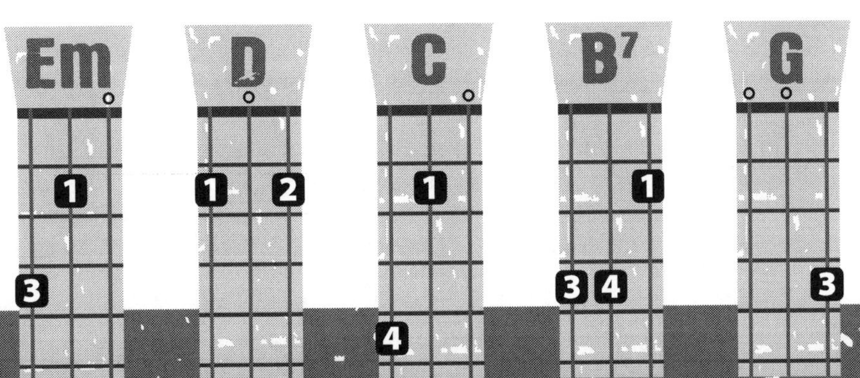

OH! SUSANNA

D
I came from A - la - ba - ma with my ban - jo on my

A7 D A7
knee, I'm goin' to Lou' - si - a - na, my Su - san - na for to

D G D A
see. Oh! Su - san - na, oh don't you cry for me, for I

D A7 D
come from A - la - ba - ma with my ban - jo on my knee.

2 I had a dream the other night
when ev'rything was still;
I thought I saw Susanna
a-comin' down the hill;
the buckwheat cake was in her mouth,
the tear was in her eye;
says I, I'm comin' from the south,
Susanna, don't you cry.
Oh! Susanna,
o, don't you cry for me ...

3 I soon will be in New Orleans,
and then I'll look around,
and when I find Susanna
I'll fall upon the ground.
And if I do not find her,
then I will surely die,
and when I'm dead and buried,
Susanna, don't you cry.
Oh! Susanna,
o, don't you cry for me ...

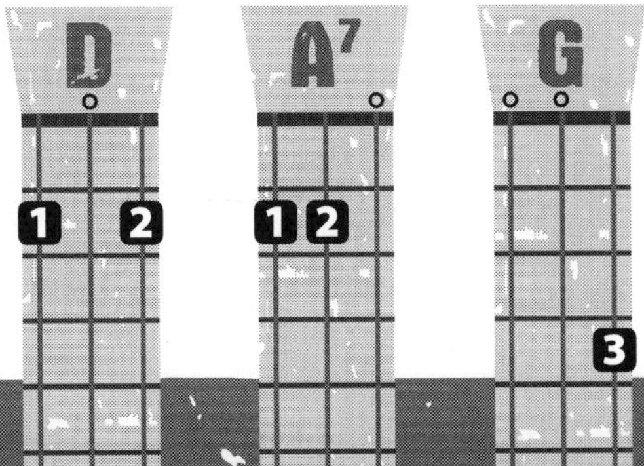

Rock My Soul

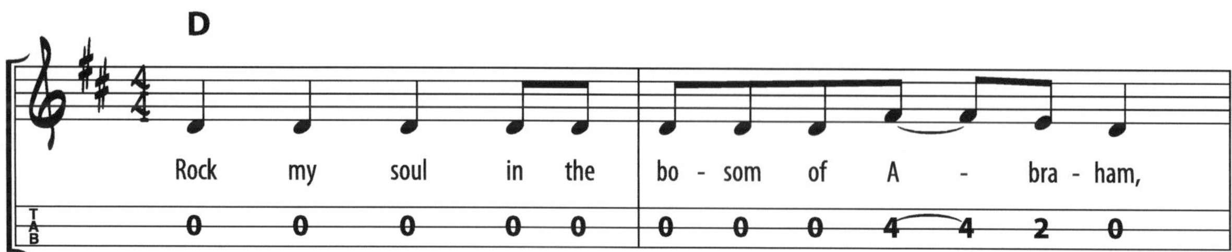
D
Rock my soul in the bo - som of A - bra - ham,

A7 D
rock my soul in the bo - som of A - bra - ham, rock my soul in the

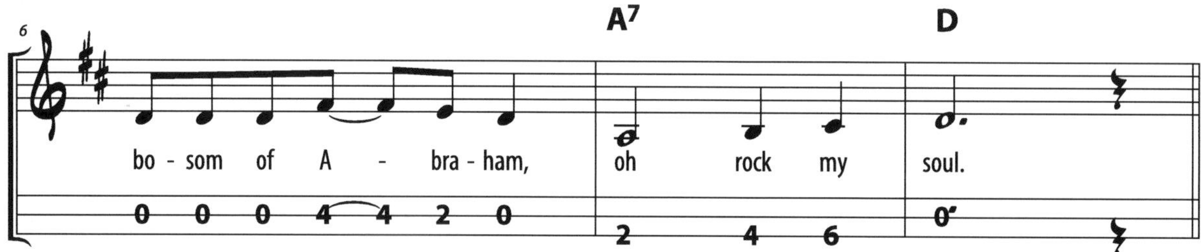
A7 D
bo - som of A - bra - ham, oh rock my soul.

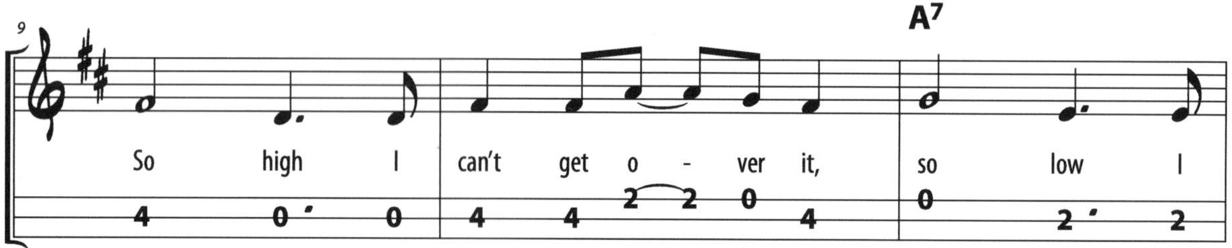
A7
So high I can't get o - ver it, so low I

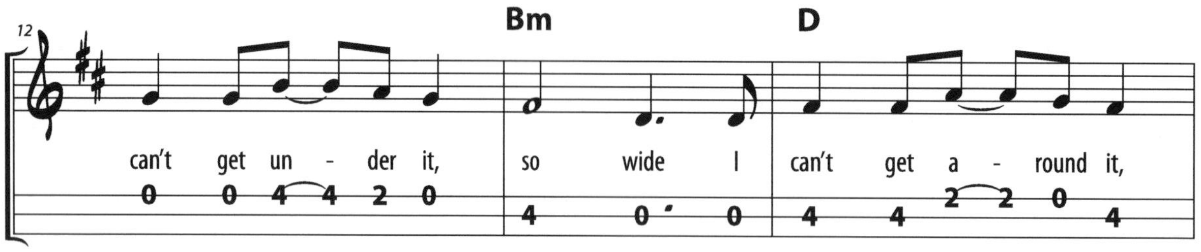
Bm D
can't get un - der it, so wide I can't get a - round it,

G A7 D
got - ta come in at the door. Rock my soul,

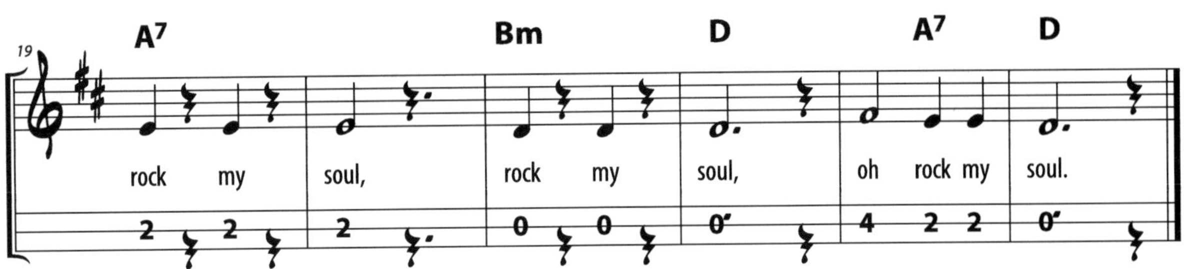

A7
Bm
D
A7
D
rock my soul, rock my soul, oh rock my soul.

STRUMMING PATTERN
Rock my soul in the

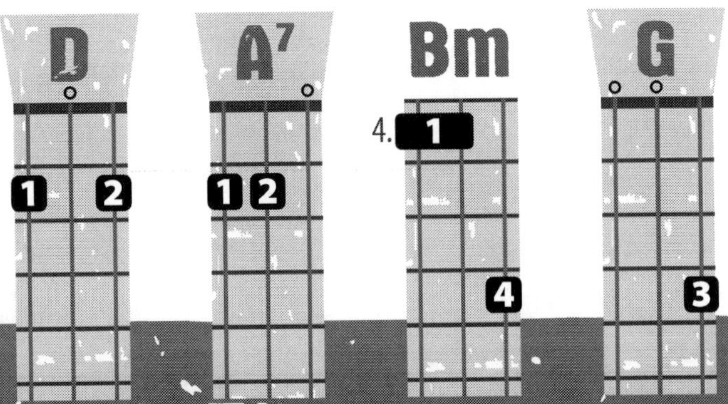

D
A7
Bm
G

POOR PADDY WORKS ON THE RAILWAY

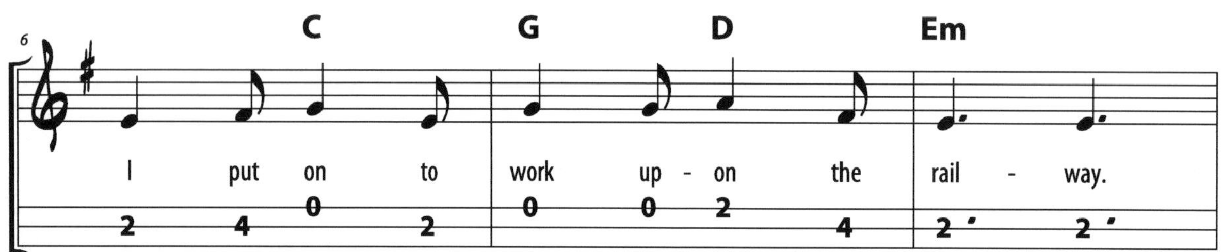

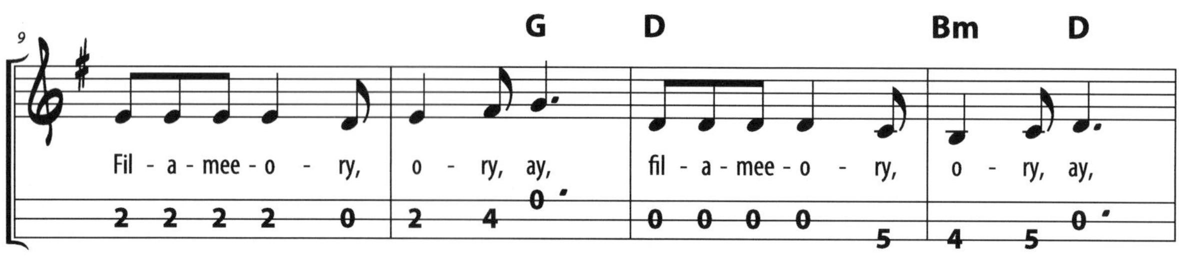

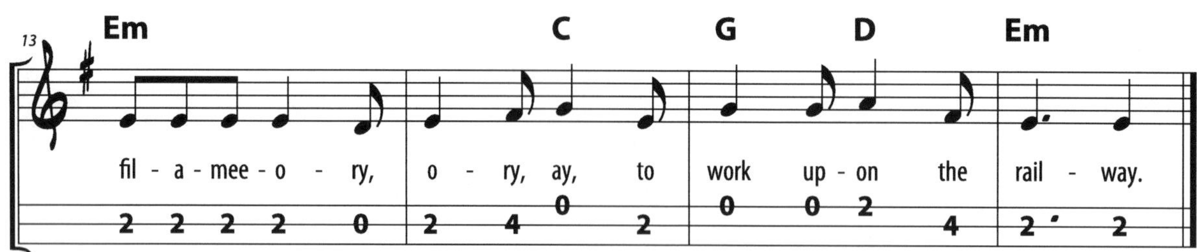

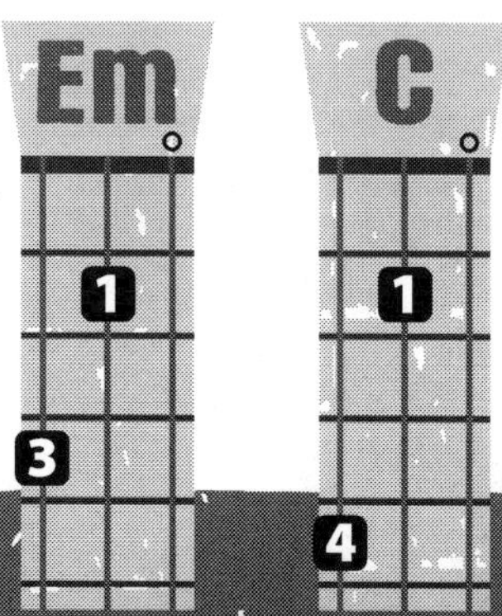

2 In eighteen hundred and forty-two
I didn't know what I should do.
I didn't know what I should do,
to work upon the railway, the railway,
I'm weary of the railway,
poor Paddy works on the railway.

3 In eighteen hundred and forty-three
I sailed away across the sea.
I sailed away across the sea,
to work upon the railway, the railway,
I'm weary of the railway,
poor Paddy works on the railway

4 In eighteen hundred and forty-four
I landed on Columbia's shore.
I landed on Columbia's shore,
to work upon the railway, the railway.
I'm weary of the railway,
poor Paddy works on the railway.

5 In eighteen hundred and forty-five
when Daniel O'Connell he was alive.
When Daniel O'Connell he was alive
to work upon the railway, the railway.
I'm weary of the railway,
poor Paddy works on the railway.

6 In eighteen hundred and forty-six
I made my trade to carrying bricks.
I made my trade to carrying bricks
for working on the railway.
I'm weary of the railway,
poor Paddy works on the railway.

7 In eighteen hundred and forty-seven
poor Paddy was thinking of going to Heaven.
poor Paddy was thinking of going to Heaven,
to work upon the railway, the railway.
I'm weary of the railway,
poor Paddy works on the railway.

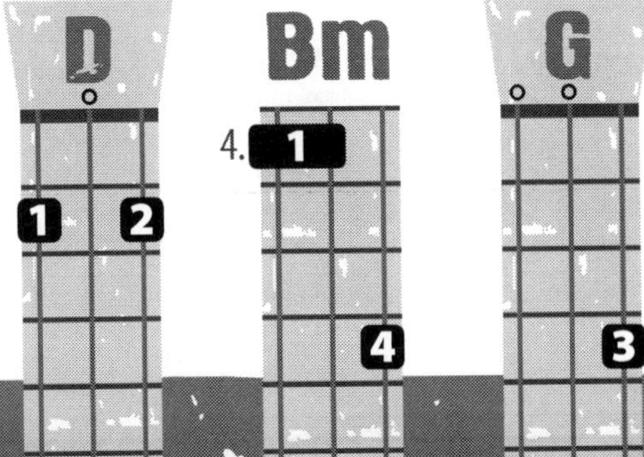

LONG JOURNEY HOME

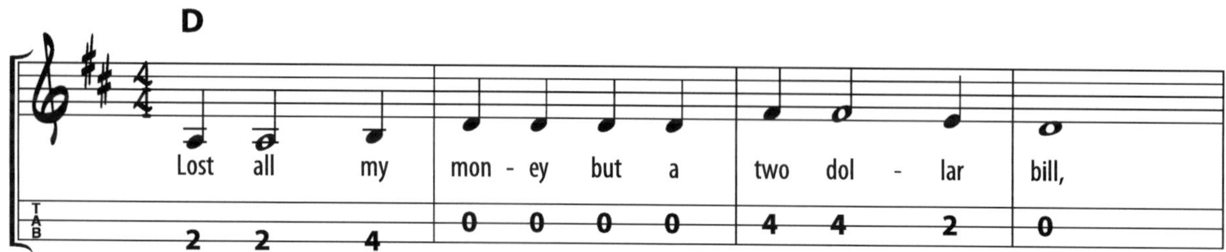

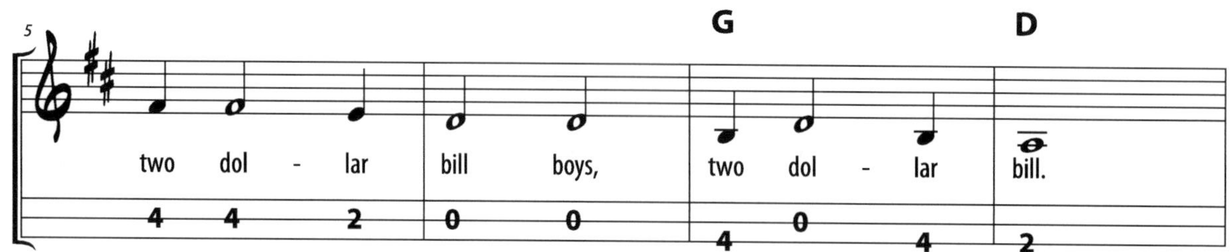

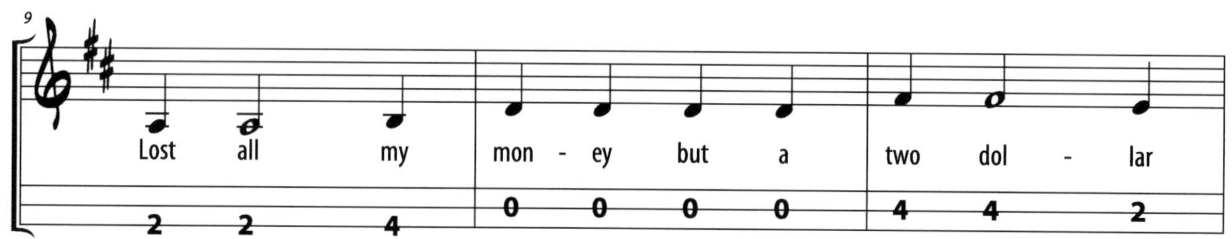

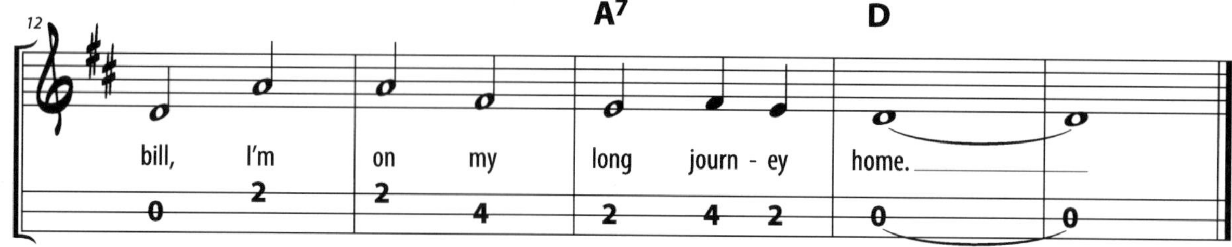

STRUMMING PATTERN

2 Cloudy in the west and it looks like rain,
looks like rain boy, looks like rain.
Cloudy in the west and it looks like rain,
I'm on my long journey home.

3 Black smoke a-rising and it surely is a train,
surely is a train boys, surely is a train.
Black smoke a-rising and it surely is a train,
I'm on my long journey home.

4 Homesick and lonesome and I'm feeling kind of blue,
feeling kind of blue boys, feeling kind of blue.
Homesick and lonesome and I'm feeling kind of blue,
I'm on my long journey home.

5 It's starting raining and I've got to go home,
I've got to go home boys, I've got to go home.
It's starting raining and I've got to go home,
I'm on my long journey home.

D G A7

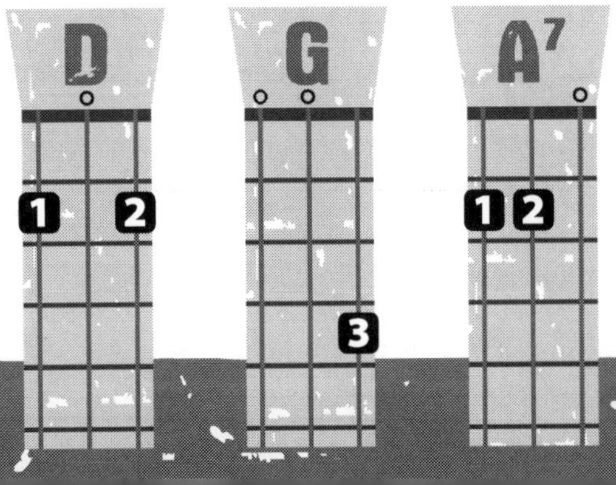

RED RIVER VALLEY

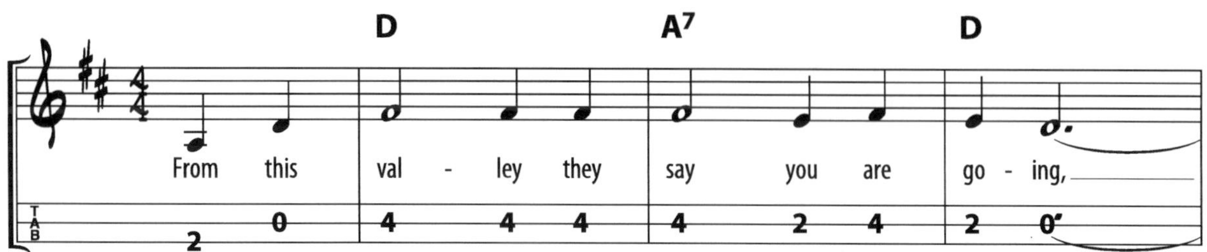

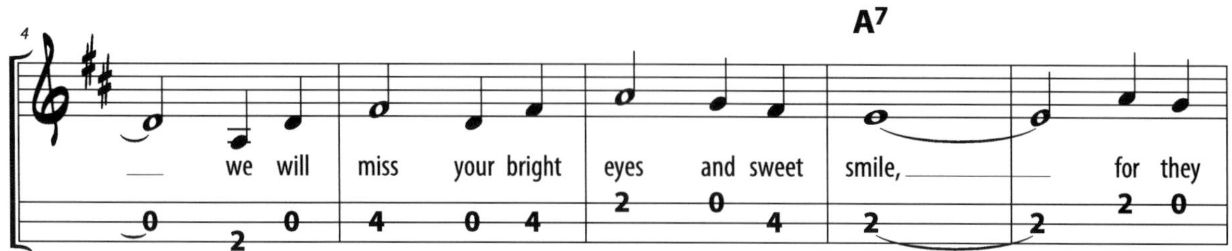

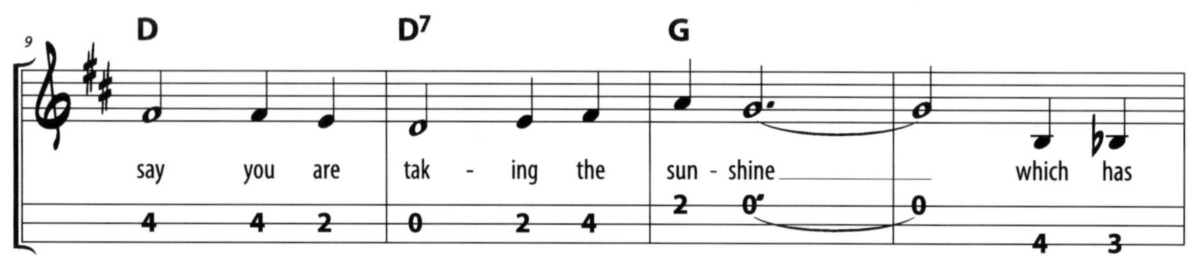

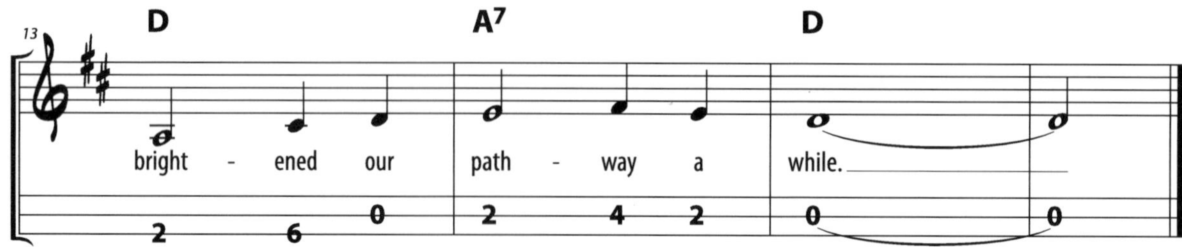

STRUMMING PATTERN

2 Come and sit by my side if you love me;
Do not hasten to bid me adieu,
but remember the Red River Valley,
and the girl that has loved you so true.

3 I've been thinking a long time, my darling,
of the sweet words you never would say,
now, alas, must my fond hopes all vanish?
For they say you are going away.

4 Won't you think of the valley you're leaving,
oh, how lonely and sad it will be,
just think of the fond heart you're breaking,
and the grief you are causing to me.

5 From this valley they say you are going,
when you go, may your darling go too?
Would you leave her behind unprotected,
when she loves no one other than you.

6 As you go to your home by the ocean,
may you never forget those sweet hours,
that we spent in the Red River Valley,
and the love we exchanged,mid the flowers.

7 I have promised you, darling, that never
will a word from my lips cause you pain,
and my life, it will be yours forever,
if you only will love me again.

8 They will bury me where you have wandered,
near the hills where the daffodils grow,
when you're gone from the Red River valley,
for I can't live without you I know.

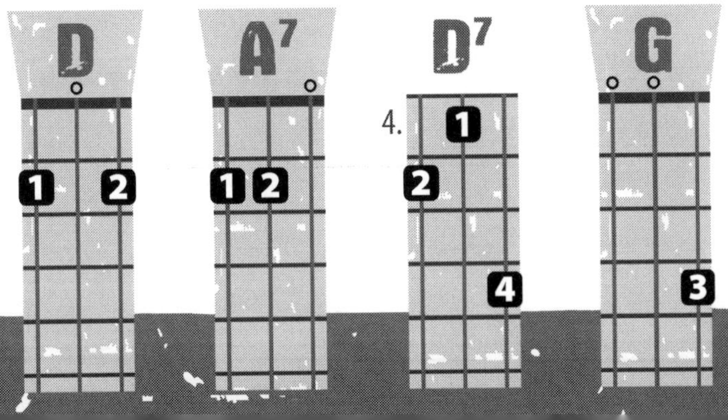

D A7 D7 G

4.

Make Me Down a Pallet

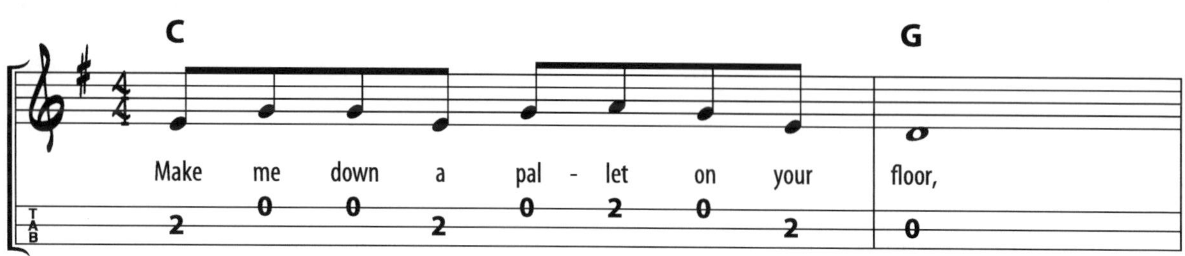

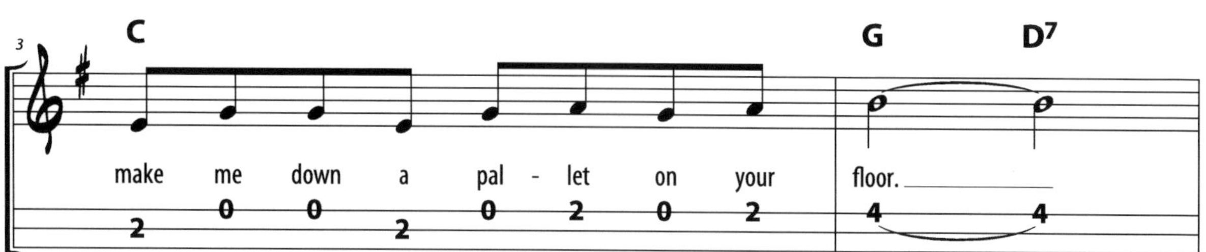

2 Up the country, where there's sleet and snow,
up the country where there's sleet and snow.
I'm goin' up the country where there's sleet and snow,
no tellin' how much further I may go.

3 Way of sleepin', my back and shoulders' tired,
Way of sleepin', my back and shoulders' tired.
This way of sleepin', my back and shoulders' tired,
Goin' turn over and try it on the side.

4 Don't you let my good girl catch you here,
please don't let my good girl catch you here.
Or she might shoot you, might cut and stab you, too,
ain't no tellin' just what she might do.

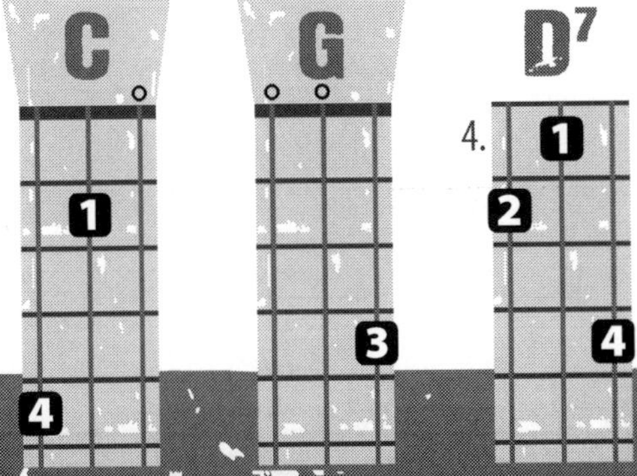

OLD BLACK JOE

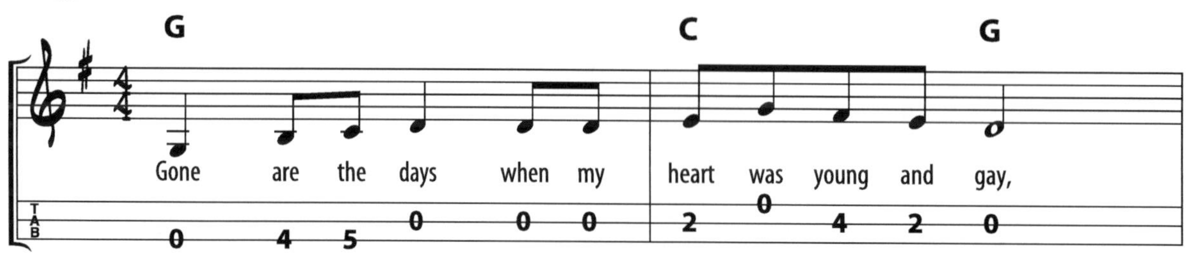

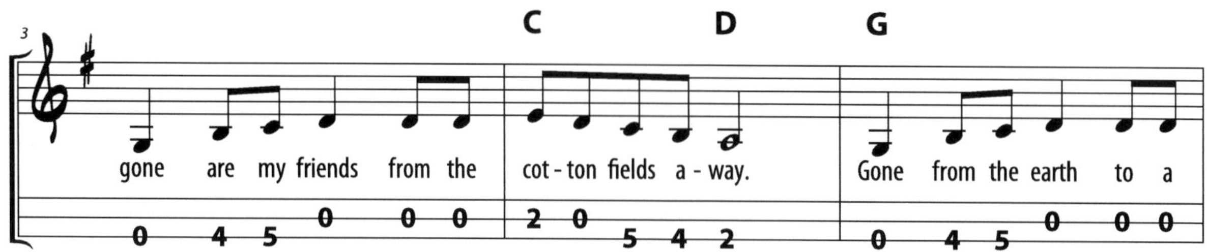

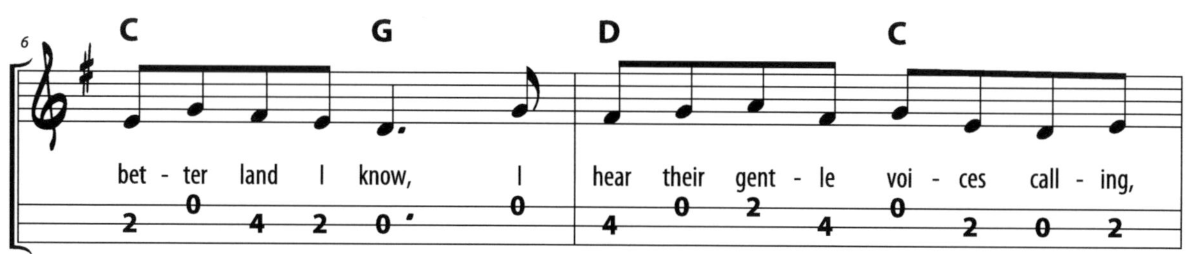

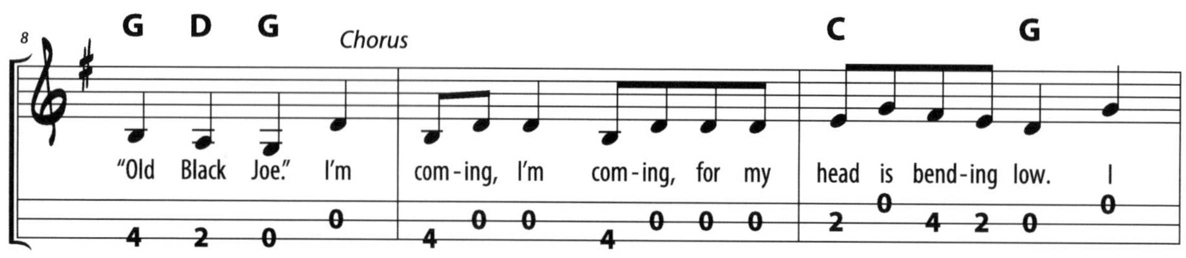

2 Why do I weep when my heart should feel no pain?
Why do I sigh that my friends come not again?
Grieving for forms now departed long ago,
I hear their gentle voices calling, "Old Black Joe."

3 Where are the hearts once so happy and so free?
The children so dear that I held upon my knee?
Gone to the shore where my soul has longed to go,
I hear their gentle voices calling, "Old Black Joe."

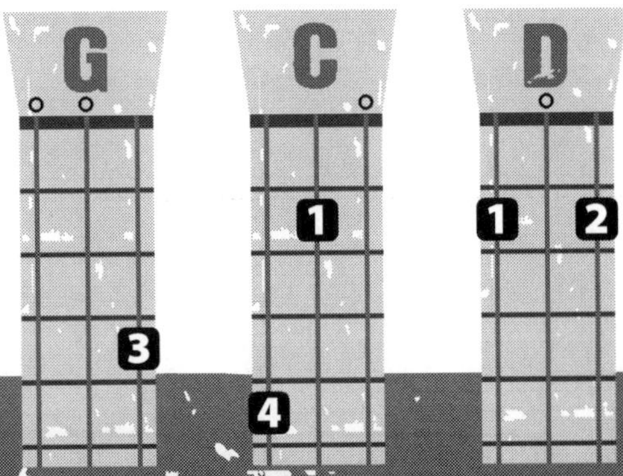

Swing Low, Sweet Chariot

C / F G / C G

Swing low, sweet chariot, comin' for to carry me home,

C / F G / C G C

swing low, sweet chariot, comin' for to carry me home. 1. I

C7 / F G / C G

looked over Jordan and what did I see, comin' for to carry me home. A

C C7 / F G / C G C

band of angels lookin' after me, comin' for to carry me home.

2 If you get there before I do,
comin' for to carry me home,
tell all o' God's children that I'm comin' too,
comin' for to carry me home.

3 I'm sometimes up, I'm sometimes down,
comin' for to carry me home,
but still my soul feels heavenly bound,
comin' for to carry me home.

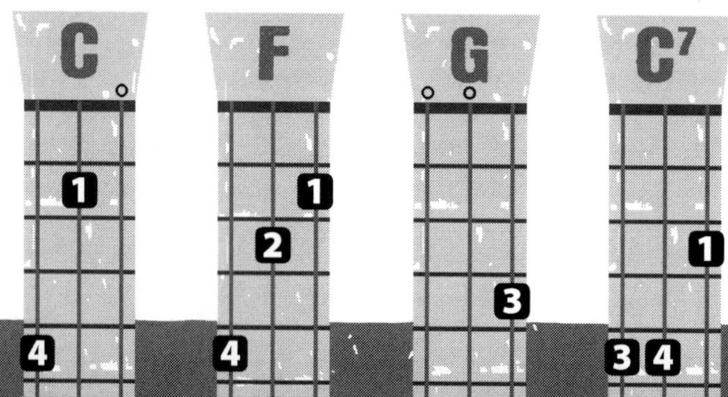

NOBODY KNOWS THE TROUBLE

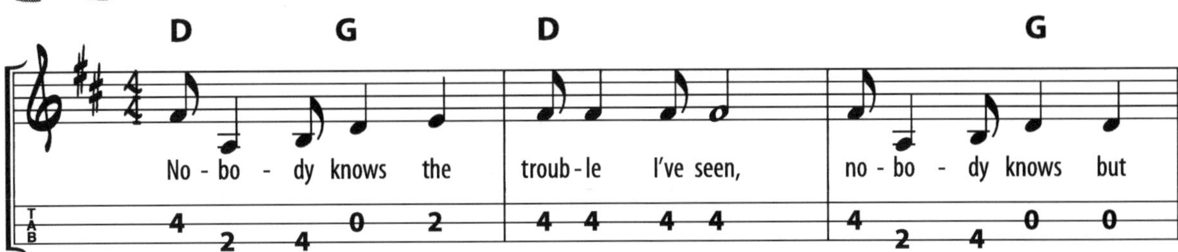

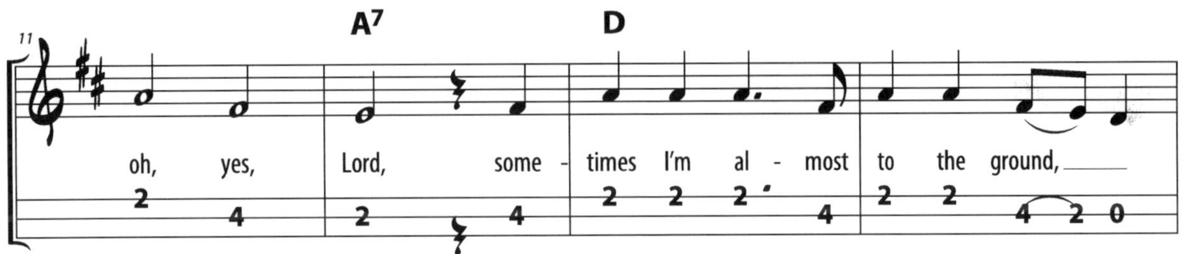

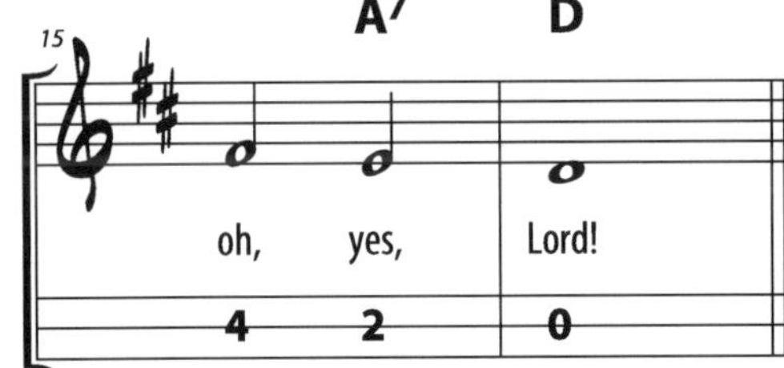

2 I never shall forget that day.
Oh, yes, Lord!
When Jesus washed my sins away.
Oh, yes, Lord!

3 Although you see me goin' so.
Oh, yes, Lord!
I have my trials here below.
Oh, yes, Lord!

D G A^7

Sometimes I Feel Like a Motherless Child

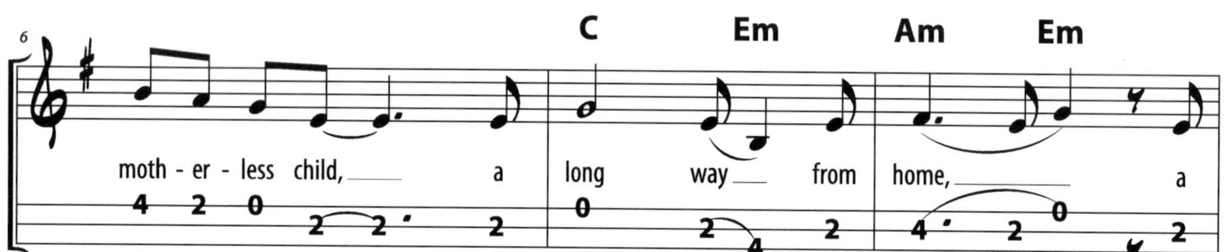

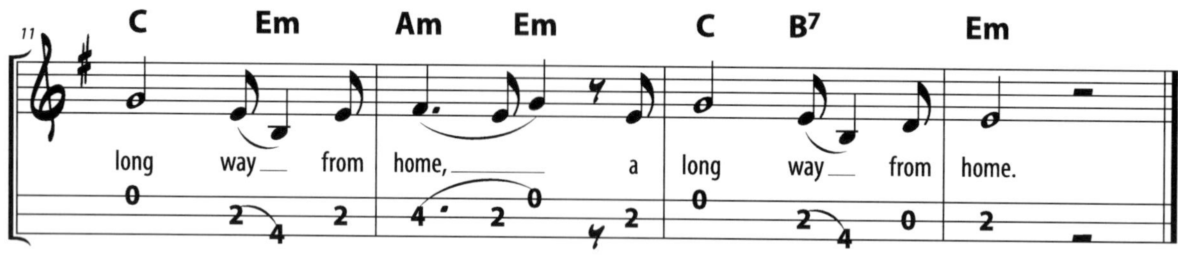

2 Sometimes I feel like I'm almost gone,
sometimes I feel like I'm almost gone,
sometimes I feel like I'm almost gone,
way up in the heavenly land (2x)
True believer,
way up in the heavenly land (2x).

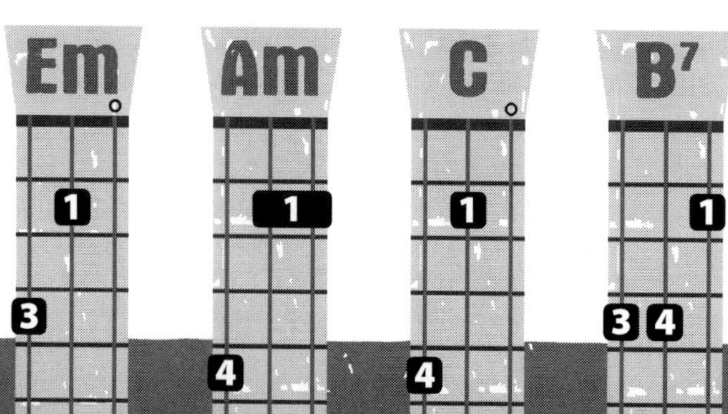

WHAT SHALL WE DO WITH THE DRUNKEN SAILOR

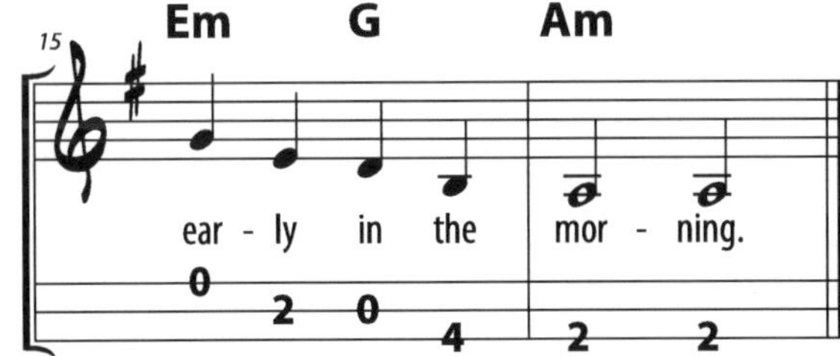

2 Give him a dose of salent water, early ...

3 Give him a dash with a besoms rubber, early ...

4 Pull out the plug and wet him all over, early ...

5 Heave him by the leg in a running bowlin', early ...

6 That's what to do with a drunken sailor, early ...

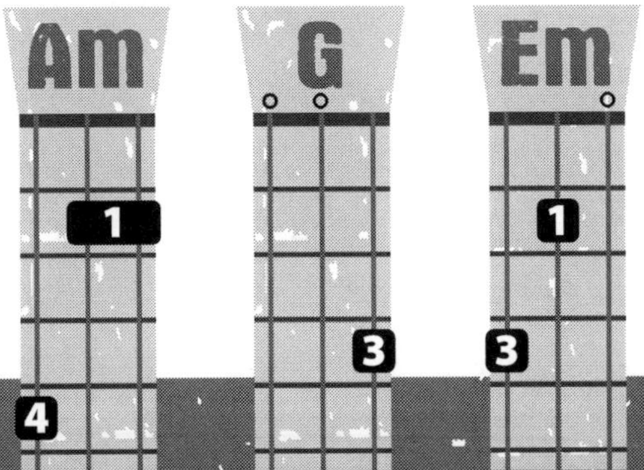

WAY DOWN THE OLD PLANK ROAD

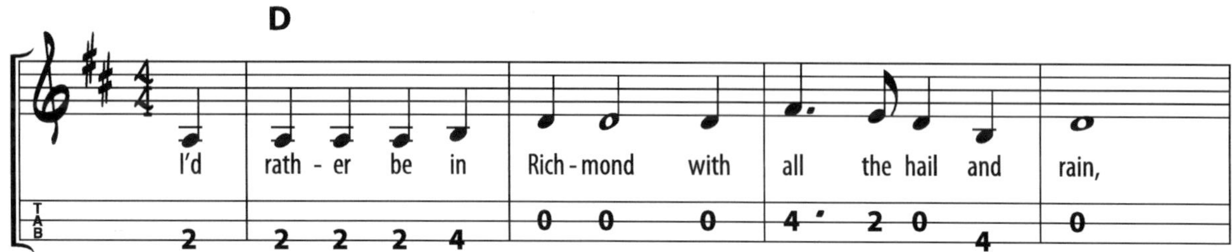

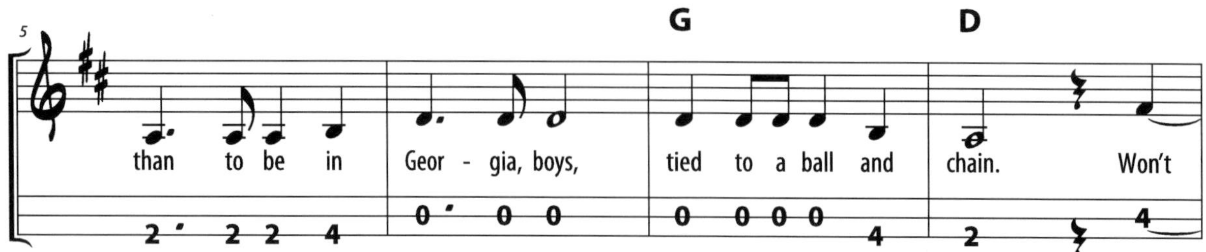

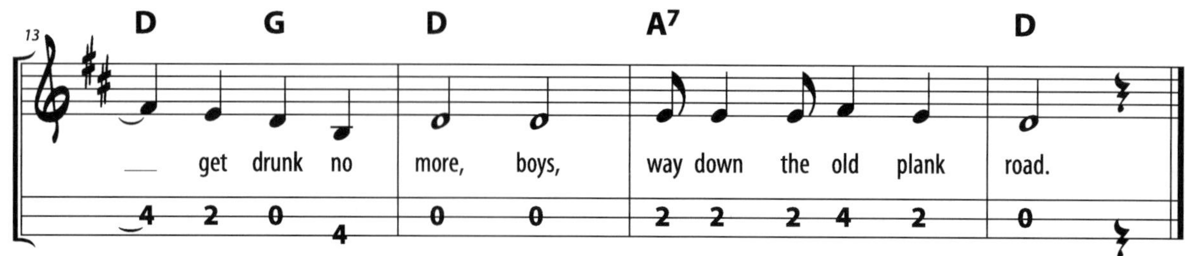

STRUMMING PATTERN

2 I went down to Mobile, but I got on the gravel train,
very next thing they heard of me, had on that ball and chain.
Won't get drunk no more, boys ...

3 Doney, oh dear Doney, what makes you treat me so,
caused me to wear that ball and chain, now my ankle's sore
Won't get drunk no more, boys ...

4 Knoxville is a pretty place, Memphis is a beauty,
wanta see them pretty girls, hop to Chattanoogie.
Won't get drunk no more, boys ...

5 I'm going to build me a scaffold on some mountain high,
so I can see my Doney girl as she goes riding by.
Won't get drunk no more, boys ...

6 My wife died on Friday night, Saturday she was buried,
Sunday was my courtin' day, Monday I got married.
Won't get drunk no more, boys ...

7 Eighteen pounds of meat a week, whiskey here to sell,
how can a young man stay at home, pretty girls look so well.
Won't get drunk no more, boys ...

D G A7

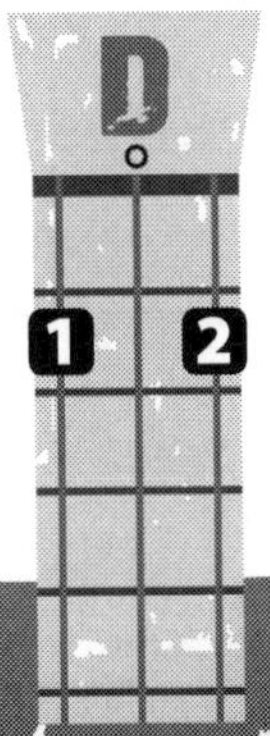

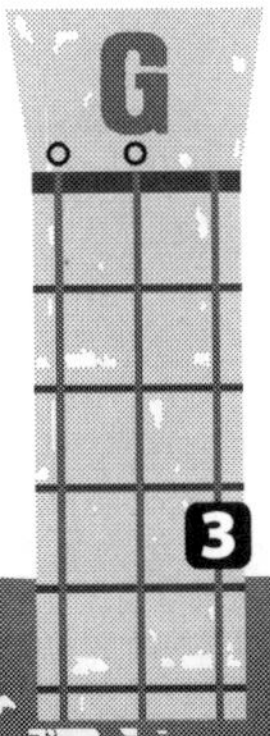

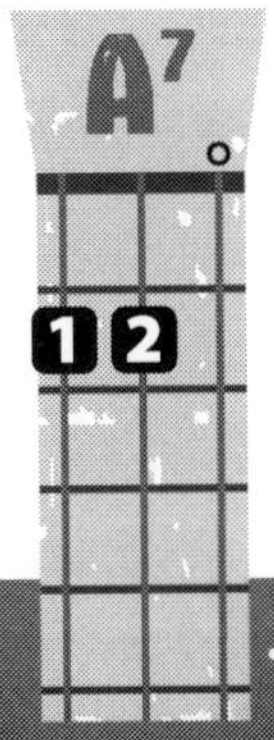

WHISKEY JOHNNY

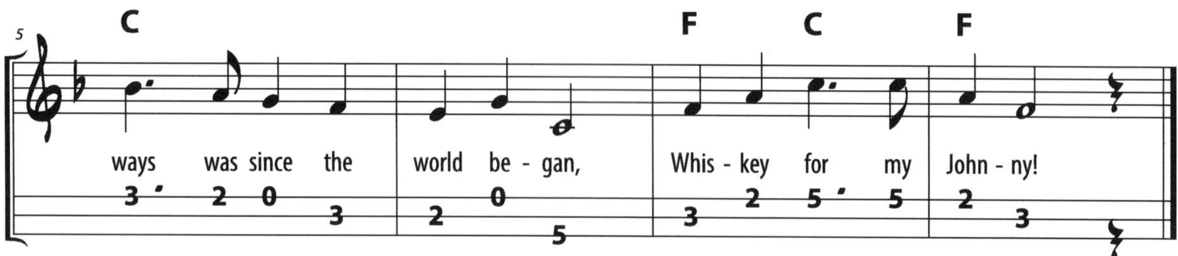

2 Whiskey here, whiskey there,
Whiskey almost everywhere.

3 Whiskey up and whiskey down,
Whiskey all around the town.

4 Whiskey killed me poor old dad,
Whiskey drove me mother mad.

5 My wife and I do not agree.
She puts whiskey in her tea.

6 I had a girl and her name was Lize.
She puts whiskey in her pies.

7 Oh whiskey straight, and whiskey strong,
Give me some whiskey and I'll sing you a song.

8 If whiskey comes too near my nose,
I tip it up and down she goes.

9 Some likes whiskey, some likes beer,
I wish I had a barrel here.

10 Whiskey made me pawn me clothes.
Whiskey gave me this broken nose.

11 Oh the mate likes whiskey, the skipper likes rum.
The sailors like both but me can't get none.

12 Whiskey is the life of man,
Whiskey from that old tin can.

13 I thought I heard the first mate say,
I treats me crew in a decent way.

14 If whiskey was a river and I could swim,
I'd say here goes and dive right in.

15 If whiskey was a river and I was a duck,
I'd dive to the bottom and never come up.

16 I wisht I knew where whiskey grew,
I'd eat the leaves and the branches too.

17 A tot of whiskey all around,
and a bottle full for the shanty man.

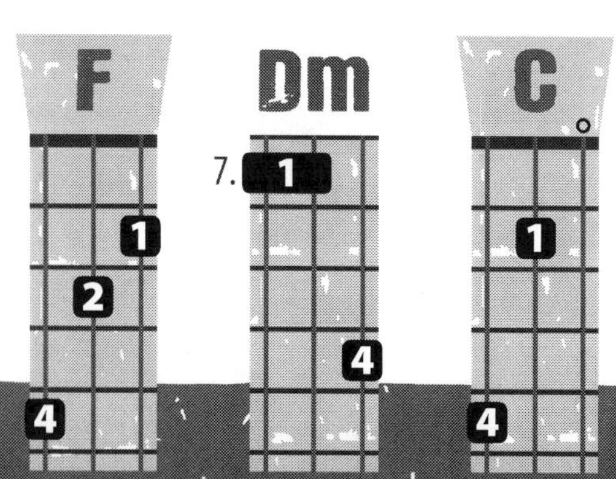

Roll in My Sweet Baby's Arms

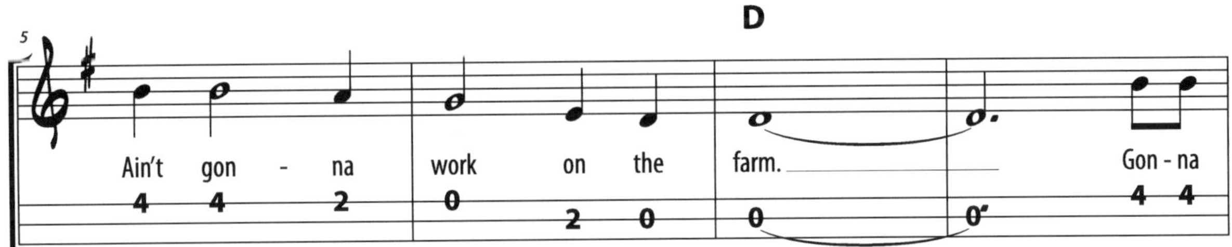

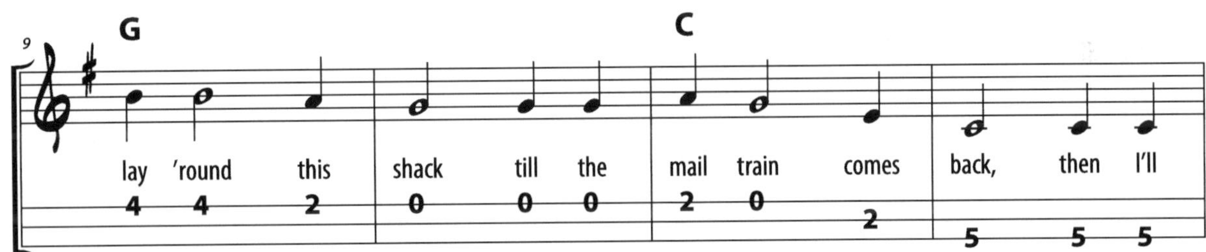

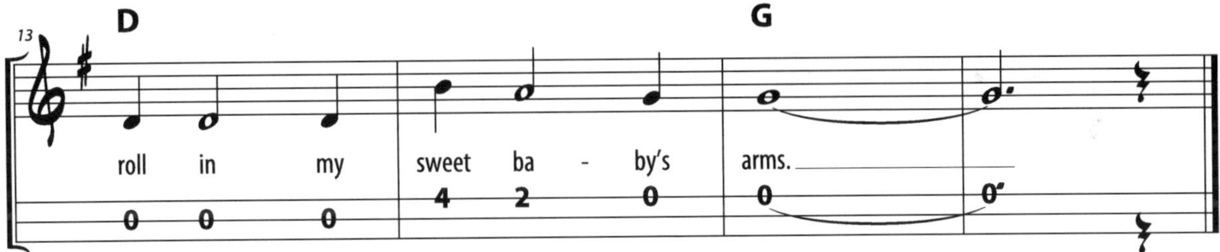

2 Now where was you last Friday night while I was lyin' in jail.
Walkin' the streets with another man you wouldn't even go my bail,
then I'll roll in my sweet baby's arms.

3 I know your parents don't like me they drove me away from your door.
And my life's too bluer never to wearing more,
then I'll roll in my sweet baby's arms.

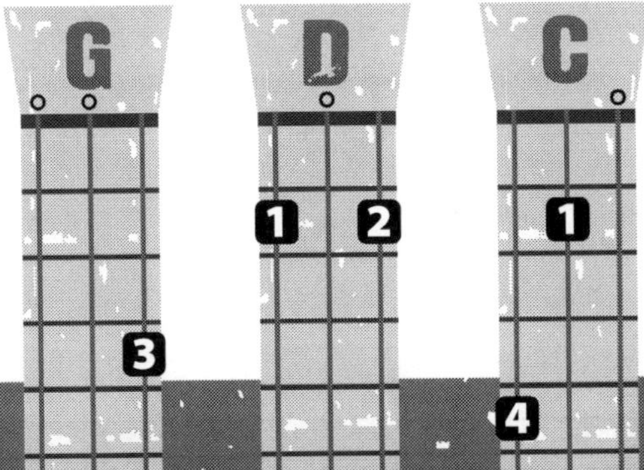

YANKEE DOODLE

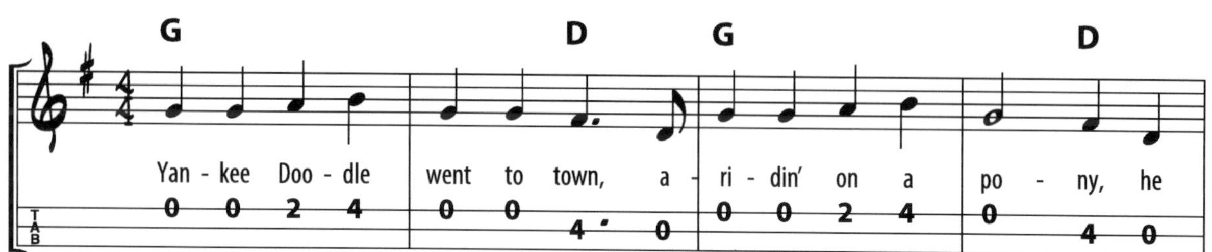

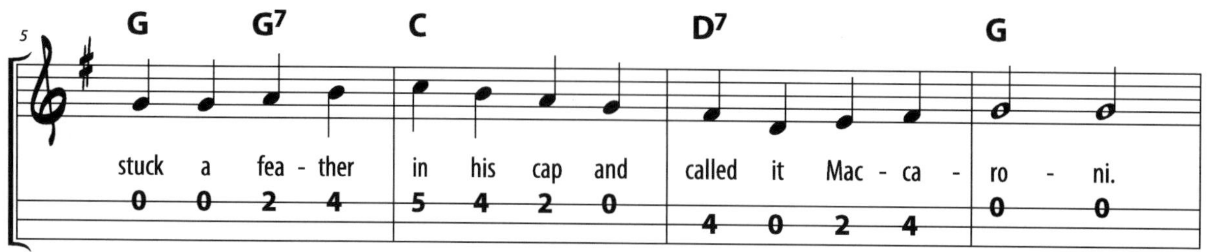

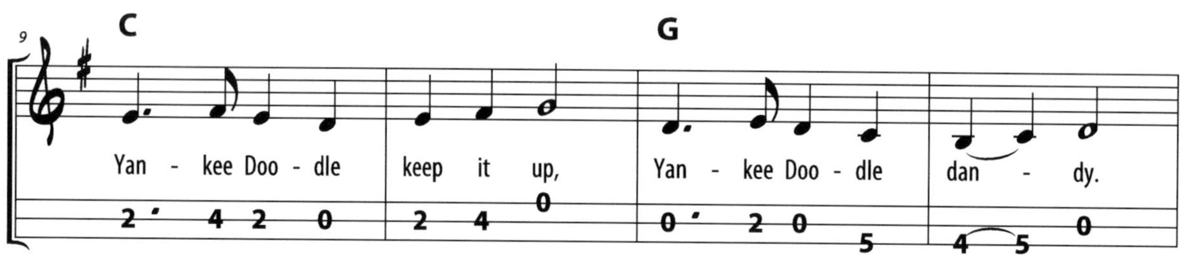

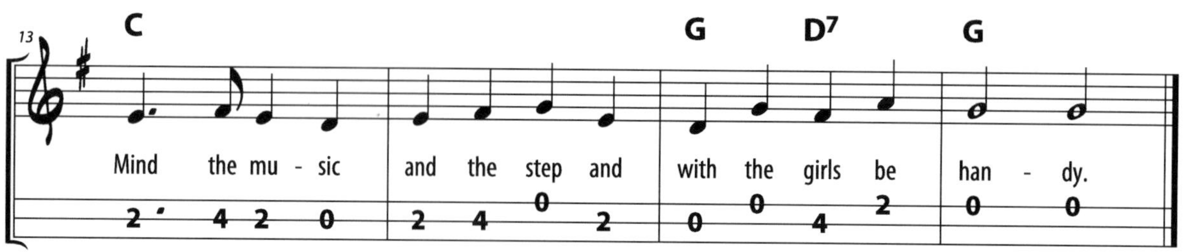

2 Father and I went down to camp,
along with Captain Gooding.
And there we saw the men and boys,
as thick as hasty pudding.
Yankee Doodle, keep it up,
Yankee Doodle dandy.
Mind the music and the step,
and with the girls be handy.

3 There was Captain Washington,
upon a slapping stallion.
A-giving orders to his men,
I guess there was a million.
Yankee Doodle, keep it up,
Yankee Doodle dandy.
Mind the music and the step,
and with the girls be handy.

4 Yankee Doodle is a tune,
that comes in mighty handy.
The enemies all run away,
at Yankee Doodle dandy!
Yankee Doodle, keep it up,
Yankee Doodle dandy.
Mind the music and the step,
and with the girls be handy.

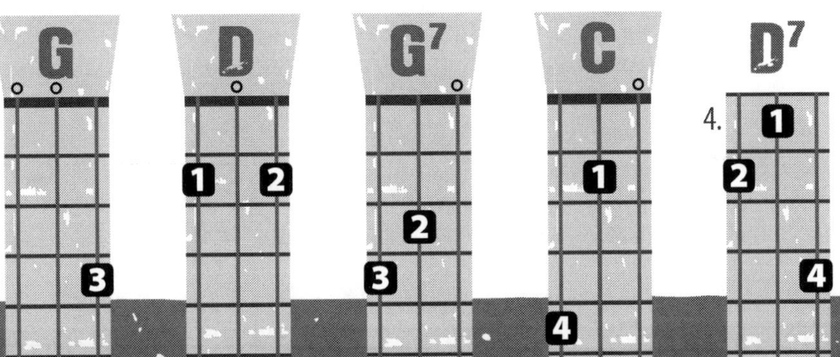

THE WABASH CANNON BALL

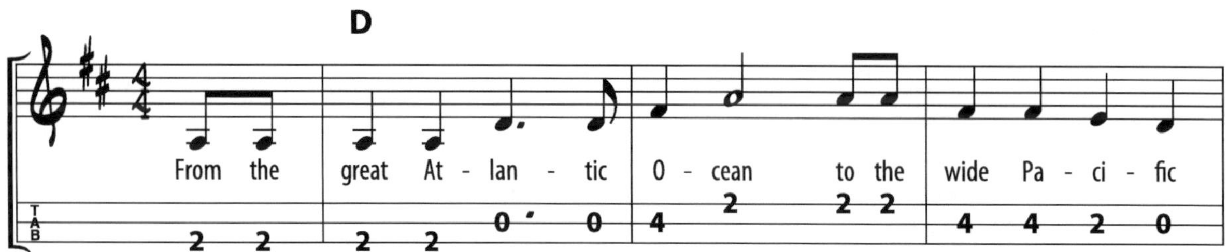

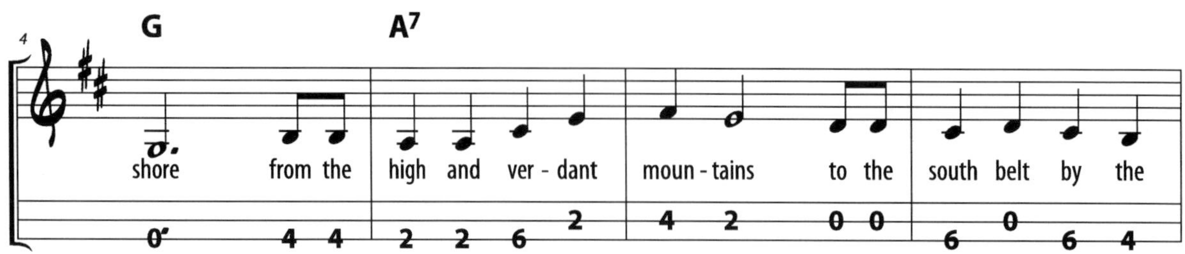

STRUMMING PATTERN

CHORUS:

Listen to the jingle, the rumble and the roar,
as she glides along the woodland, through the hills and by the shore.
Hear the mighty rush of the engine, hear that lonesome hobo squall.
You're travelling through the jungles on the Wabash Cannonball.

2 She came down from Birmingham, one cold December day,
as she rolled into the station, you could hear all the people say,
"There's a girl from Tennessee, she's long and she's tall
She came down from Birmingham on the Wabash Cannonball."

3 Our the Eastern states are dandy so the people always say,
"From New York to St. Louis and Chicago by the way
from the hills of Minnesota where the rippling waters fall,
no changes can be taken on that Wabash Cannonball."

4 Here's to daddy Claxton, may his name forever stand
and always be remembered 'round the courts of Alabam'.
His earthly race is over and the curtains 'round him fall.
We'll carry him home to victory on the Wabash Cannonball.

D G A^7

1 2 3

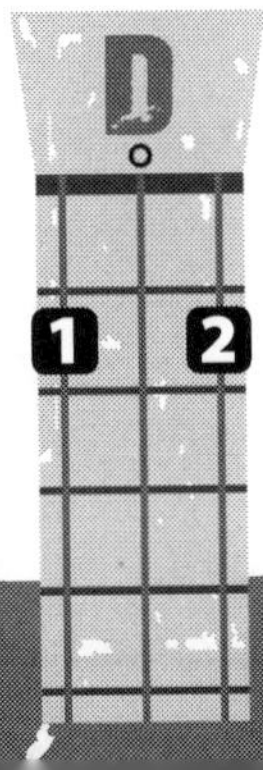

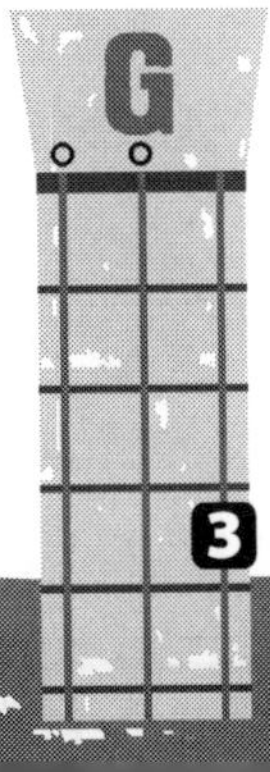

ACRES OF CLAMS

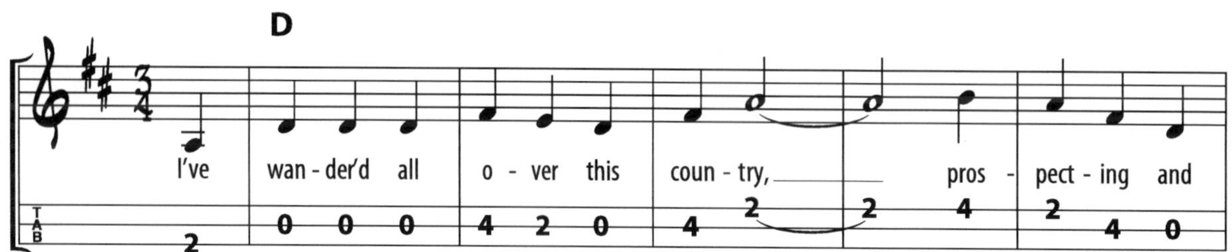

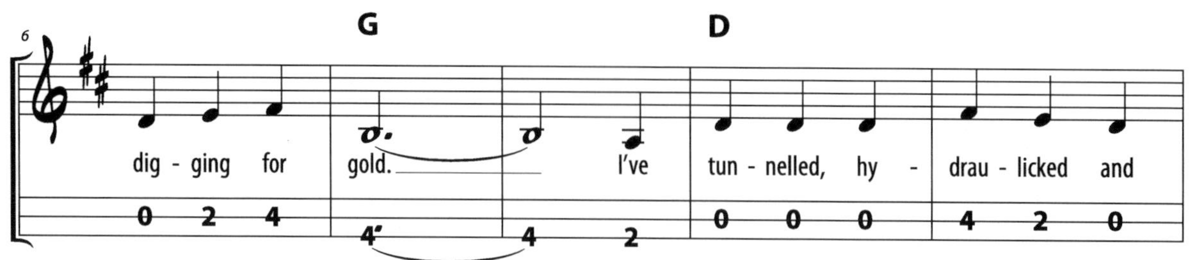

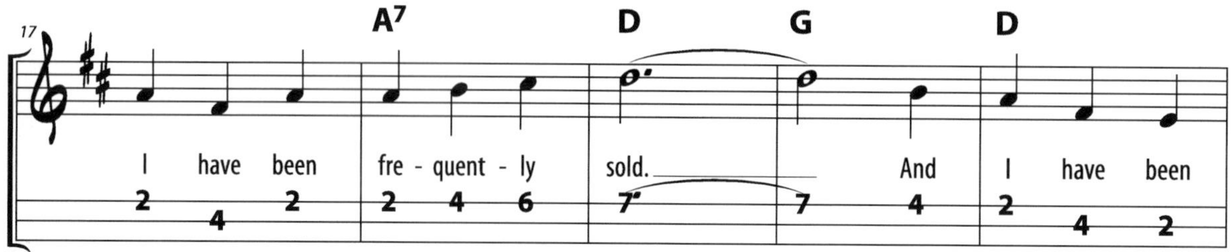

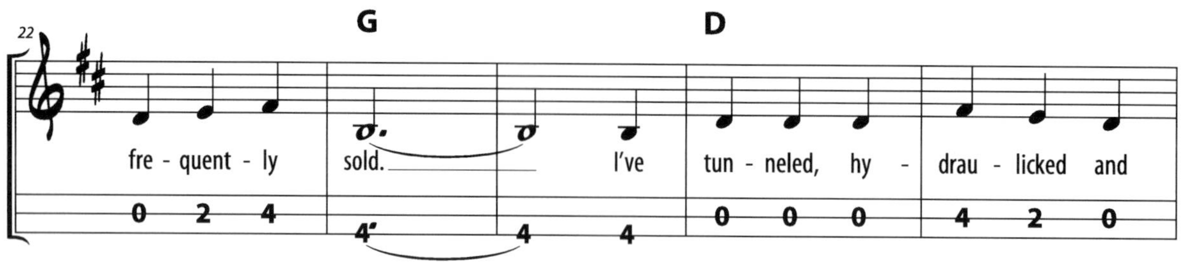

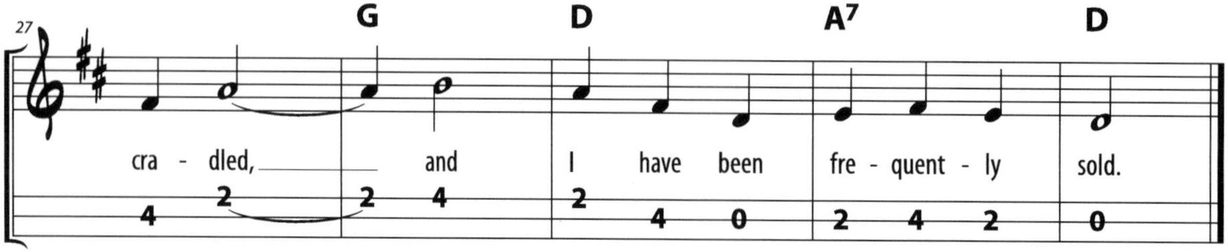

2 For one who got wealthy by mining,
I saw many hundreds get poor.
I made up my mind to go digging,
for something a little more sure.
For something a little more sure ...

3 I rolled up my grub in my blanket,
I left all my tools on the ground.
I started one morning to shank it,
For the country they call Puget Sound.
For the country they call Puget Sound ...

4 No longer a slave of ambition,
I laugh at the world and its shams.
And I think of my happy condition,
surrounded by acres of clams.
Surrounded by acres of clams ...

D G A7

1 2
3
1 2

AMERICA THE BEAUTIFUL

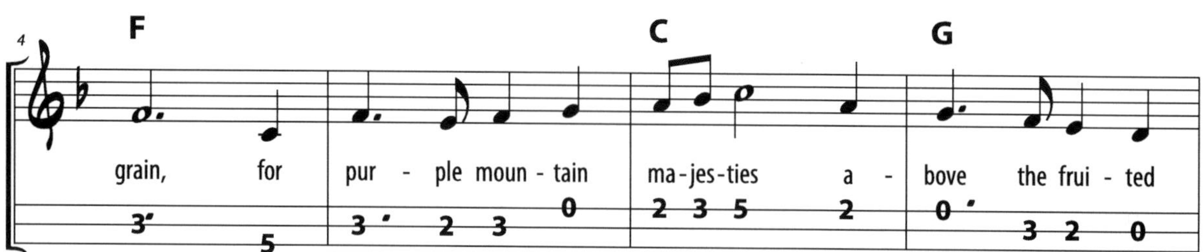

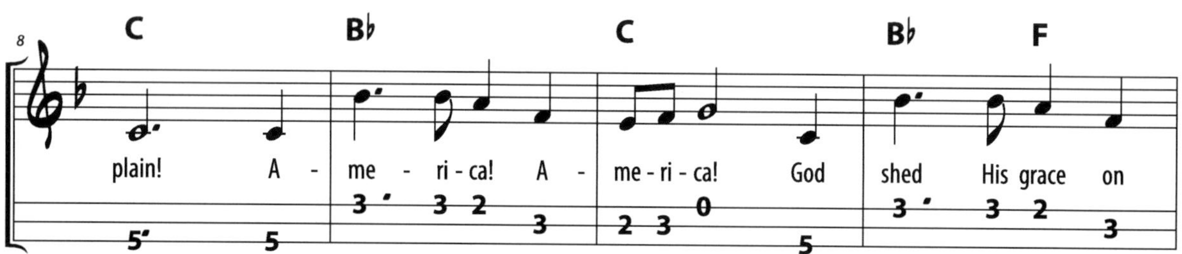

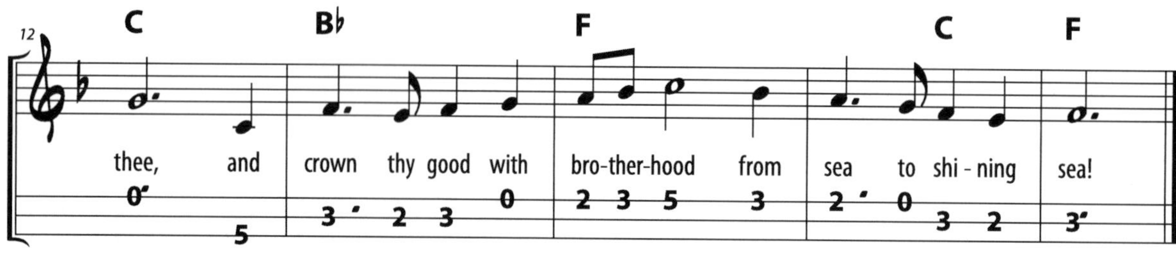

STRUMMING PATTERN

F C G B♭

7.

2 O beautiful for pilgrim feet,
whose stern impassioned stress.
A thoroughfare of freedom beat
across the wilderness!
America! America!
God mend thine every flaw,
confirm thy soul in self-control,
thy liberty in law!

3 O beautiful for heroes proved,
in liberating strife.
Who more than self their country loved,
and mercy more than life!
America! America!
May God thy gold refine,
till all success be nobleness,
and every gain divine!

4 O beautiful for patriot dream,
that sees beyond the years,
thine alabaster cities gleam,
undimmed by human tears!
America! America!
God shed his grace on thee,
and crown thy good with brotherhood
from sea to shining sea!

5 O beautiful for halcyon skies,
for amber waves of grain,
for purple mountain majesties
above the enameled plain!
America! America!
God shed his grace on thee,
till souls wax fair as earth and air,
and music-hearted sea!

6 O beautiful for pilgrim feet,
whose stem impassioned stress
a thoroughfare for freedom beat
across the wilderness!
America! America!
God shed his grace on thee,
till paths be wrought through wilds of thought
by pilgrim foot and knee!

7 O beautiful for glory-tale
of liberating strife,
when once and twice, for man's avail
men lavished precious life!
America! America!
God shed his grace on thee,
till selfish gain no longer stain
the banner of the free!

8 O beautiful for patriot dream,
that sees beyond the years,
thine alabaster cities gleam
undimmed by human tears!
America! America!
God shed his grace on thee,
till nobler men keep once again
thy whiter jubilee!

BURY ME BENEATH THE WILLOW

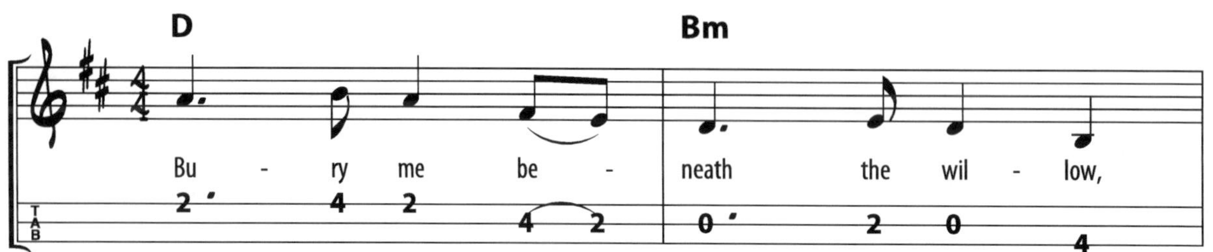

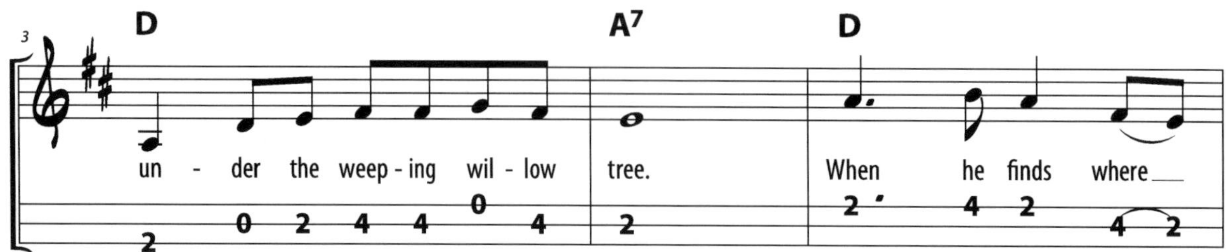

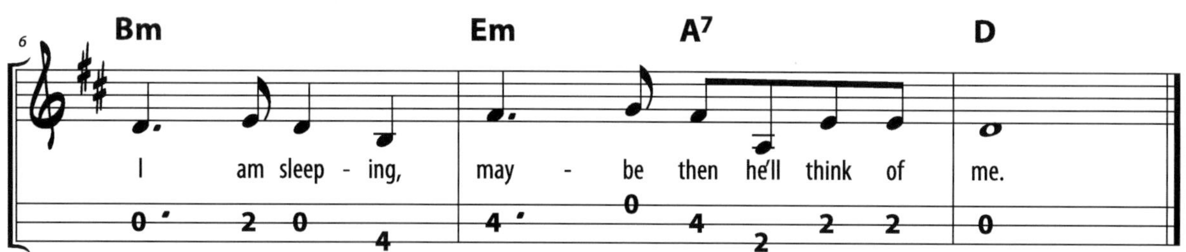

2 My heart is sad I am lonely,
for the only one I love.
When shall I see her oh no never,
'til we meet in heaven above.

3 She told me that she dearly loved me.
How could I believe it untrue,
until the angels softly whispered,
she will prove untrue to you.

4 Tomorrow was to be our wedding,
God, oh God, where can she be.
She's out a-courting with another,
and no longer cares for me

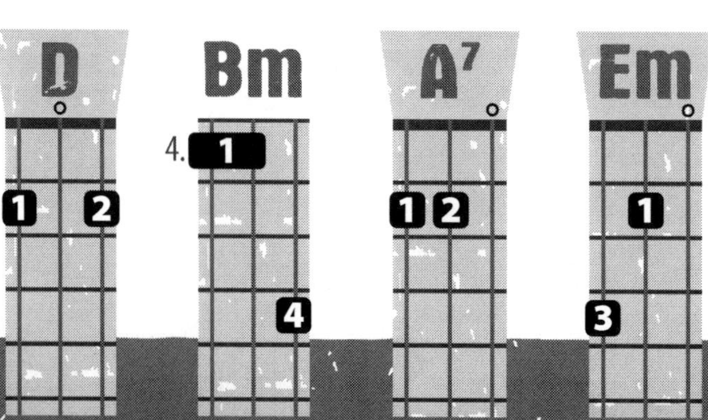

FOGGY MOUNTAIN TOP

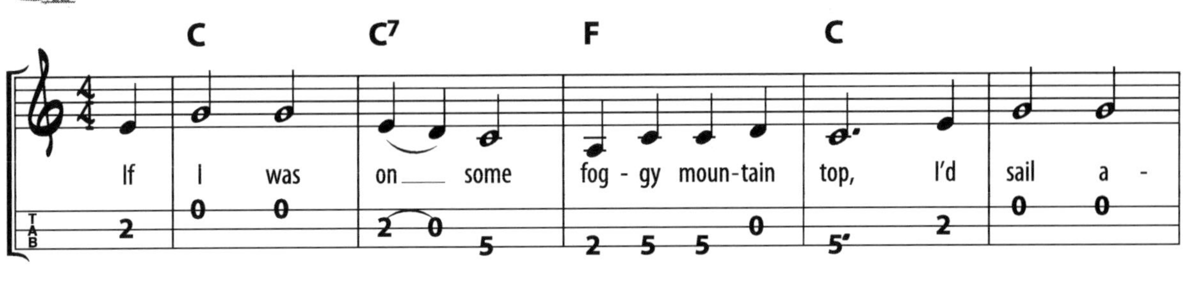

2 If I'd only listened to what my mama said,
I would not be here today.
Lying around this old jailhouse,
wasting my poor life away.
If I was on some foggy mountain top ...

3 Oh she caused me to weep, she caused me to mourn,
she caused me to leave my home.
Oh the lonesome pines and the good old times,
I'm on my way back home.
If I was on some foggy mountain top ...

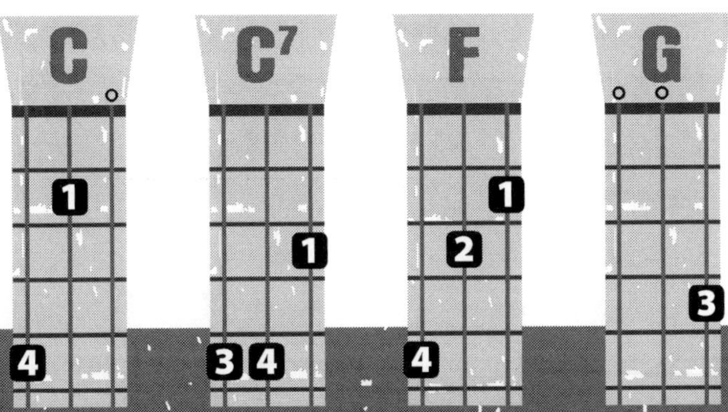

Give Me That Old Time Religion

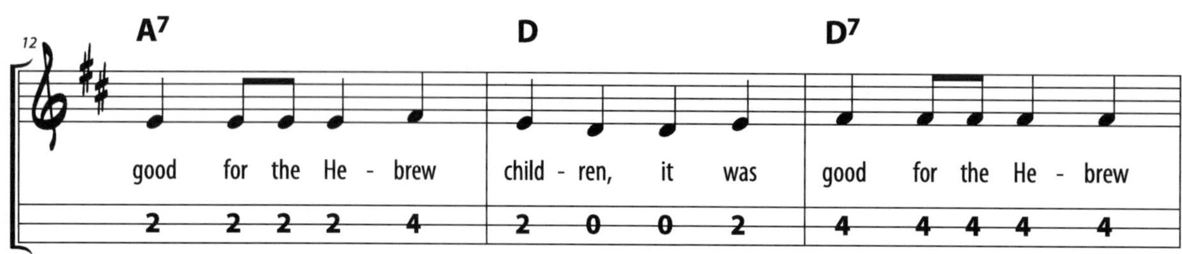

2 It will do when the world's on fire,
it will do when the world's on fire,
it will do when the world's on fire,
and it's good enough for me.

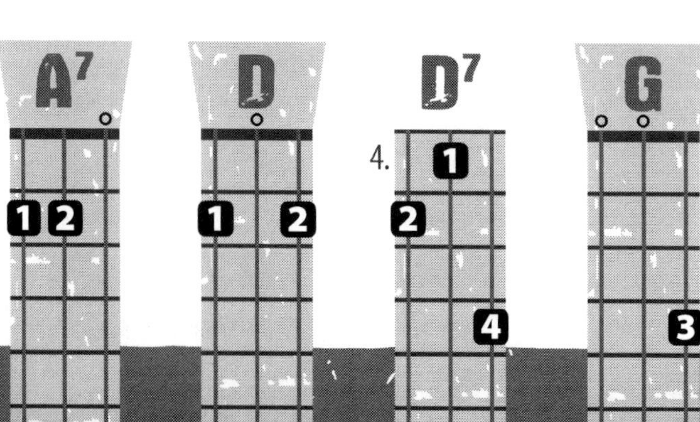

He's Got the Whole World in His Hands

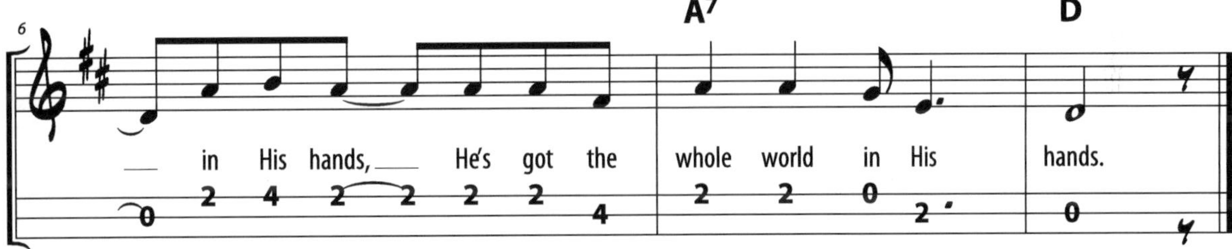

2 He's got the tiny little baby in His hands.

3 He's got you and me brother in His hands.

4 He's got the son and the father in His hands.

5 He's got the mother and her daughter in His hands.

6 He's got everybody here in His hands.

7 He's got the sun and the moon in His hands.

8 He's got the whole world in His hands.

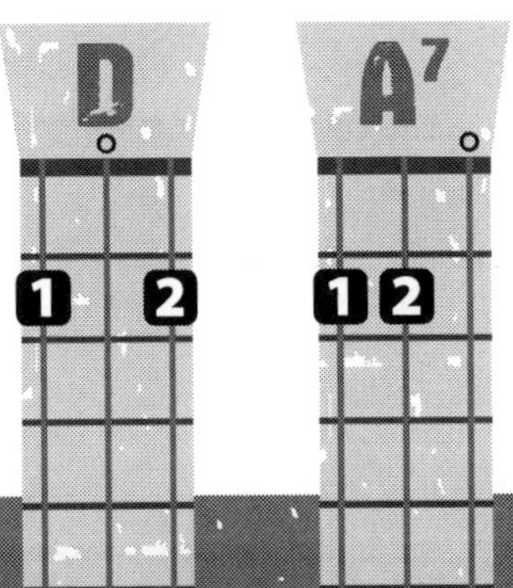

HOUSE OF THE RISING SUN

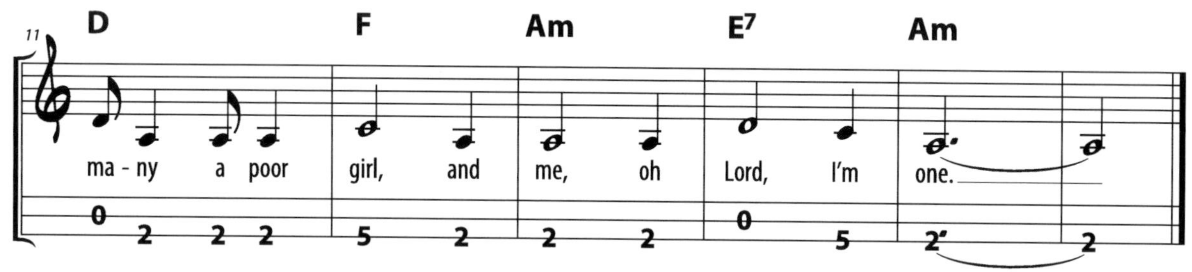

STRUMMING PATTERN

2 If I had listened what Mamma said,
I'd been at home today.
Being so young and foolish, poor boy,
let a rambler lead me astray.

3 Go tell my baby sister,
never do like I have done,
to shun that house in New Orleans,
they call the Rising Sun.

4 My mother she's a tailor;
She sold those new blue jeans.
My sweetheart, he's a drunkard, Lord,
drinks down in New Orleans.

5 The only thing a drunkard needs,
is a suitcase and a trunk.
The only time he's satisfied,
is when he's on a drunk.

6 Fills his glasses to the brim,
passes them around.
Only pleasure he gets out of life,
is hoboin' from town to town.

7 One foot is on the platform,
and the other one on the train.
I'm going back to New Orleans,
to wear that ball and chain.

8 Going back to New Orleans,
my race is almost run.
Going back to spend the rest of my life,
beneath that Rising Sun.

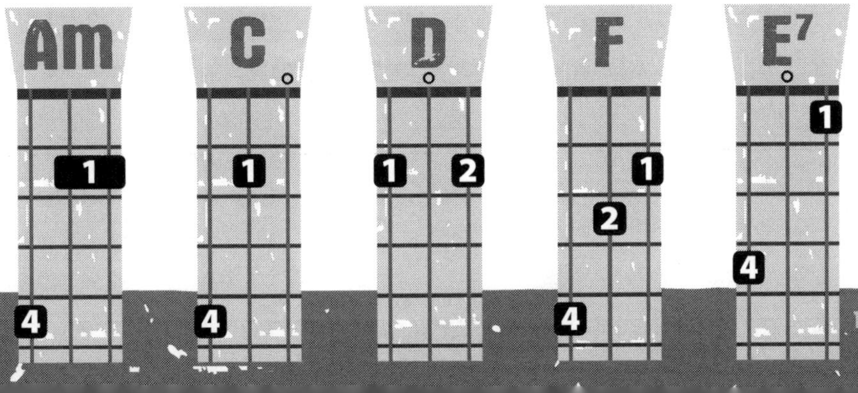

Am C D F E^7

My Home's Across the Smoky Mountains

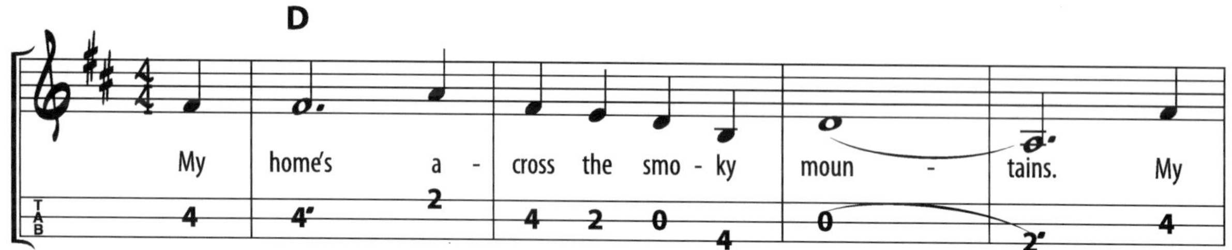

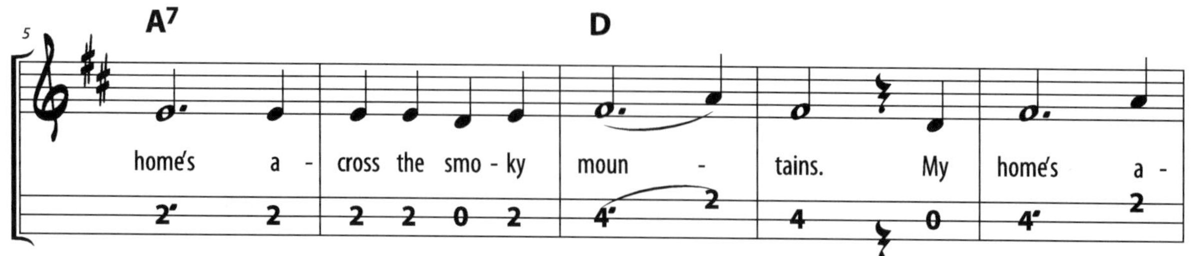

2 Goodbye honey, sugar darling.
Goodbye honey, sugar darling.
Goodbye honey, sugar darling,
and I'll never get to see you any more, more, more,
I'll never get to see you any more.

3 Rock my baby, feed her candy.
Rock my baby, feed her candy.
Rock my baby, feed her candy,
and I'll never get to see you any more, more, more,
I'll never get to see you any more.

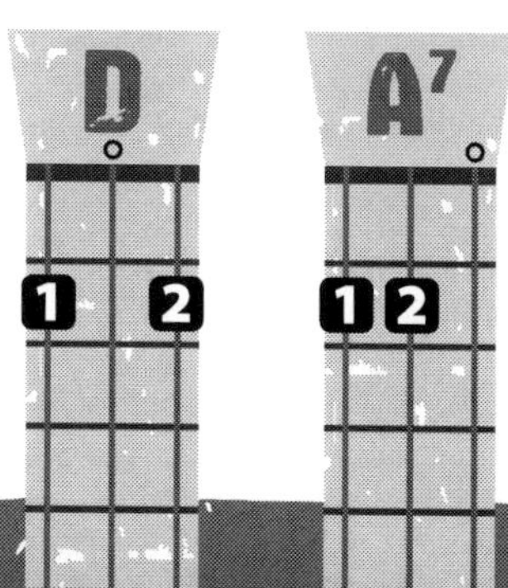

Will the Circle Be Unbroken

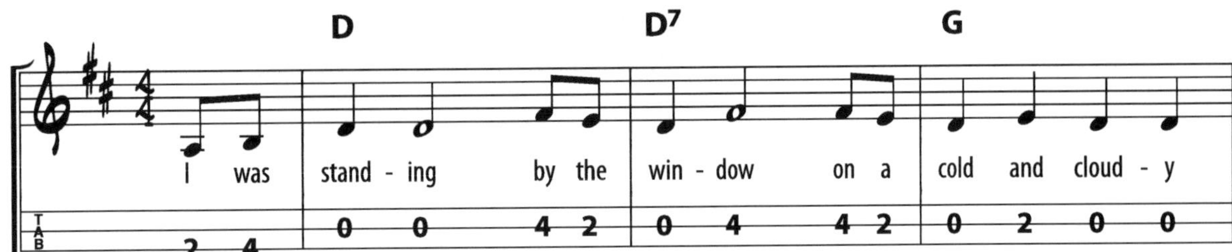

2 I said to the undertaker,
"Undertaker please drive slow.
For that body you are carrying,
Lord, I hate to see her go."

3 Well I followed close behind her,
tried to hold up and be brave.
But I could not hide my sorrow,
when they laid her in that grave.

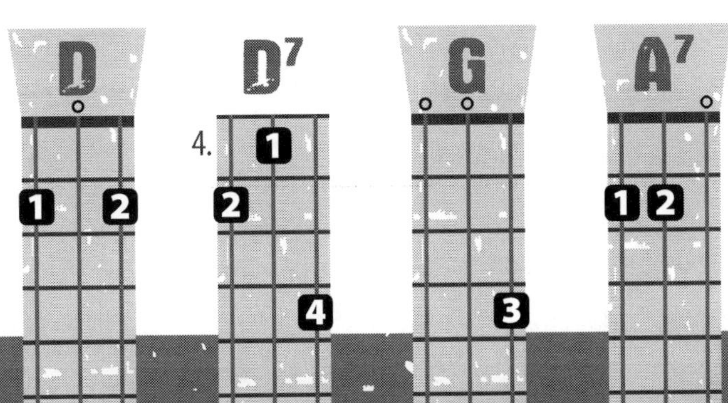

4 I went back home, Lord,
that home was lonesome.
Since my mother, she was gone,
all my brothers and sisters crying.
What a home so sad and alone.

The Last Rose of Summer

2 I'll not leave thee, thou lone one!
To pine on the stem;
Since the lovely are sleeping,
go, sleep thou with them.
Thus kindly I scatter,
thy leaves o'er the bed,
where thy mates of the garden
lie scentless and dead.

3 So soon may I follow,
when friendships decay,
and from Love's shining circle
the gems drop away.
When true hearts lie withered,
and fond ones are flown.
Oh! who would inhabit
this bleak world alone?

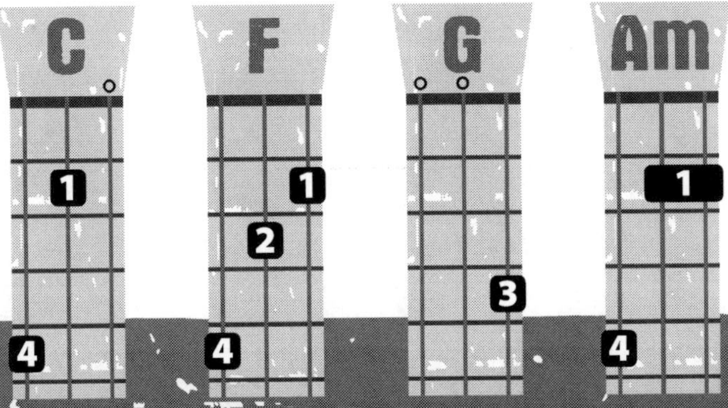

Go, Tell It On The Mountain

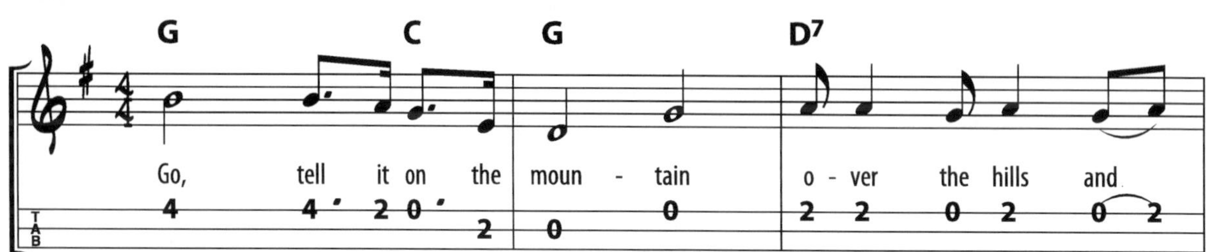

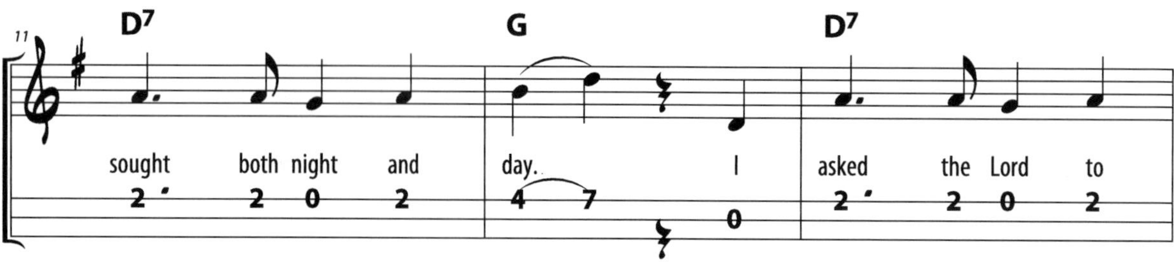

2 He made me a watchman upon the city wall,
and if I am a Christian I am the least of all.

3 'T was a lowly manger that Jesus Christ was born.
The Lord sent down an angel that bright and glorious morn'.

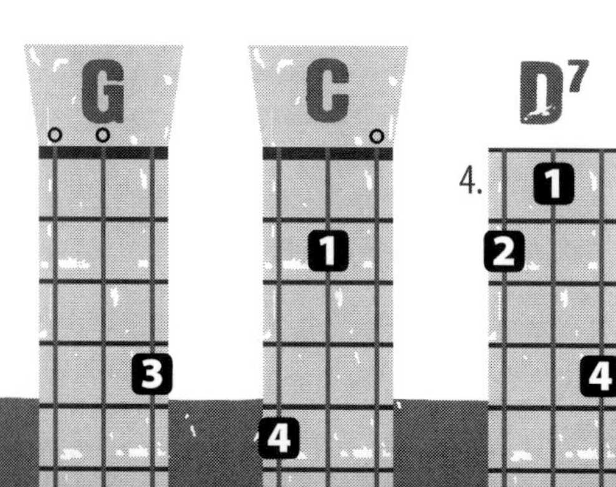

CARELESS LOVE

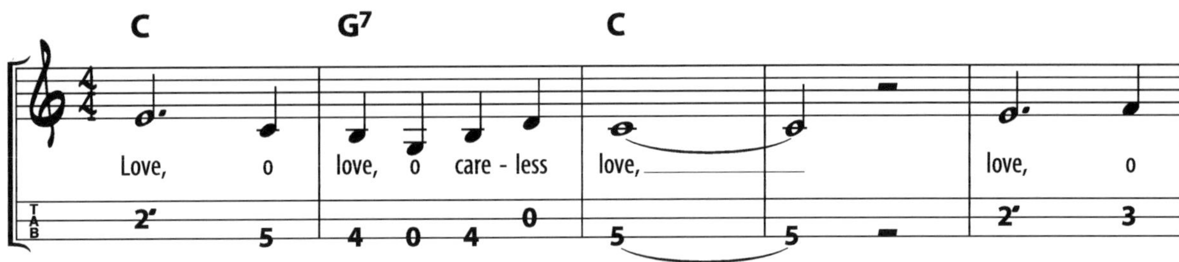

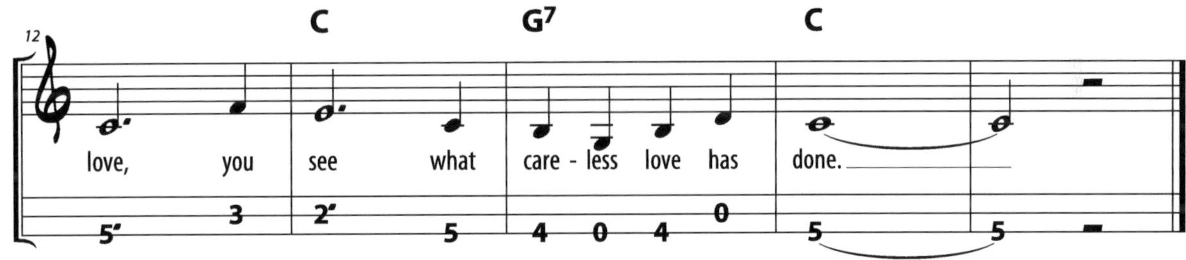

2 Once I wore my apron low,
once I wore my apron low,
once I wore my apron low,
you'd follow me through rain and snow.

3 Now I wear my apron high,
now I wear my apron high,
now I wear my apron high,
you'll see my door and pass it by.

4 How I wish that train would come,
how I wish that train would come,
how I wish that train would come,
take me back where I come from.

5 I love my mother and father too,
I love my mother and father too,
I love my mother and father too,
But I'd leave them both to got with you.

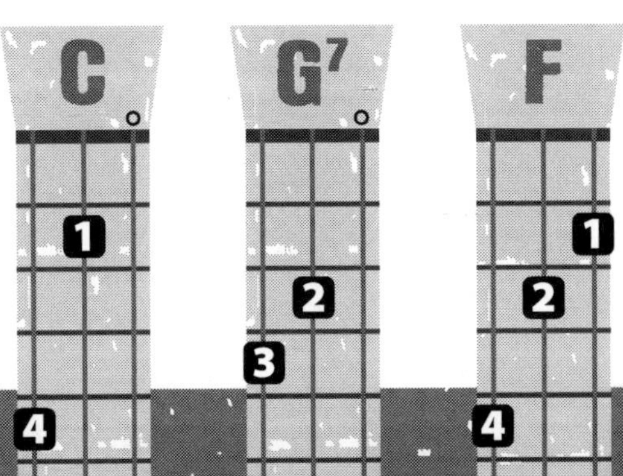

OVER THE RIVER AND THROUGH THE WOODS

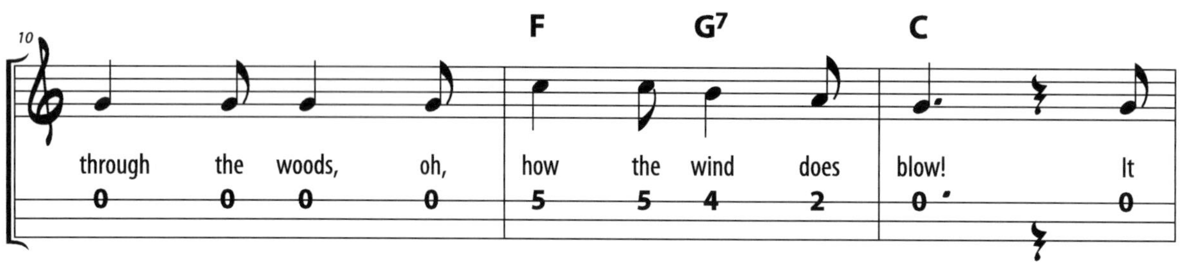

2 Over the river and through the woods,
to have a first-rate play;
Oh, hear the bells ring, "Ting-a-ling-ling!"
Hurrah for Thanksgiving Day!
Over the river and through the woods,
trot fast, my dapple gray!
Spring over the ground, Like a hunting hound!
For this is Thanksgiving Day.

3 Over the river and through the woods,
and straight through the barnyard gate.
We seem to go extremely slow
it is so hard to wait!
Over the river and through the woods,
now Grandmother's cap I spy!
Hurrah for the fun! Is the pudding done?
Hurrah for the pumpkin pie!

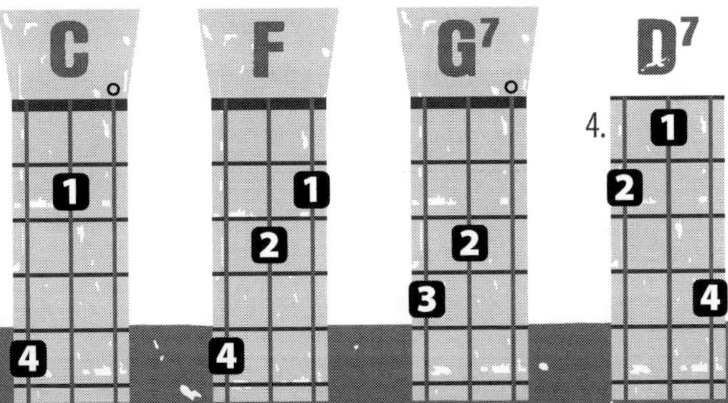

THE BALLAD OF JOHN HENRY

2 The captain said to John Henry:
"Gonna bring that steam drill 'round,
gonna bring that sterm drill out on the job,
gonna whop that steel on down, Lord, Lord,
gonna whop that steel on down."

3 John Henry told his captain:
"A man ain't nothing but a man,
nut before I let your steam drill beat me down,
I'd die with a hammer in my hand, Lord, Lord,
I'd die with a hammer in my hand."

4 John Henry said to his shaker:
"Shaker, why don't you sing?
I'm throwin' thirty pounds from my hips on down,
just listen to that cold steel ring, Lord, Lord,
just listen to that cold steel ring."

5 John Henry said to his shaker:
"Shaker, you'd better pray,
'cause if I miss that little piece of steel,
tomorrow be your buryin' day, Lord, Lord,
tomorrow be your buryin' day."

6 The shaker said to John Henry:
"I think this mountain's cavin' in!"
John Henry said to his shaker, "Man,
that ain't nothin' but my hammer suckin' wind! Lord, Lord,
that ain't nothin' but my hammer suckin' wind!"

7 Now the man that invented the steam drill,
thought he was mighty fine.
But John Henry made fifteen feet,
the steam drill only made nine, Lord, Lord,
the steam drill only made nine.

8 John Henry hammered in the mountains,
his hammer was striking fire.
But he worked so hard, he broke his poor heart,
he laid down his hammer and he died, Lord, Lord,
he laid down his hammer and he died.

9 John Henry had a little woman,
her name was Polly Ann.
John Henry took sick and went to his bed,
Polly Ann drove steel like a man, Lord, Lord,
Polly Ann drove steel like a man.

10 John Henry had a little baby,
you could hold him in the palm of your hand.
The last words I heard that poor boy say:
"My daddy was a steel driving man, Lord, Lord,
my daddy was a steel driving man."

11 They took John Henry to the graveyard,
and they buried him in the sand.
And every locomotive comes a-roaring by
says "There lies a steel-driving man, Lord, Lord,
there lies a steel-driving man."

12 Well every Monday morning,
when the bluebirds begin to sing,
you can hear John Henry a mile or more,
you can hear John Henry's hammer ring, Lord, Lord,
you can hear John Henry's hammer ring.

G D C

1 2

1

3

4

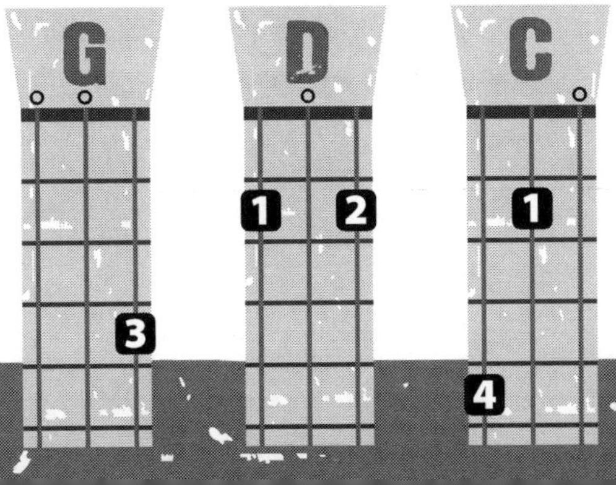

OLD FOLKS AT HOME

2 All 'round the little farm I wandered,
when I was young.
Then many happy days I squandered,
many the songs I sung,
when I was playing with my brother,
happy was I.
Oh, take me to my kind old mother,
there let me live and die.

3 One little hut among the bushes,
one that I love,
still sadly to my mem'ry rushes,
no matter where I rove,
when shall I see the bees a-humming,
all 'round the comb,
when shall I hear the banjo strumming,
down by my good old home.

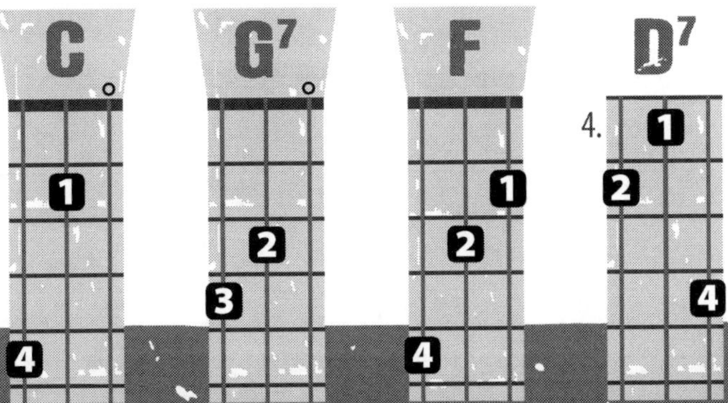

MAMA DON'T 'LOW

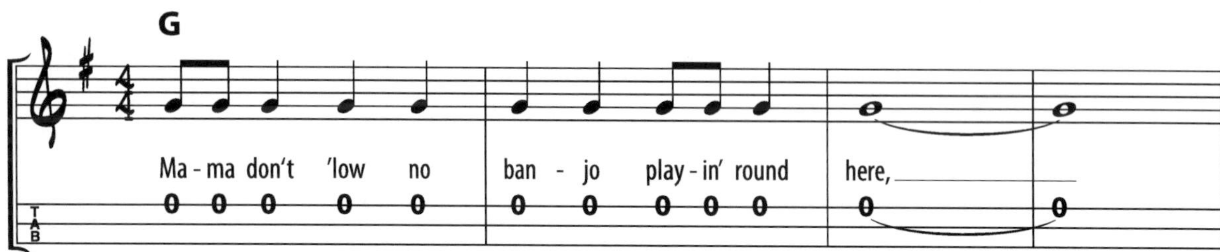

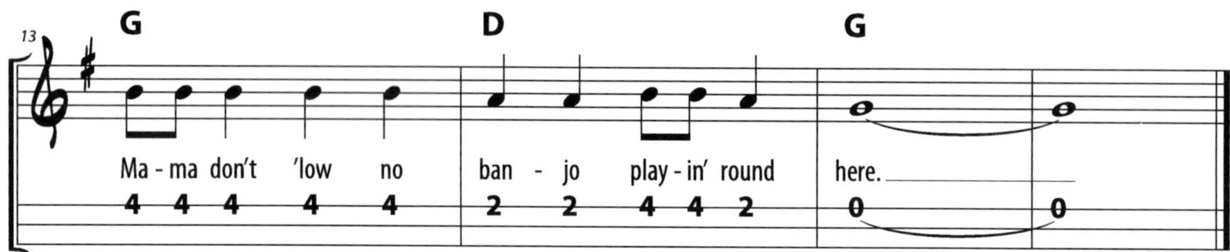

2 Mama don't 'low no guitar playin' round here,
Mama don't 'low no guitar playin' round here,
I don't care what Mama don't 'low,
gonna play my guitar anyhow,
Mama don't 'low no guitar playin' round here.

3 Mama don't 'low no talkin' round here,
Mama don't 'low no talkin' round here,
I don't care what Mama don't 'low,
gonna shoot my mouth off anyhow,
Mama don't 'low no talkin' round here.

4 Mama don't 'low no singin' round here,
Mama don't 'low no singin' round here,
I don't care what Mama don't 'low,
gonna sing my head off anyhow,
Mama don't 'low no singin' round here.

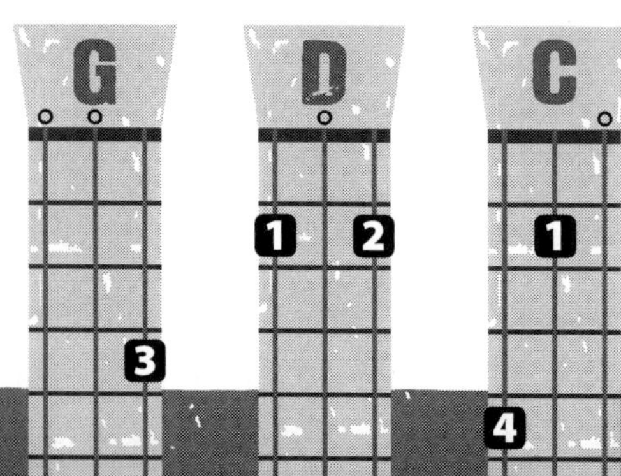

OLD MAC DONALD HAD A FARM

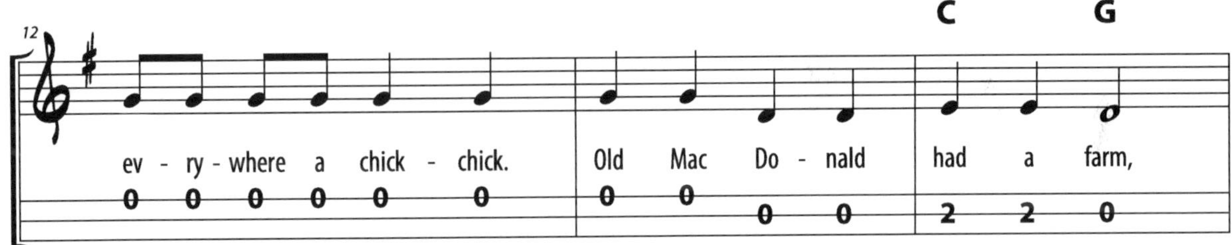

2 ... he had some geese ...
With a gabble-gabble here ...

3 ... he had a pig ...
With an oinck-oink here ...

4 ... he had some ducks ...
With a quack-quack here ...

5 ... he had a cow ...
With a moo-moo here ...

G C D7

4.

Git Along, Little Dogies

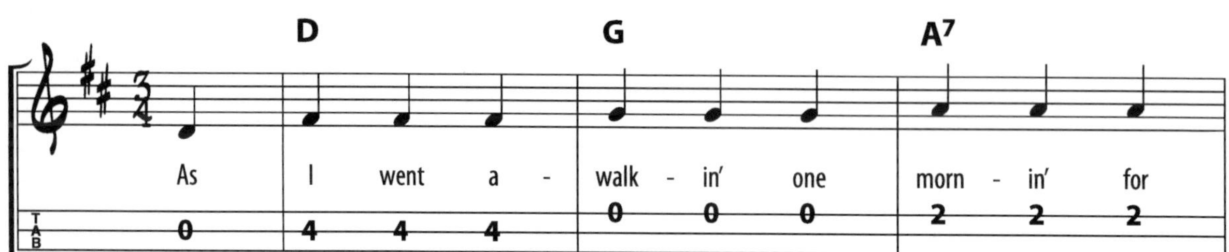

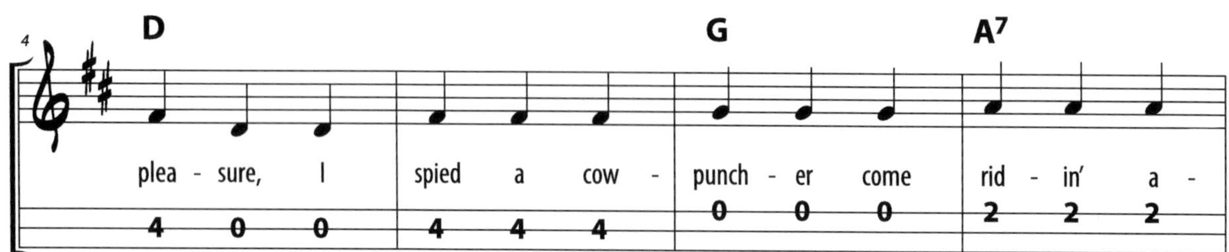

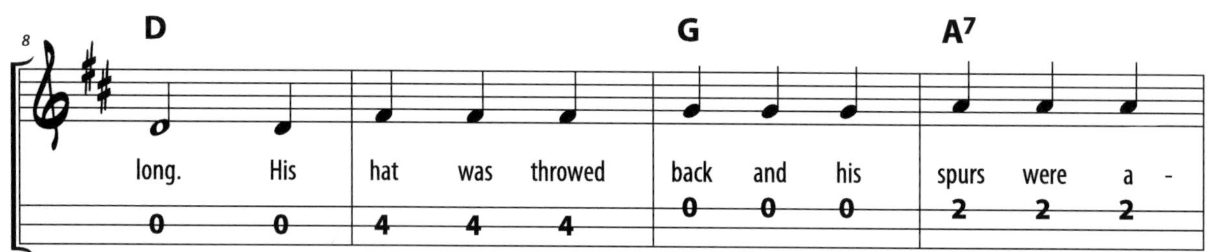

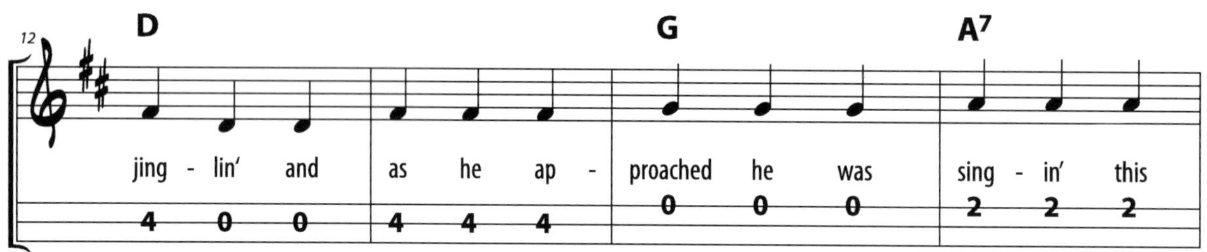

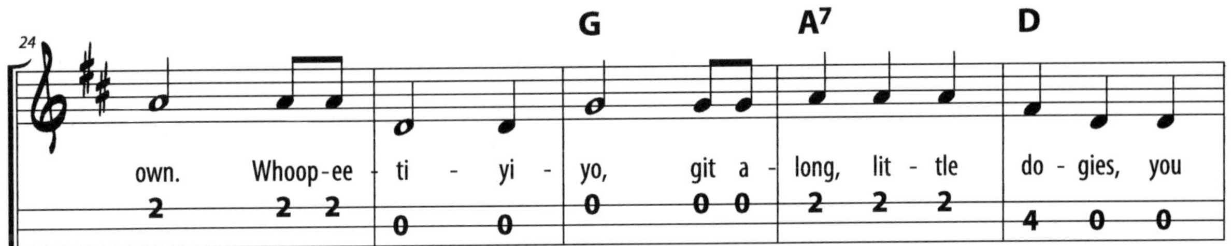

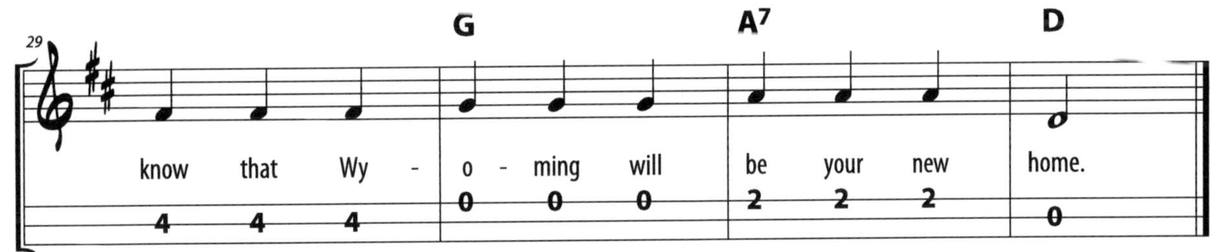

2 It's early in spring that we round up the dogies,
and mark 'em and brand 'em and bob off their tails;
We round up our horses and load the chuckwagon,
and then throw them dogies out onto the trail.
Whoopee-ti-yi-yo, git along ...

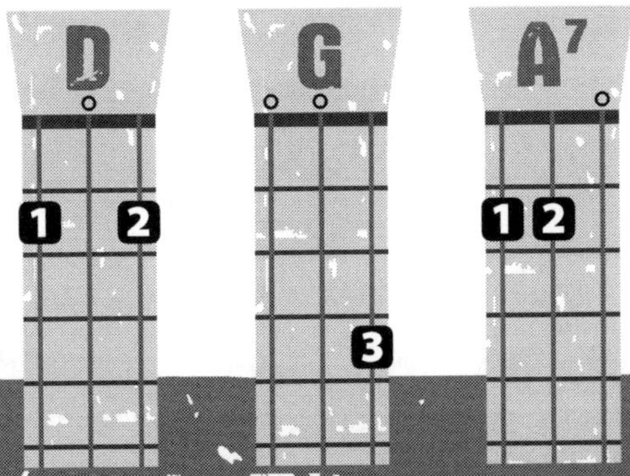

THE JOHN B. SAILS

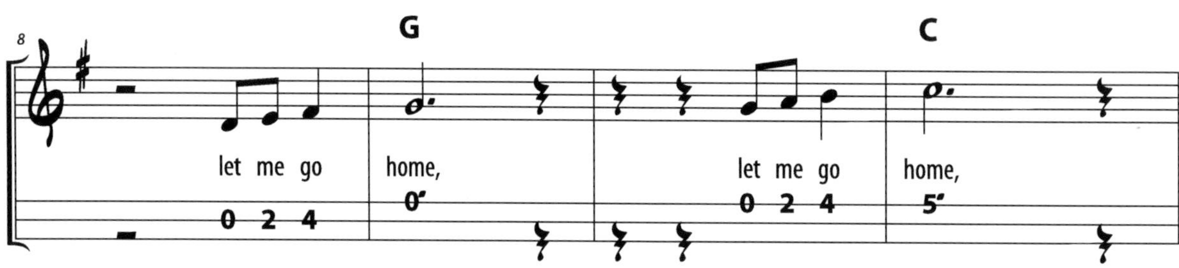

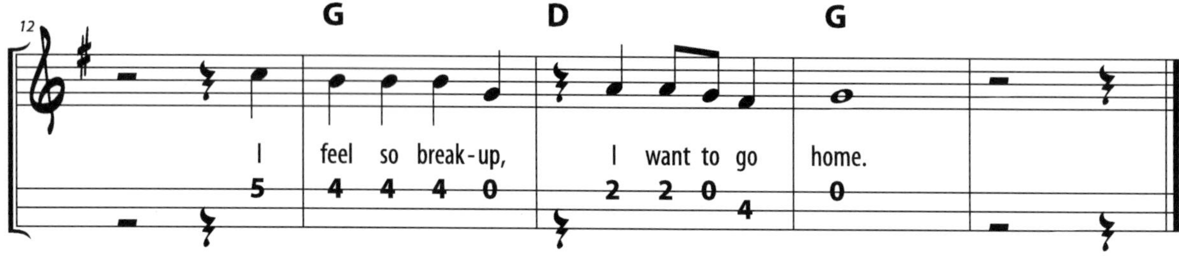

1 Come on the sloop John B.,
my grandfather and me,
round Nassau town we did roam.
Drinking all night, we got in a fight,
we feel so break-up, we want to go home.

CHORUS

So hoist up the John B. sails,
see how the mainsail set,
send for the captain ashore, let me go home,
let me go home, let me go home,
I feel so break-up, I want to go home.

2 The first mate he got drunk,
break up the people trunk,
constable come aboard, take him away,
Mr. Johnstone, leave me alone,
I feel so break-up, I want to go home.

3 The poor cook got the fits,
throw away all o' my grits,
captain's pig done eat up all o' my corn.
Lemme go home, I want to go home,
I feel so break-up, I want to go home.

4 Steamboat go by steam,
sailboat go by sail,
my girl's hat ain't got no tail.
Lemme go home, I want to go home,
I feel so break-up, I want to go home.

5 Send all the things from ashore,
let all the breezes blow,
I'm so sorry that I can longer stay,
good-by to you, Tra-la-la-lu,
this is the worst trip since I was born.

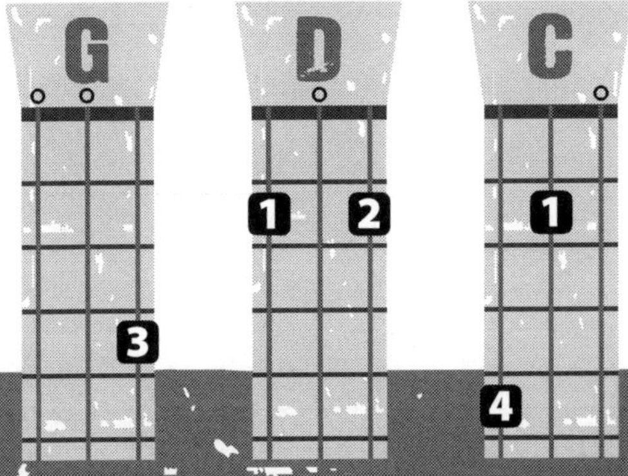

John Hardy

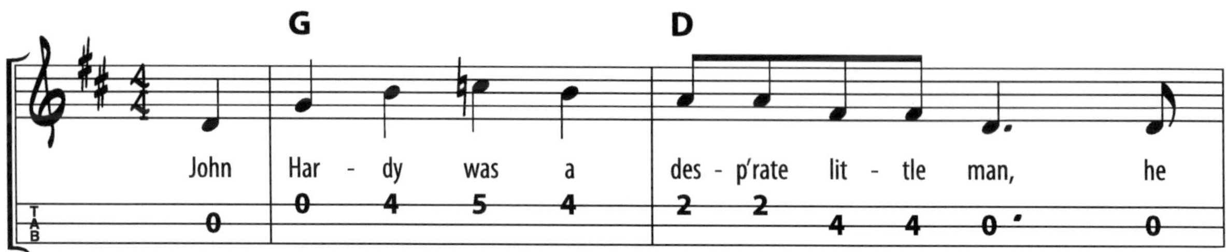
G D
John Har - dy was a des - p'rate lit - tle man, he
0 0 4 5 4 2 2 4 4 0 0

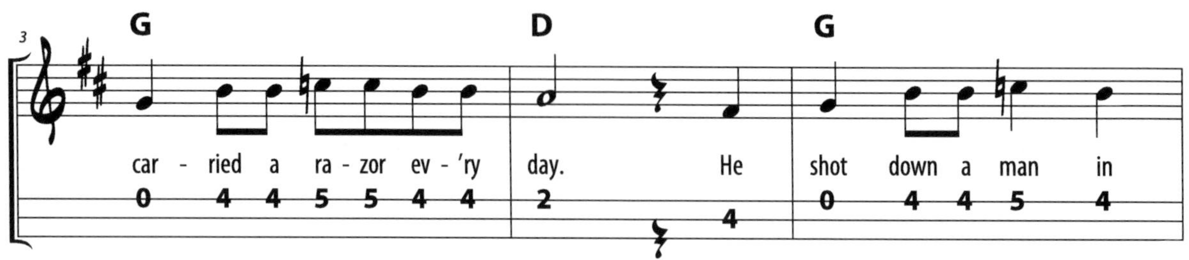
3
G D G
car - ried a ra - zor ev - 'ry day. He shot down a man in
0 4 4 5 5 4 4 2 4 0 4 4 5 4

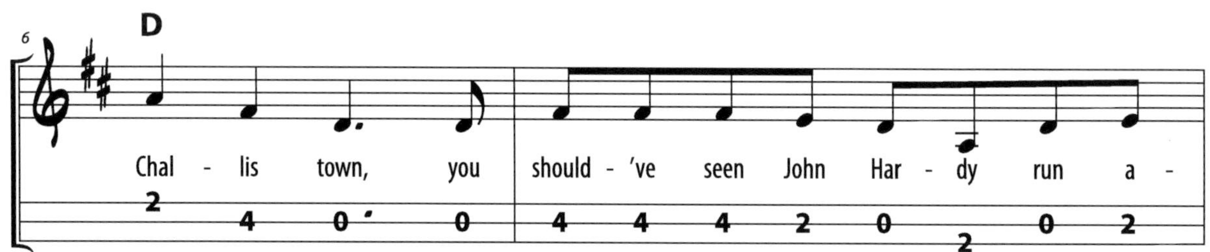
6
D
Chal - lis town, you should - 've seen John Har - dy run a -
2 4 0 0 4 4 4 2 0 2 0 2

8
A7 D
way, poor boy, you should' - ve seen John Har - dy run a - way.
4 4 0 0 4 4 4 2 6 2 4 2 0

2 John Hardy stood in that old barroom,
so drunk that he could not see.
And a man walked up and took him by the arm.
He said Johnny, come and go along with me,
Johnny, come and walk along with me.

3 John Hardy stood in his old jail cell,
the tears running down from his eyes.
He said I've been the death of many a poor boy,
but my six-shooters never told a lie,
but my six-shooters never told a lie.

4 The first one to visit John Hardy in his cell,
was a little girl dressed in blue.
She came down to that old jail cell,
she said Johnny, I've been true to you,
she said, Johnny, I've been true to you.

5 The next one to Visit John Hardy in his cell,
was a little girl dressed in red.
She come down to that old jail cell,
she said, Johnny, I had rather see you dead,
she said, Johnny, I had rather see you dead

6 I've been to the East and I've been to the West,
I've traveled this wide world around.
I've been to that river and I've been baptized,
so take me to my burying ground,
so take me to my burying ground.

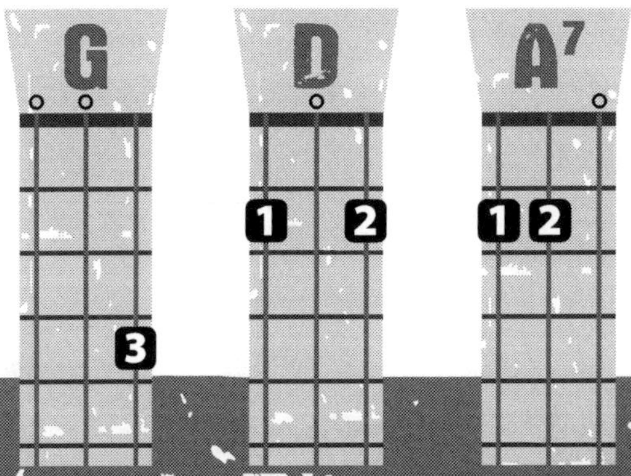

JOSHUA FIT THE BATTLE OF JERICHO

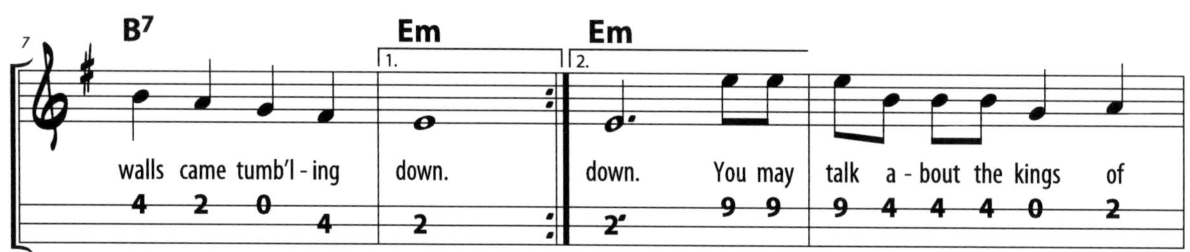

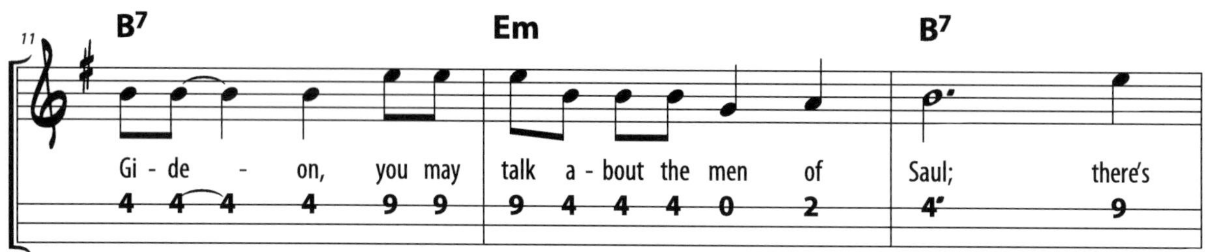

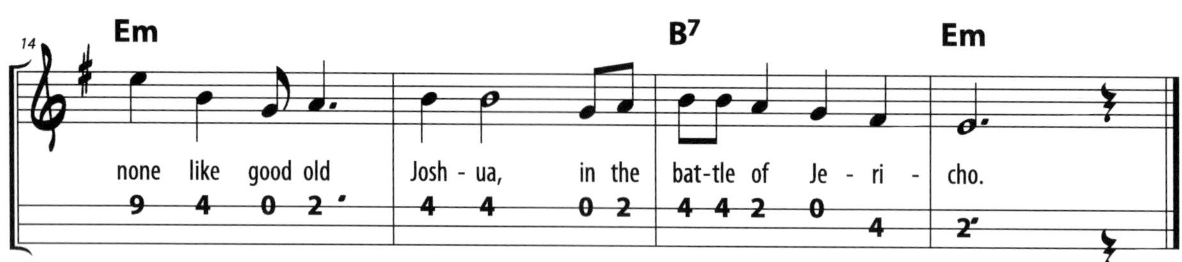

2 Right up to the walls of Jericho.
He marched with spear in Hand.
Go, blow dat ram's horn, Joshua cried,
'cause de battle am in my hand.

3 Then de lamb ram sheep horns begin a blow.
Trumpets begin to sound.
Joshua commanded de children to shout,
and de walls came tumbling down.

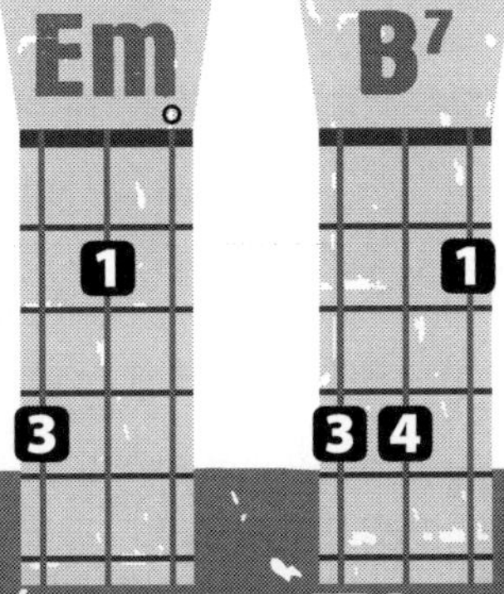

LITTLE BESSIE

STRUMMING PATTERN

2 Something hurts me here, dear mother,
like a stone upon my breast.
Oh I wonder, wonder, mother,
why it is I cannot rest.

3 All the day as you were working,
and I lay upon my bed.
I was trying to be patient,
and to think of what you said.

4 How the King, Blessed Jesus,
loves His lambs to watch and keep.
Oh, I wish He would come and take me
In His arms that I might sleep.

5 Just before the lamps were lighted,
just before the children came.
While the room was very quiet,
I heard someone call my name.

6 All at once a window opened,
one so bright upon me smiled
And I knew it must be Jesus,
when He said come here, my child.

7 Come up here, little Bessie,
come up here and live with me.
Where little children never suffer,
suffer through eternity.

8 Then I thought of all you told me,
of that bright and happy land.
I was going when you called me,
when you came and kissed my hand.

9 And at first I felt so sorry
you had called, I would go.
Oh, to sleep and never suffer,
mother, don't be crying so.

10 Hug me close dear mother closer,
put your arms around me tight.
Oh how much I love you mother,
and how strong I feel tonight

11 And her mother pressed her closer,
to her own dear burdened breast.
On the heart so near its breaking,
Lay the heart so near its rest.

12 At the solemn hour of midnight,
in the darkness calm and deep.
Laying on her mother's bosom,
Little Bessie fell asleep.

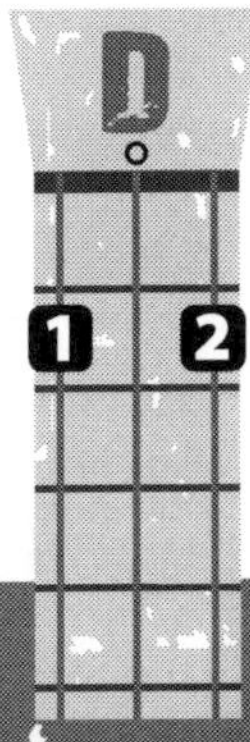

D

A^7

MORNING HAS BROKEN

C Dm G F C

T
A
B
5 2 0 | 5 | 7 | 4 2 0 | 2 4 2 | 0

7 Am D7 G

5 0 2 | 0 | 2 | 0 0 2 | 0 |

13 C F C Am G

0 2 0 | 5 | 2 | 0 2 5 | 5 0 5 | 0

19 C F G C

0 2 0 | 0 | 2 | 0 2 0 | 5 | 5

STRUMMING PATTERN

T
A
B
5 2 0 | 5

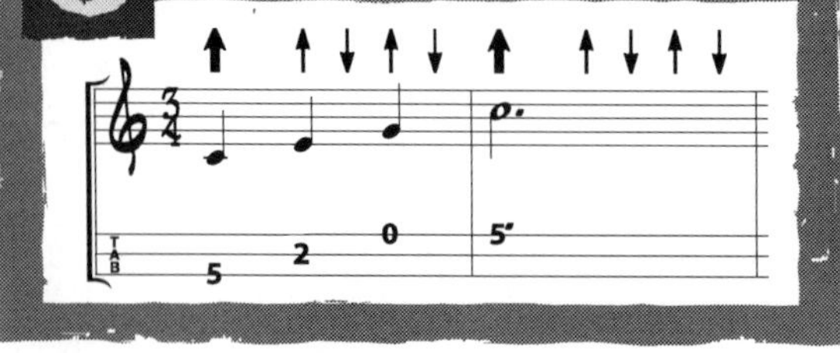

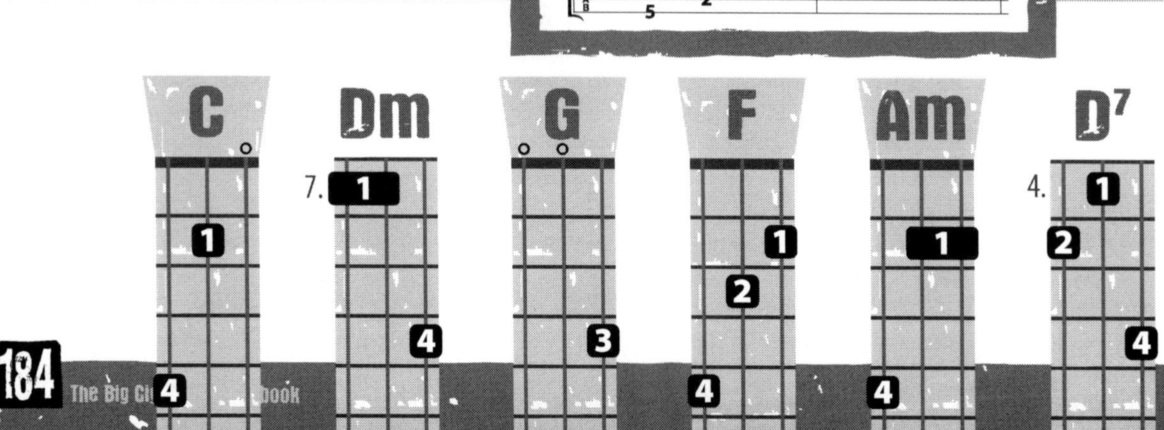

BASIC CHORDS

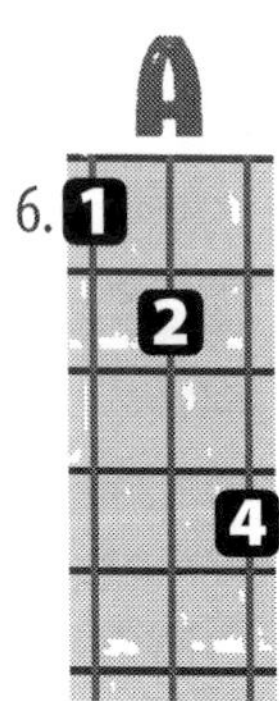

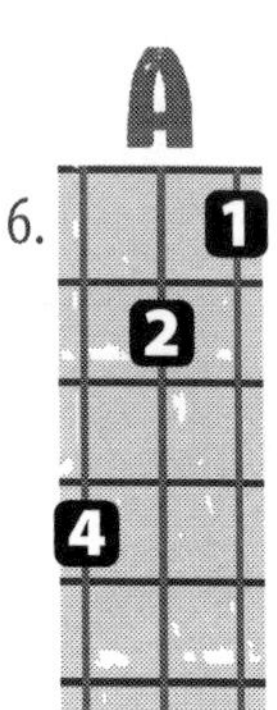

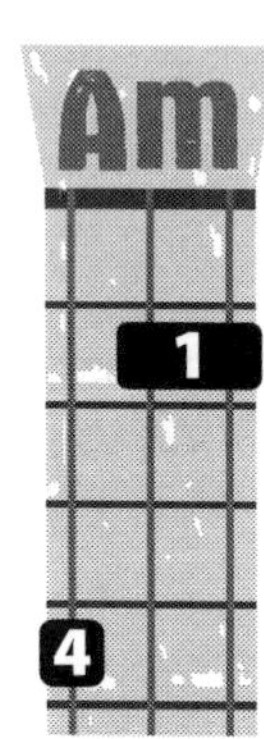

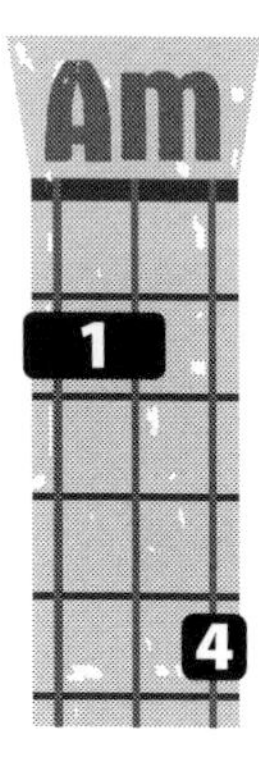

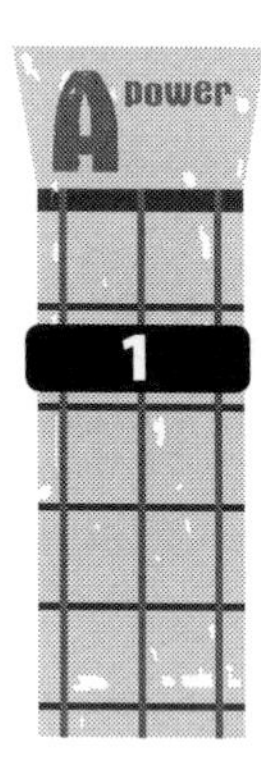

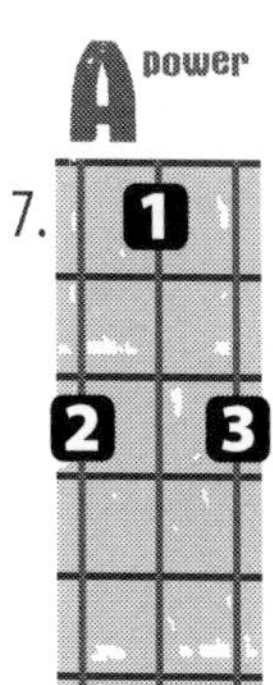

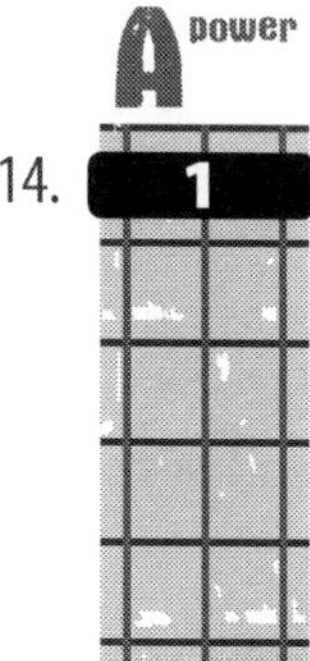

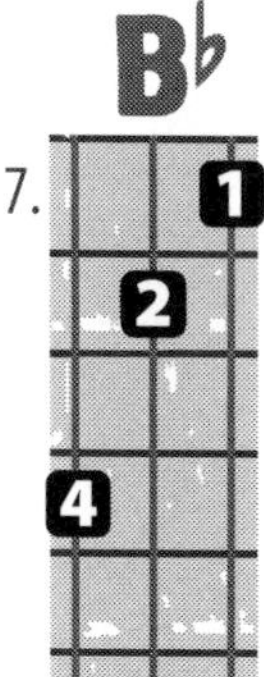

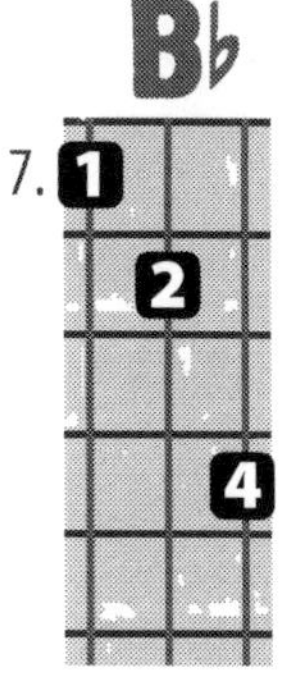

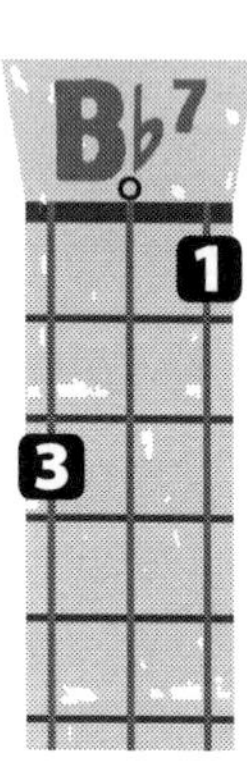

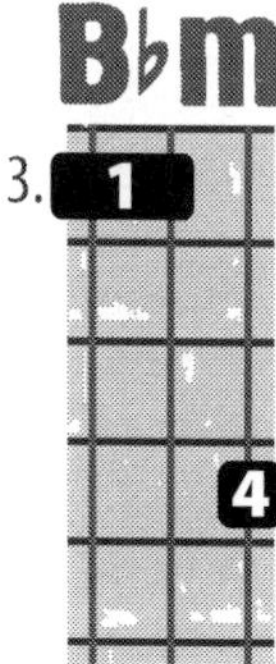

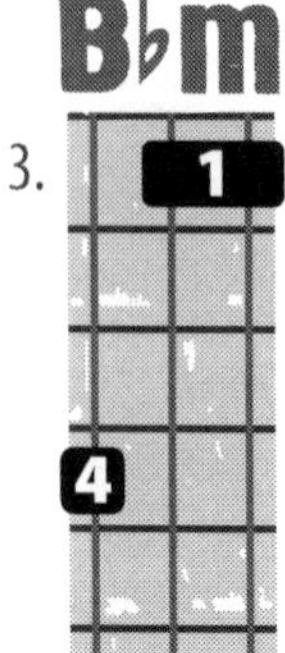

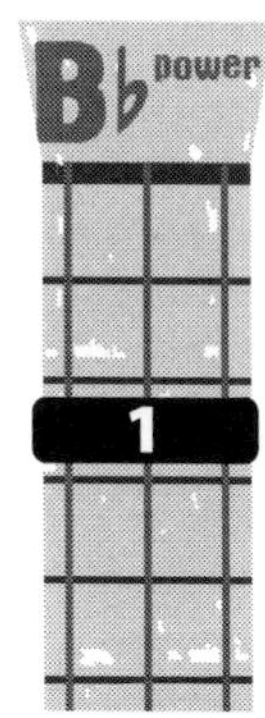

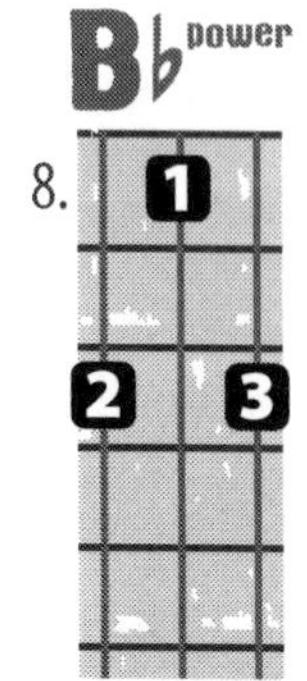

B
8.

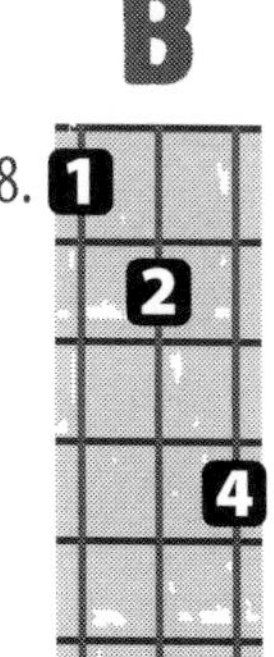

The "power" chord is a simplified version that can be substituted for the „normal" chord form.

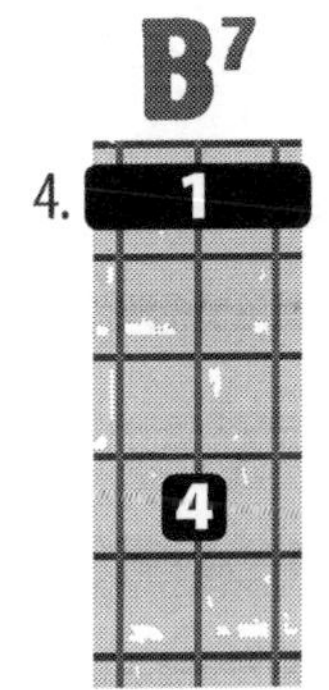

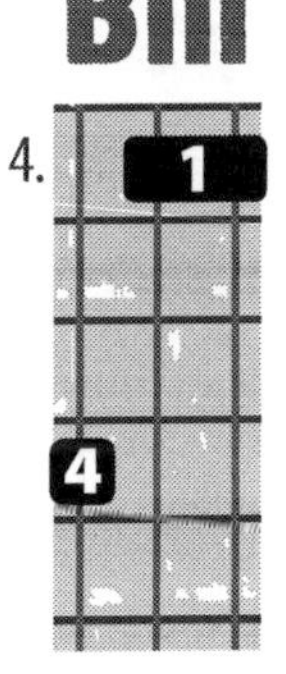

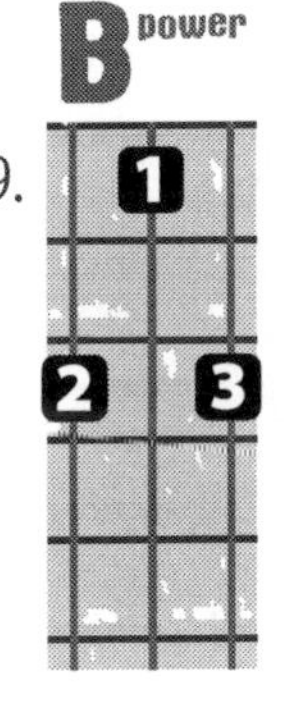

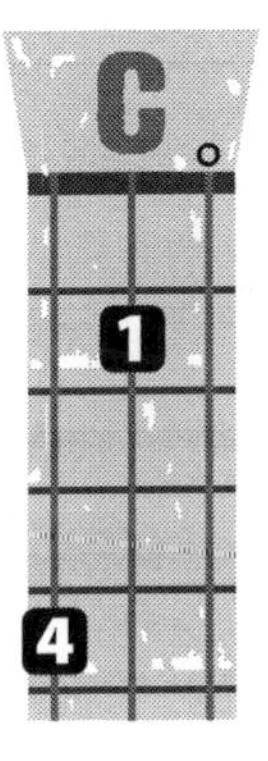

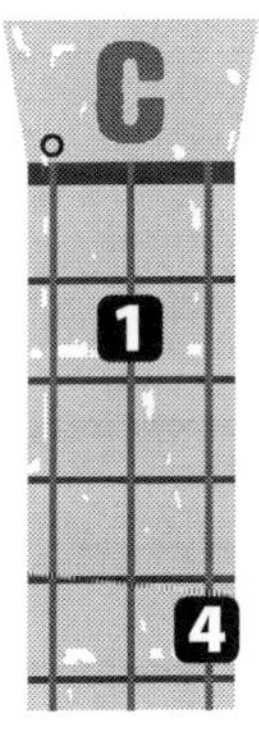

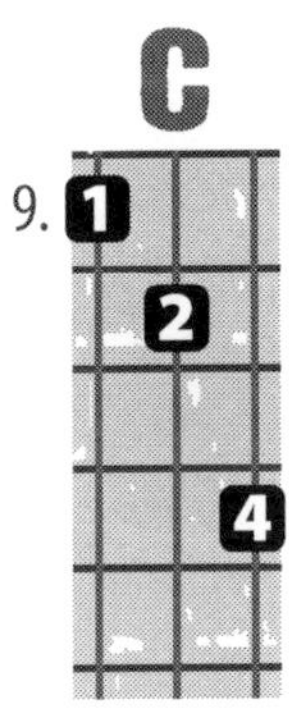

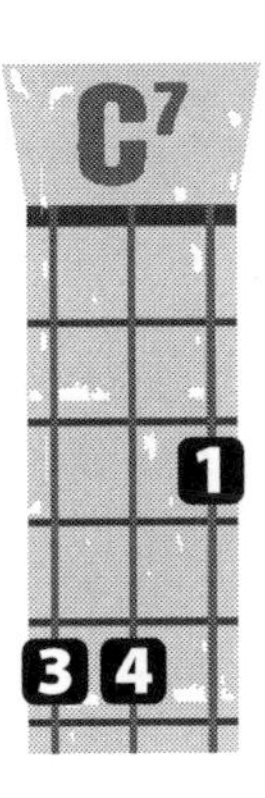

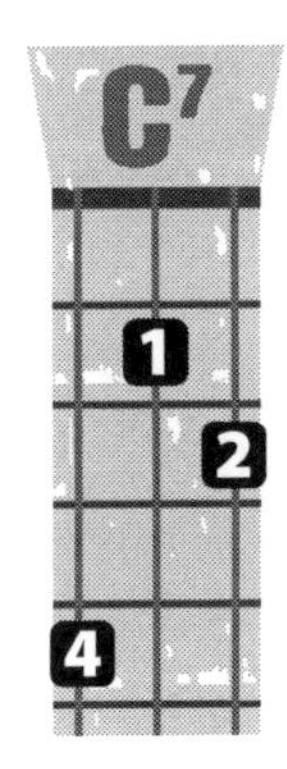

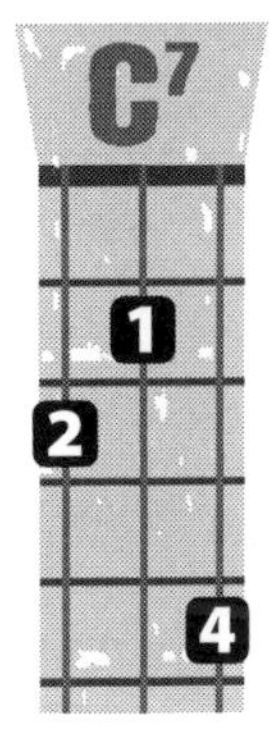

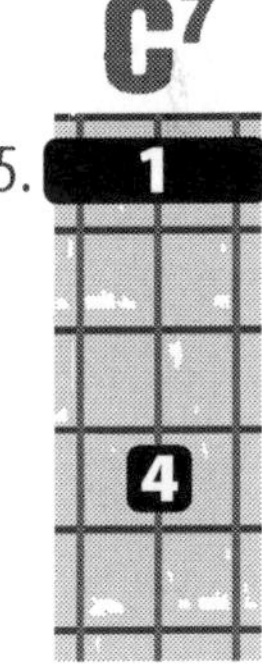

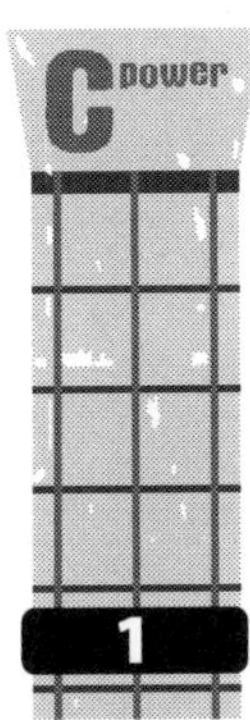

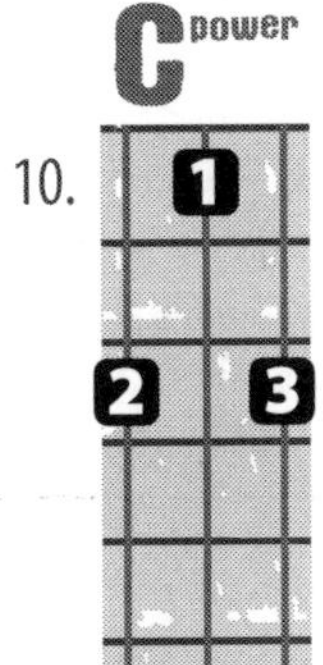

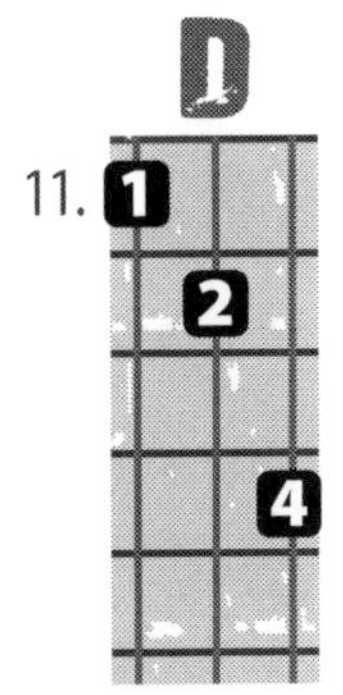

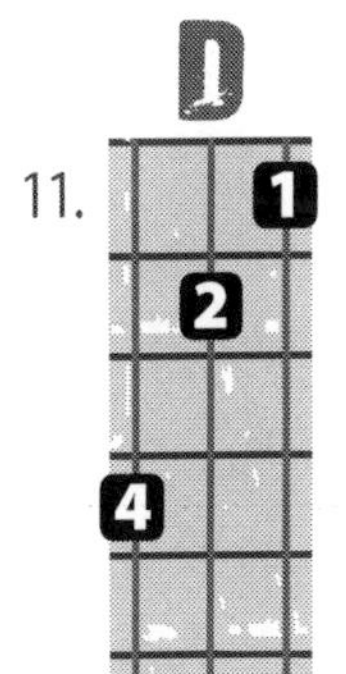

D7

4.

The "power" chord is a simplified version that can be substituted for the „normal" chord form.

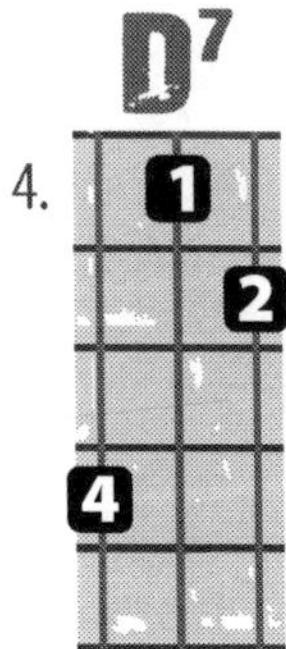

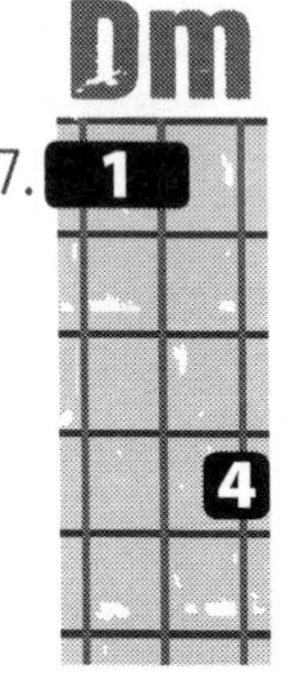

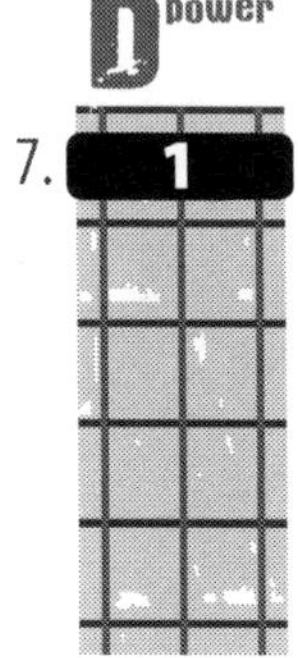

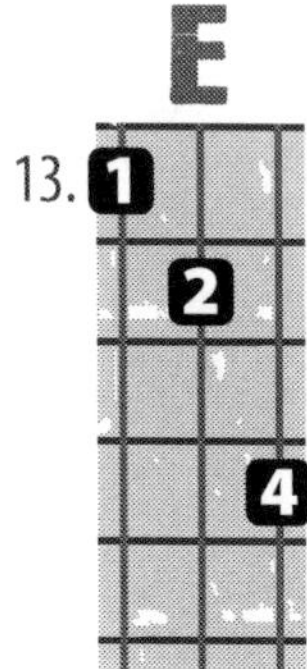

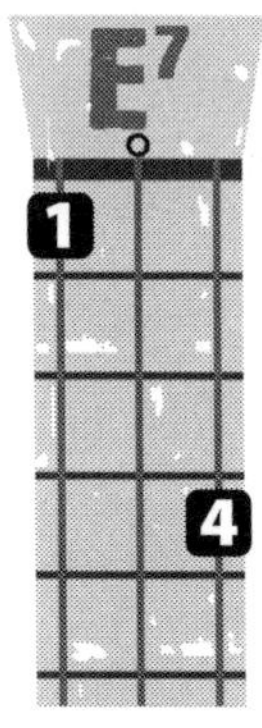

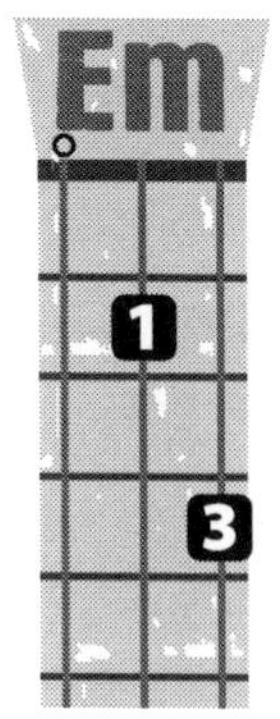

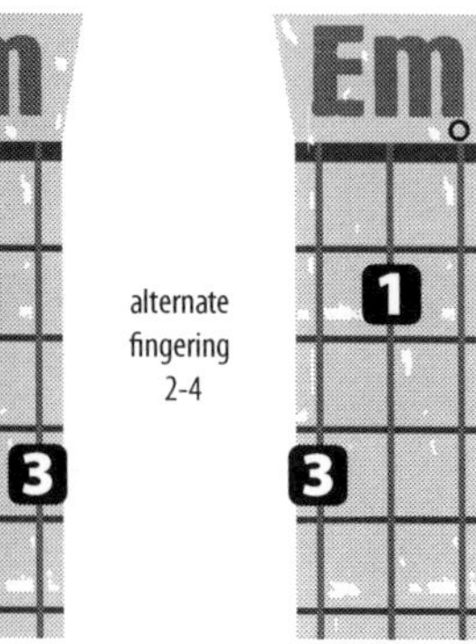

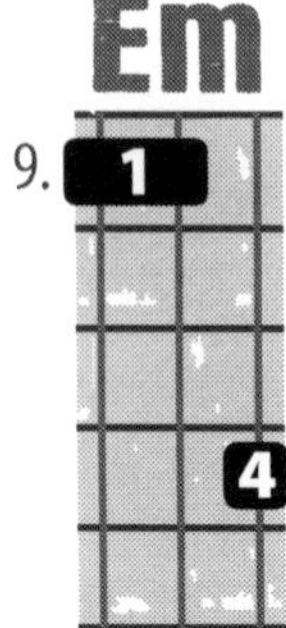

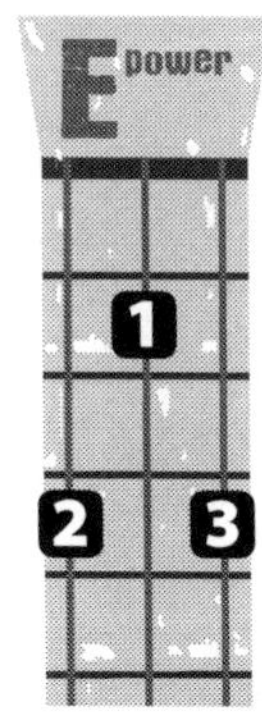

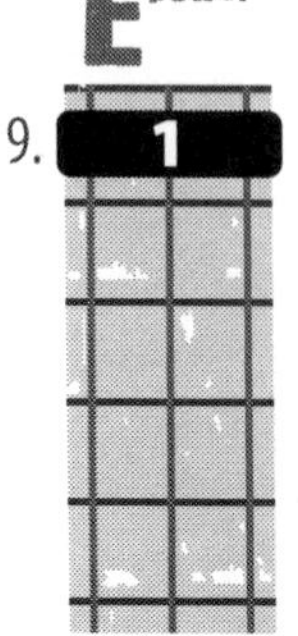

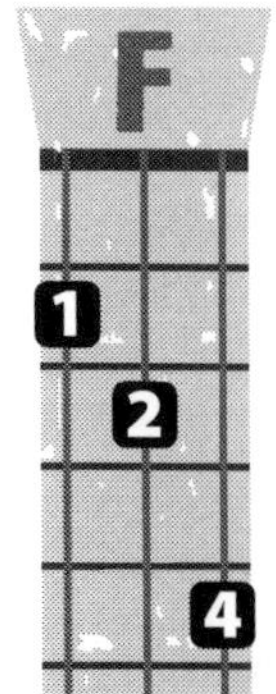

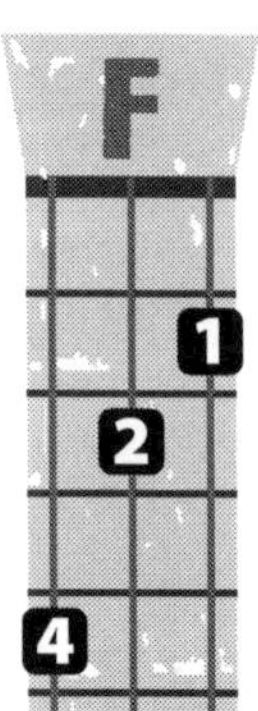

The "power" chord is a simplified version that can be substituted for the „normal" chord form.

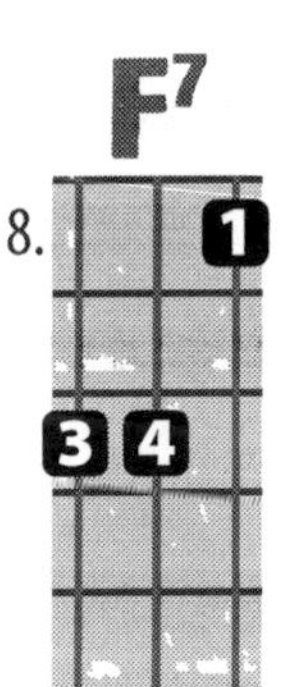

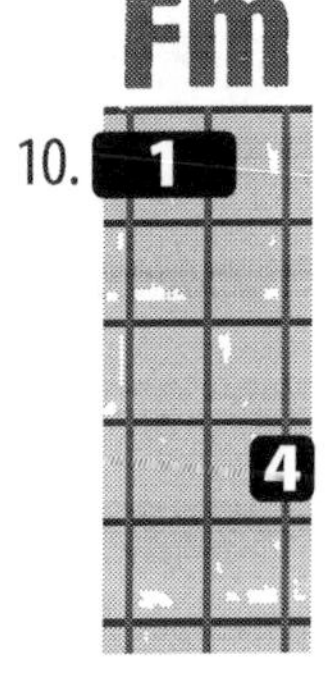

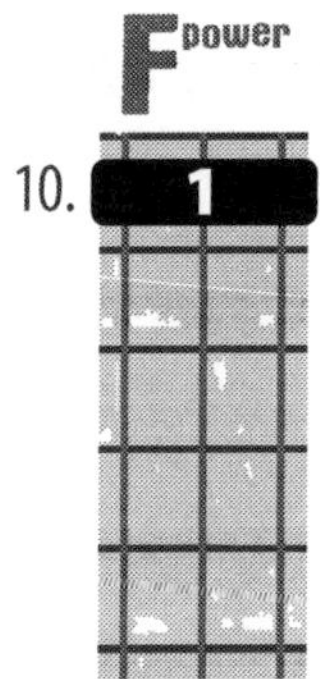

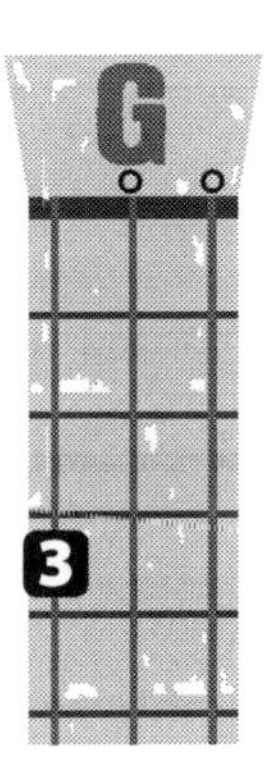

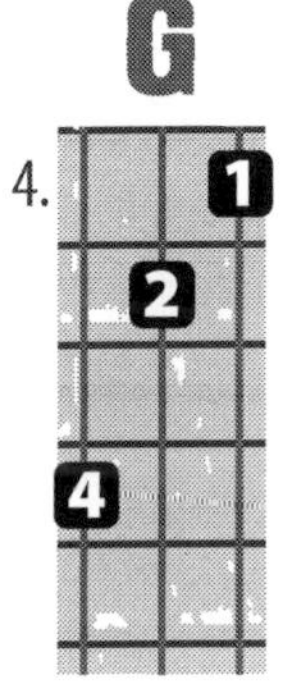

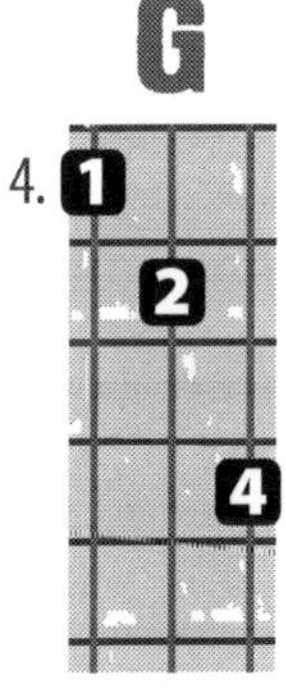

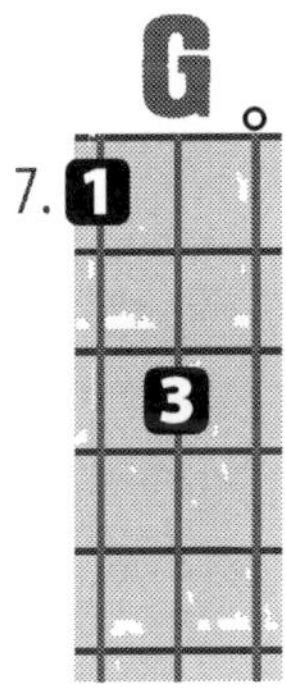

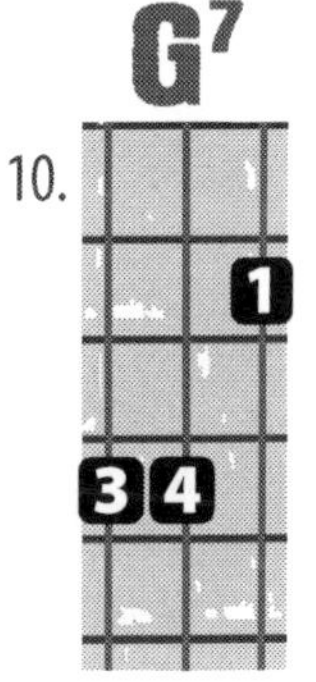

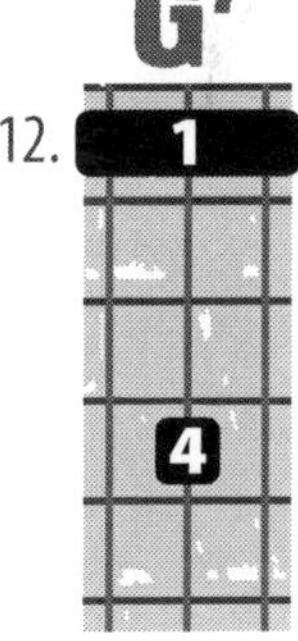

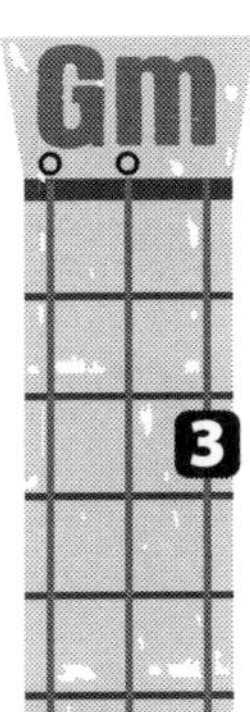

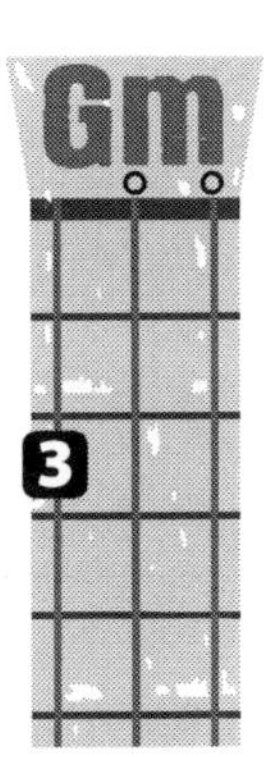

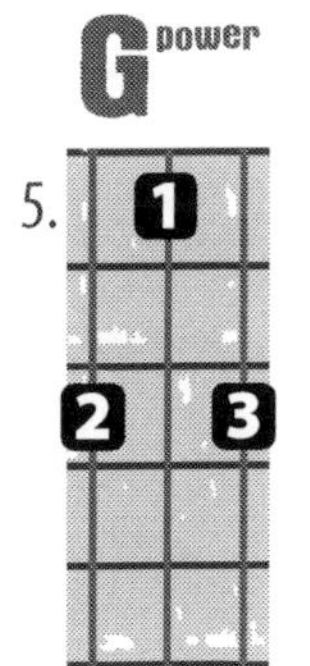

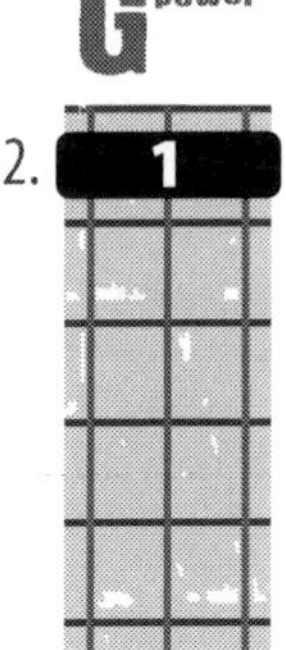

The "power" chord is a simplified version that can be substituted for the „normal" chord form.

STRUMMING PATTERNS

The following is a selection of basic strumming patterns which you can use for song accompaniment. These are just for starters–you'll soon use other, more elaborate patterns or invent your own. Feel free to use a pick or your finger(s) for strumming–basically whatever feels best.

Here's how they're read:

- The horizontal lines represent the strings of your CBG.
  Downstroke (strumming in the direction of the floor): arrow upward
  Upstroke: arrow downward.
- The length of the arrows indicates which strings to strum.
- Each of these pattern shows a whole measure.

For song accompaniment you can choose (and also combine) whatever pattern feels best to you, but keep in mind to match the pattern's time to the time of the song, e.g. for a song in 4/4 time only use strumming patterns in 4/4 time. Songs in 2/2 time can be played using strumming patterns in 4/4 time.
Practice any strumming pattern until it runs "on auto-pilot" (e.g. without any thinking), so you can concentrate on other things like changing chords and singing.

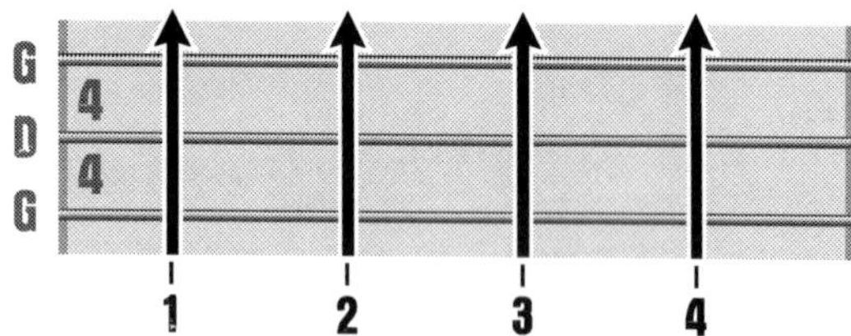

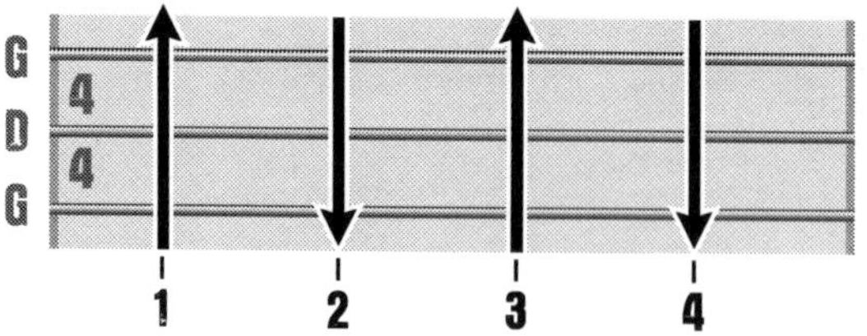

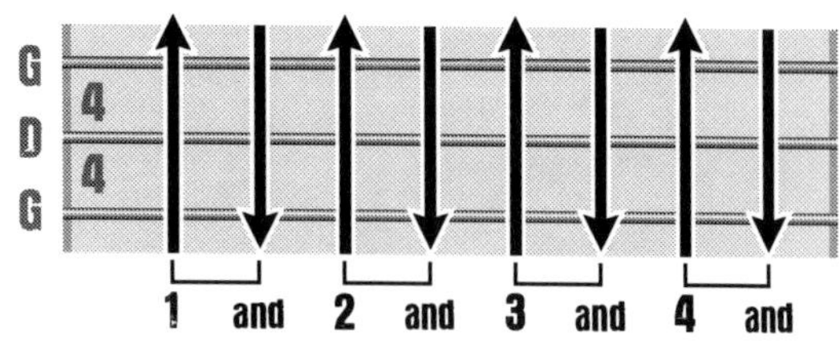

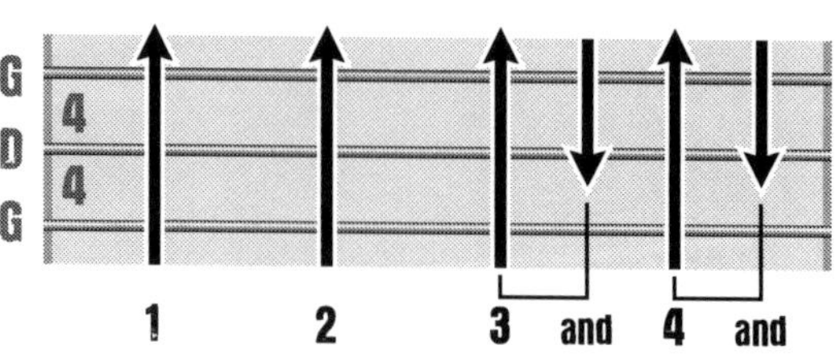

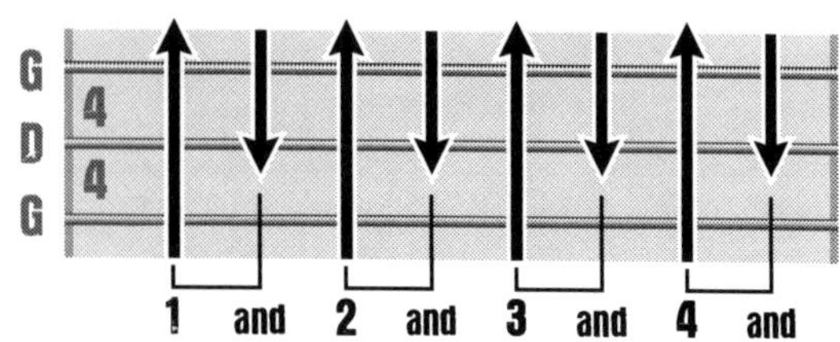

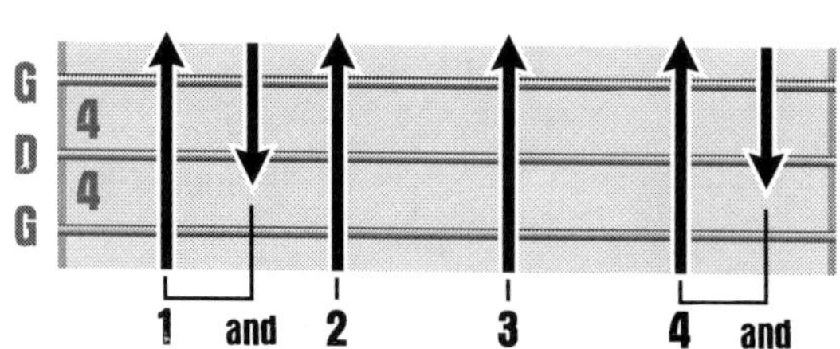

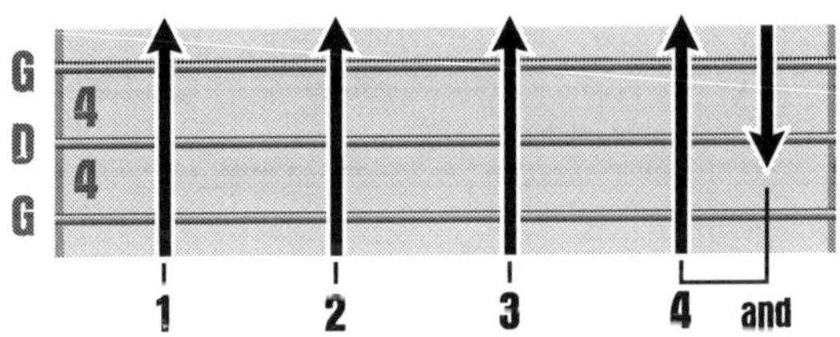
G
D
G
4
4
1
2
3
4 and

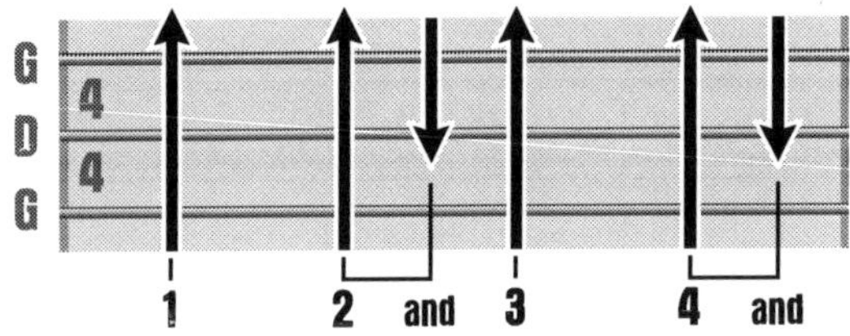
G
D
G
4
4
1
2 and
3
4 and

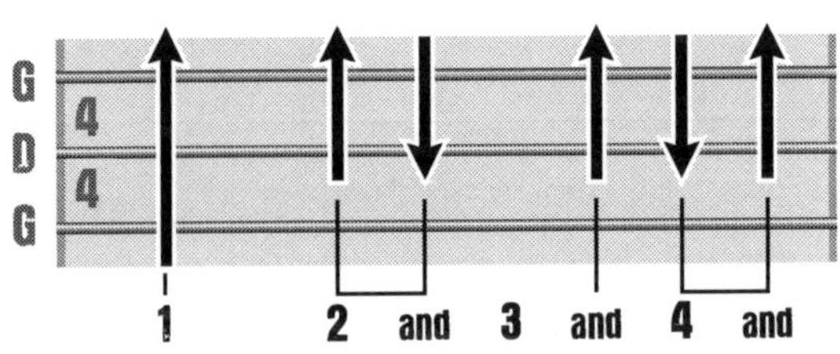
G
D
G
4
4
1
2 and
3 and
4 and

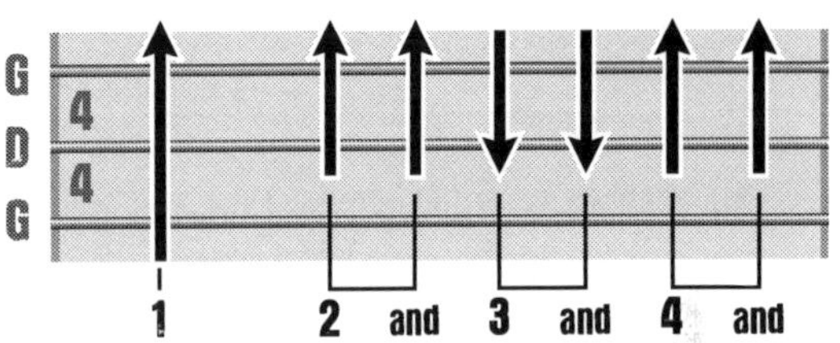
G
D
G
4
4
1
2 and
3 and
4 and

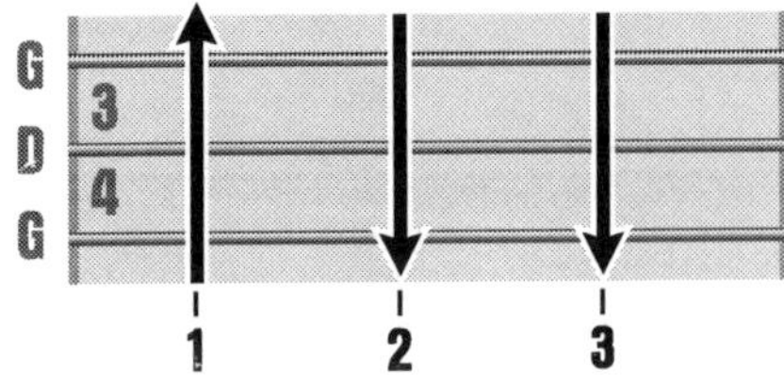
G
D
G
3
4
1
2
3

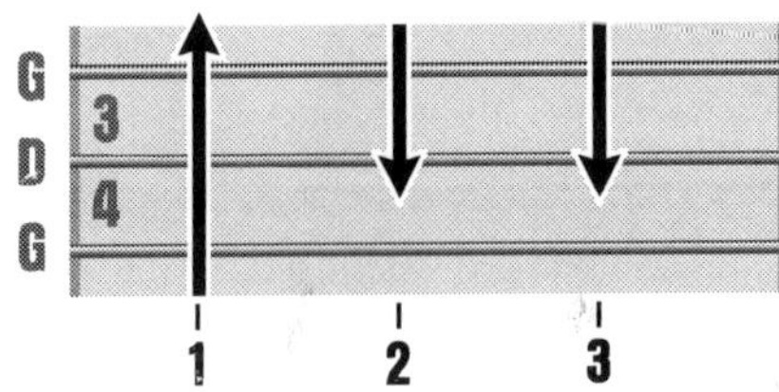
G
D
G
3
4
1
2
3

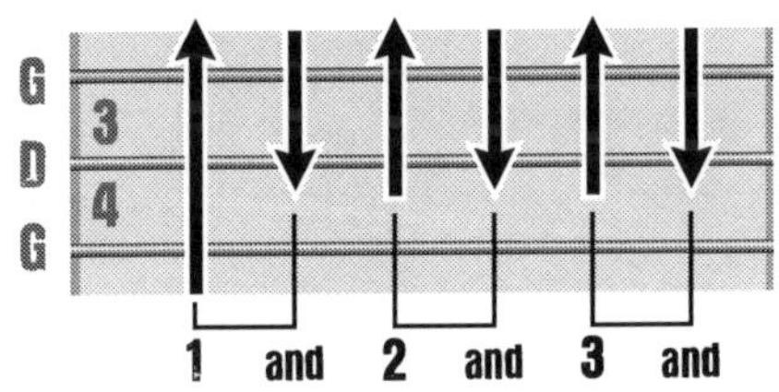
G
D
G
3
4
1 and
2 and
3 and

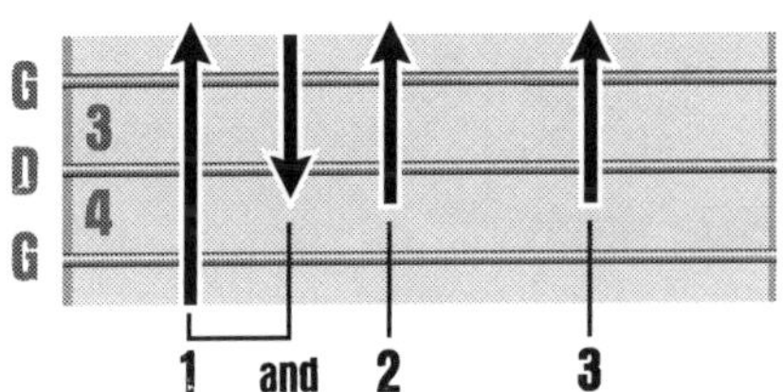
G
D
G
3
4
1 and
2
3

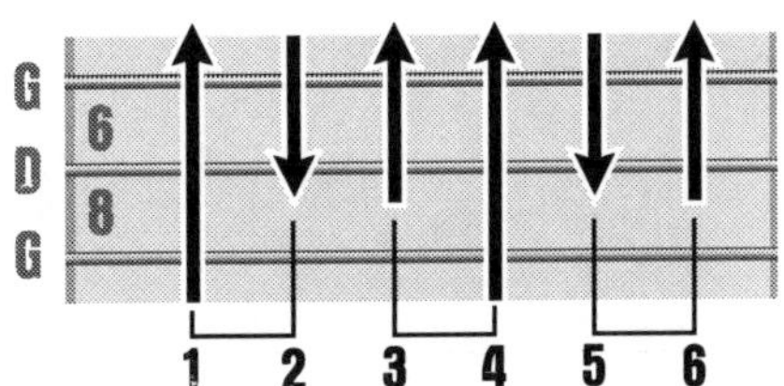
G
D
G
6
8
1
2
3
4
5
6

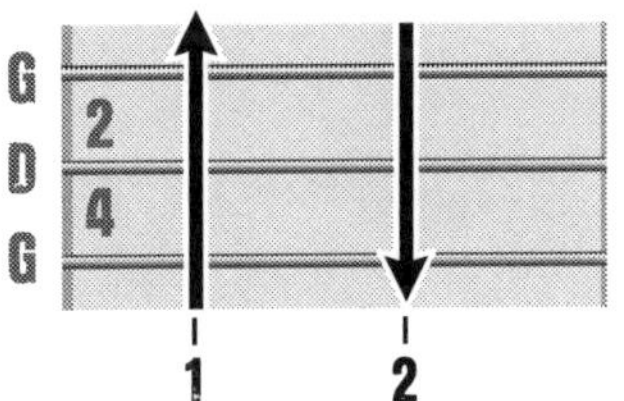
G
D
G
2
4
1
2

PICKING PATTERNS

Many songs sound particularly good when played using a picking pattern. The basic ideas is this: instead of picking all the notes of a chord simultaneously with your finger(s) or a pick, you play them successively, one after the other. Picking patterns are commonly used for longer musical sections (or even whole songs) and adapted to the chord changes if necessary.

As in tablature, horizontal lines represent the strings of your CBG. The time signature is notated at the beginning of the pattern as a fraction (e.g. 4/4 for songs in 4/4 time).
The letters T, I and M indicate the fingers of the picking hand.
There are a few things to keep in mind when using picking patterns:
Obviously, the pattern's time signature has to match that of the song. In some cases, the pattern may have to be adapted to a certain chord or a chord change, but most of the time you can use the following simple rule:

- pick the G (melody) string with your middle finger
- pick the D string with your index finger
- pick the G string (bass string) with your thumb

One of the best ways to practise picking patterns is to play them on open strings until the movement of your fingers becomes second nature–practicing this way ensures you'll be able to concentrate on more important things when it's time to play the song. When the picking pattern has been "automized" to a certain degree it's time to add chords and chord changes. Take your time because nothing sounds worse than a "stuttering" picking pattern interfering with a smooth chord change.
On the next page you'll find some basic picking patterns. These are of course just a small selection from the multitude of possible patterns, meant to whet your appetite–you'll soon find varying patterns and inventing new ones can be lots of fun!

For a start, you may want to try:
- Combining different picking patterns
  (e. g. one for the verse and one for the chorus).
- Combining picking patterns with strumming patterns.
- Mixing picking patterns with melody lines and damping techniques.

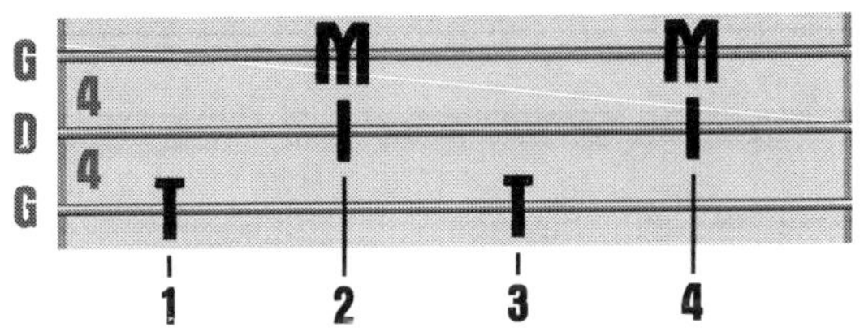
G
D
G
4
4
M
M
I
I
T
T
1
2
3
4

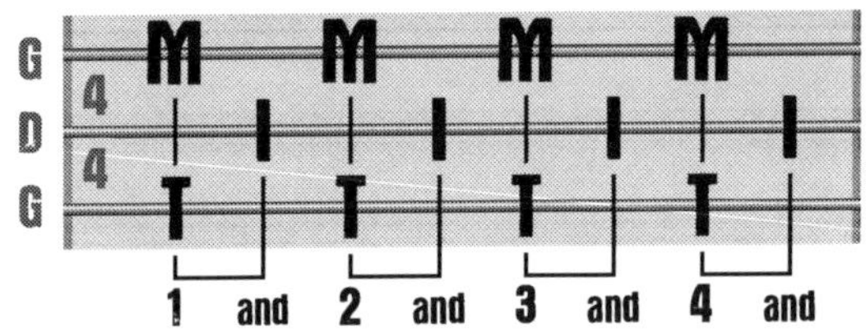
G
D
G
4
4
M M M M
I I I I
T T T T
1 and 2 and 3 and 4 and

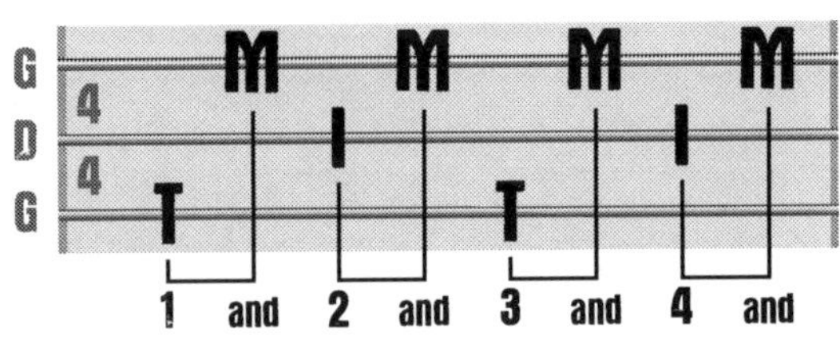
G
D
G
4
4
M M M M
I I
T T
1 and 2 and 3 and 4 and

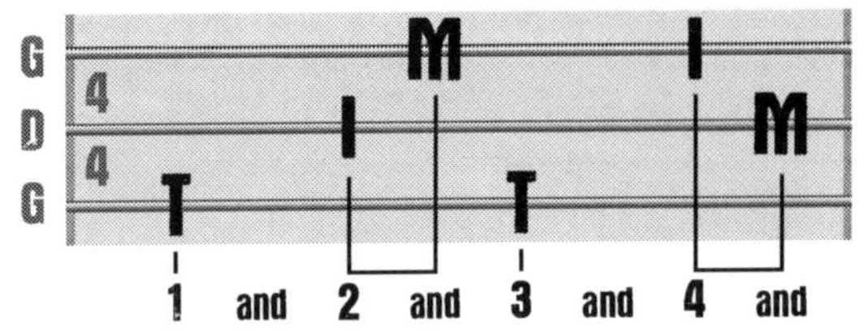
G
D
G
4
4
M I
I M
T T
1 and 2 and 3 and 4 and

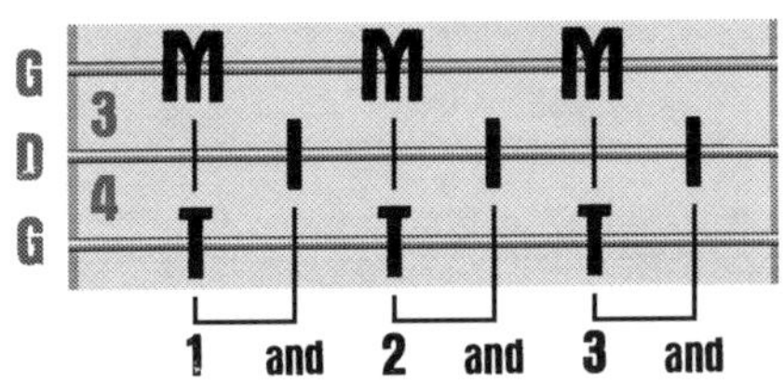
G
D
G
3
4
M M M
I I I
T T T
1 and 2 and 3 and

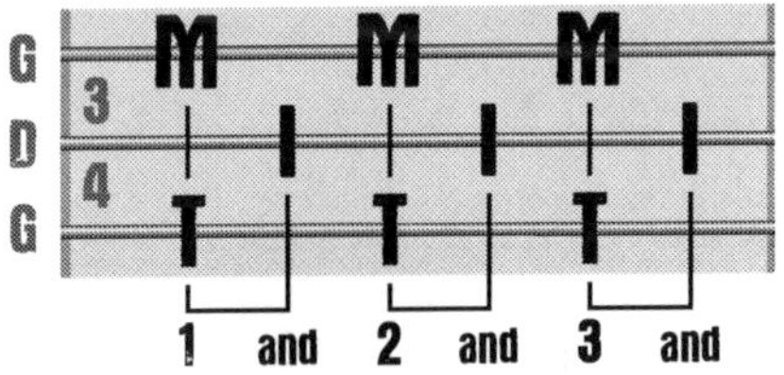
G
D
G
3
4
M M M
I I I
T T T
1 and 2 and 3 and

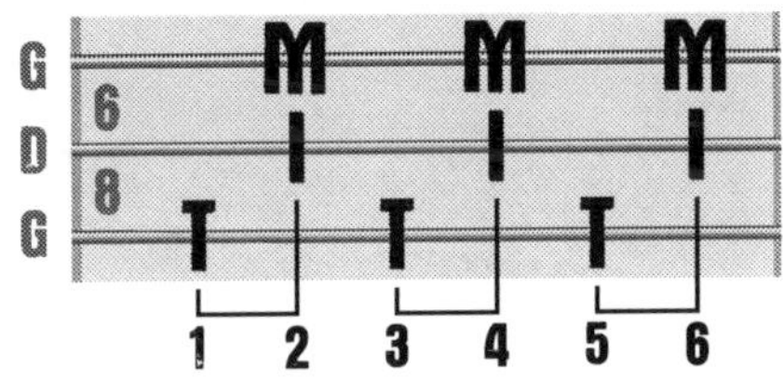
G
D
G
6
8
M M M
I I I
T T T
1 2 3 4 5 6

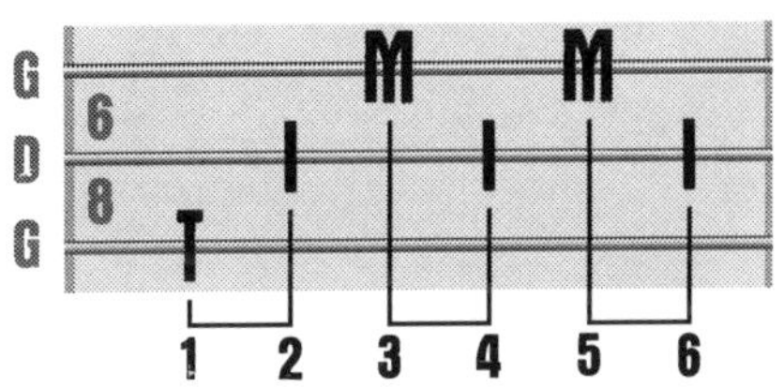
G
D
G
6
8
M M
I I I
T
1 2 3 4 5 6

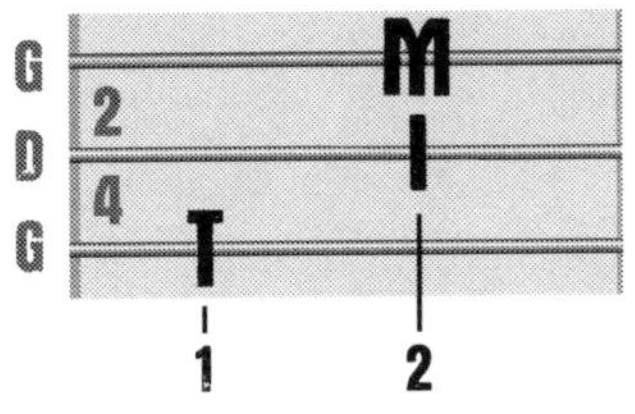
G
D
G
2
4
M
I
T
1
2

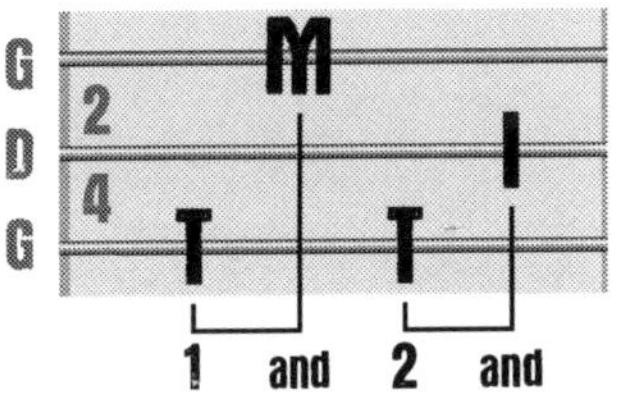
G
D
G
2
4
M
I
T T
1 and 2 and

HOW TO READ MUSIC

On the following pages I've compiled the most important basics of music notation. Don't worry if this all sounds a bit greek to you–you don't need to know this to play the songs in this book. Instead, these pages are intended for those who want to delve into the basics of reading music.

The staff

The **staff** is used to write down music. The staff is a group of five horizontal lines and the four spaces between them. It is read from left to right. At the end of the line you jump to the beginning of the next line. Notes can be written on the lines or the spaces in between.

Notes

There are different kind of notes, but they have one thing in common: Every note has a **notehead**. Most notes also have a **stem** and some of them an additional **flag** or a **beam**.

Pitch

Notes are written on the staff. You can tell the pitch of a note by its position on the staff.
Notes from the third line on upwards have their stem pointing down. The stem of all other notes is pointing up.
Notes that are too low or high for the staff are notated on **ledger lines**. You can think of ledger lines as a kind of abridged note lines.

Note value

You can tell the note value (duration of the note) by its shape. The next smaller note duration is derived by dividing the note value by two. For example: A half note is half the length of a whole note and two half notes once again add up to a whole note.

Rests

Rests are signs telling you to pause (e.g. play nothing) for a given period of time. For every note value, there's a corresponding rest. Don't mistake the whole rest for the half rest as they look quite similar!

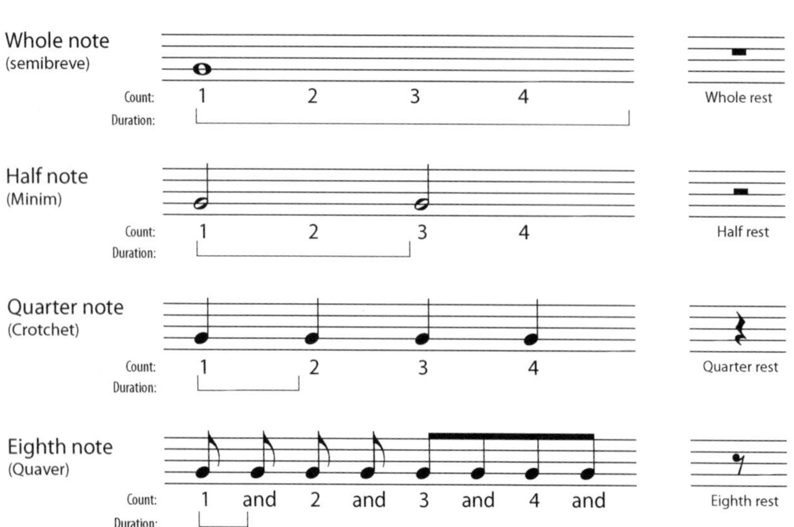

Tip: Groups of eighth notes are usually notated using a beam–they're far easier to read this way.

Clef

The clef tells you the position of a reference note used to determine the positions of all other notes. If you see a G-clef, you can simply count: one note up from G = A; one note down from G = F and so on (see below).

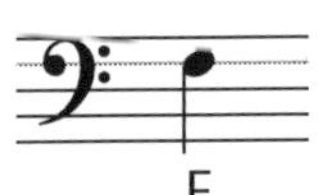

This is an **F-clef**, telling you the position of the note F: the note F is located on the second line (counting from top to bottom).

This is a **G-clef**. It is the most common clef and tells you the position of the note G: the note G is located on the second line (counting from bottom to top).

Note names

There are seven different note names: A, B, C, D, E, F, G. After the seventh note, the note names repeat: A, B, C, D, E, F, G etc.
These seven notes are also called **natural notes** or **naturals**.

To the right you can see one of the reasons there are several clefs: depending on the instrument, using another clef minimizes the number of ledger lines, making for a better readable notation.

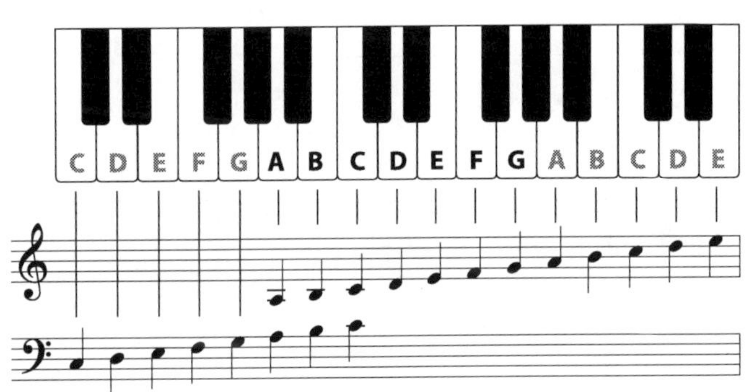

Accidentals

Take a look at the keyboard below. You'll see the note names you already know (white keys) but you'll also notice some new note names (the black keys). These new notes are created by raising or lowering one of the seven old notes.

Writing a ♯ (sharp) before a note raises it by a half-step.
The note name is extended by an added "sharp" (e. g. G sharp).

Writing a (flat) before a note lowers it by a half-step.
The note name is extended by the word "flat" (e.g. G flat).

Here are all the notes on a piano keyboard–memorize them carefully!

There are two ways to name the notes of the black keys. For instance, the black key between F and G can either be called F sharp or G flat. Don't let this confuse you–it's the same pitch nevertheless!

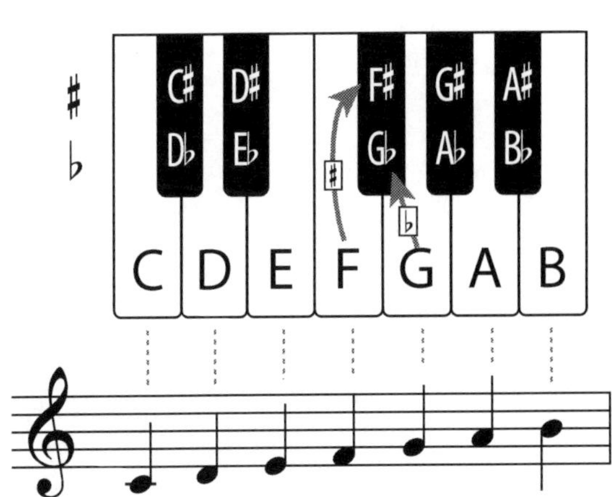

Key Signature

The **key signature** is a set of sharps (♯) or flats (♭) notated at the beginning of the staff immediately after the time signature. It designates notes that have to be played higher or lower than the corresponding natural notes. A sharp on a line or space raises all the notes on that line or space by a semitone. A flat on a line or space lowers all notes on that line or space by a semitone.

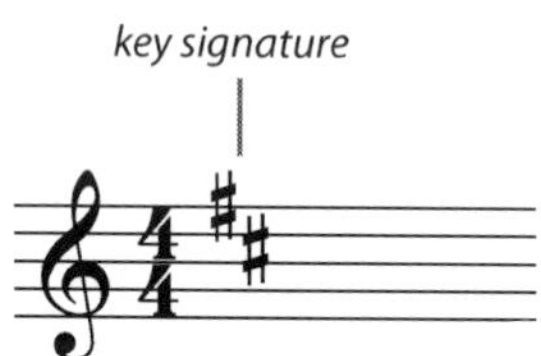

Bar (measure)

Notated music is divided into **bars** (or measures) by **bar lines**. The first note in every bar is accentuated slightly. The **time signature** at the beginning of the piece tells you how many notes make up a bar in this piece (here: 4 quarter notes). This time signature is called "Four-Four time". The end of a piece of music is indicated by a **final bar line**.

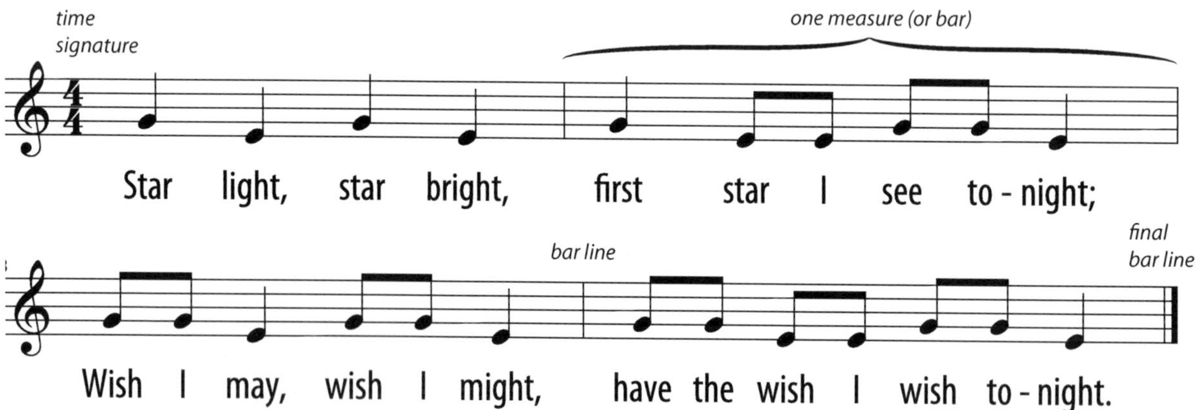

Time Signature

The time signature is notated at the beginning of the staff. It tells you how many beats each bar contains and which note value is equivalent to one beat. Here are some common time signatures and how to count them:

Ties and slurs

Two notes of the same pitch can be connected by a curved line, the **tie**. The second note is not played separately. Instead, its duration is simply added to the duration of the first note (e.g. two tied quarter notes have the same duration as a half note).

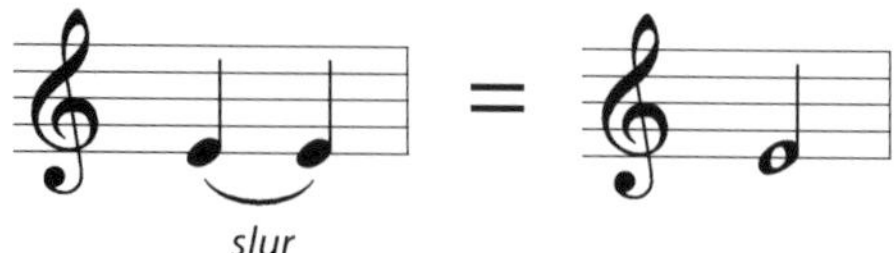

There's another musical sign looking very similar to the tie, the **slur**.
Two or more notes connected by a slur are meant to be played independently, but seamlessly after another (also called legato playing).
The distinction between the tie and the slur is easy, however. While the tie connects notes of the **same pitch and name**, the slur is only used on notes of **different pitches and names**.

Dotted notes

A dot behind a note increases the duration of that note by half its original length. This sounds much more complicated than it actually is:

A dotted half note has the duration of a half note plus a quarter note.

A dotted quarter note has the duration of a quarter note plus as eighth note.

Triplets

Dividing a note value by three instead of two is called a triplet. This sounds way more complicated than it actually is. Have a look at the graphic to the right. In standard notation, triplets are notated by the number "3" and often grouped with a small bracket.
A common way to count triplets is:
"1-and-e, 2-and-e".

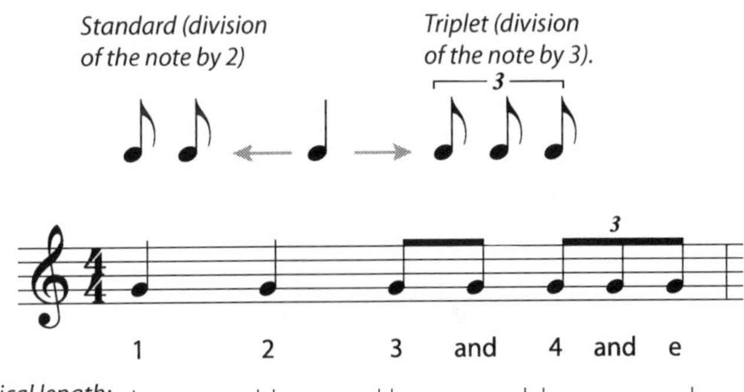

Repeat signs

tell you to repeat parts of a piece of music (or even the whole piece).

Here the whole song is played twice: 1 2 3 4 5 6 7 8 **1 2 3 4 5 6 7 8**

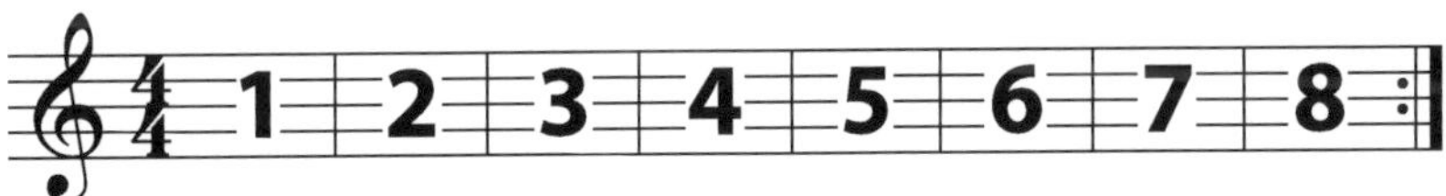

Measures 3 and 4 are repeated once: 1 2 3 4 **3 4** 5 6 7 8

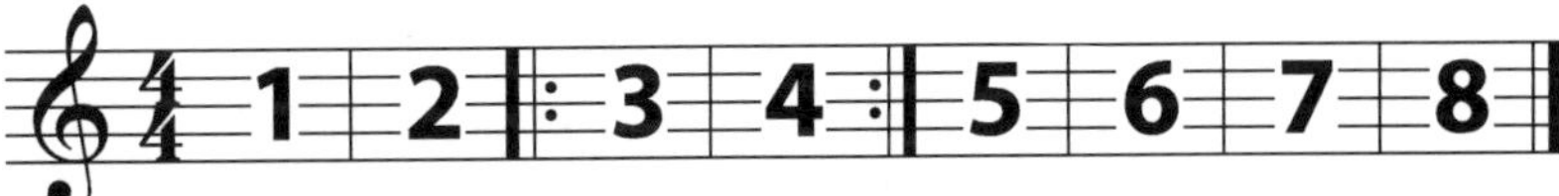

Repeat with first and second ending (or volta brackets): 1 2 3 4 5 6 **1 2 3 4** 7 8

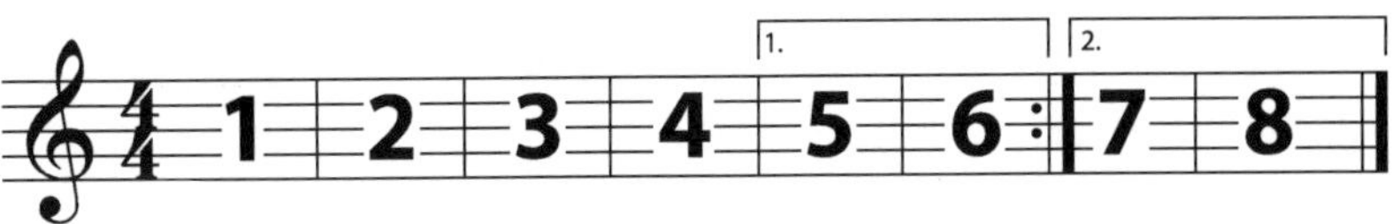

PLAYING WITH A CAPODASTER

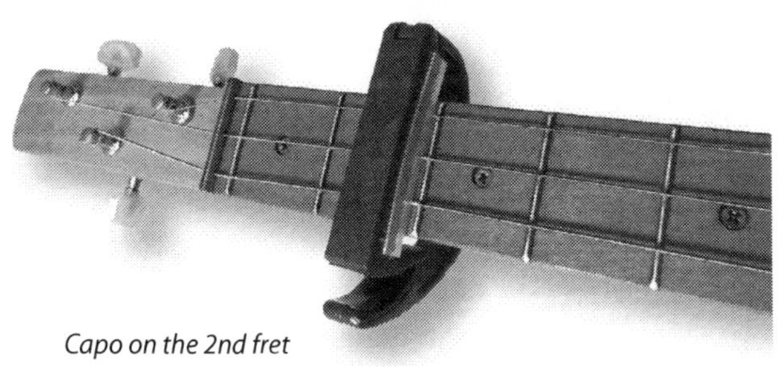
Capo on the 2nd fret

The **capodaster** (or capo for short) is a simple mechanical device that clamps down on the neck of your CBG. It shortens the length of the vibrating strings, thus raising their pitch. Think of the capo as a fast and effective way of retuning, with the capo replacing the saddle of your CBG.

Using a capo enables you to play in keys normally hard to play and what's better still: you don't have to learn new fingerings!

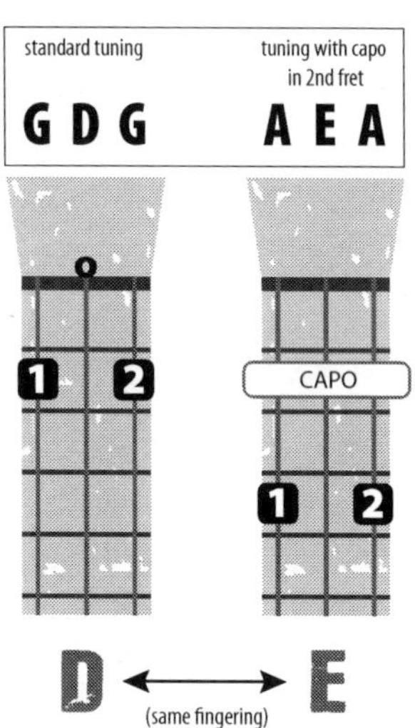

Here's an example: You know a song in the key of D and want to play it in the key of E (if, for instance, D is too low for you to sing). Put a capo on the 2nd fret. Using the same fingerings you used to play in D you're now playing in E (because your CBG has been „tuned" two frets higher by the capo).

You can use any capo that fits your CBG. Guitar capos are a good starting point, but a capo for ukulele or banjo will work, too. Try and see what you like.

Transposing a song to another key

This is another way to play a song in another key (without using a capo).
Transposing simply means playing a song in another key. You may want to do this because you/the singer can't sing it in the original key or because it simply sounds better to you in another key. Here's how it's done:

Suppose the song's key is D and the chords are D, G and A. You want to play this song in the key of G.

- Using the chart on the right, search for the note D in the first row.
- Now go down the columns until you reach the note G, five columns down from D.
- Now look for the chord G (the second chord in the original key) in the first row and count down exactly as many columns as you did from D to G (five).
- You'll arrive at the note C, so the second chord in the new key is C.

Using the same principle, the last chord (A) becomes a D in the new key.
So, the chords D, G and A of the original key (D) become G, C and D in the key of G.
But what about the chord extensions like major, minor, seventh?
That's simple: The chord **type** (major, minor, seventh chord, 7#9 or whatever) stays the same, the chord **name** (A, B, D etc.) changes. In other words: If the chord was a minor chord before, it's still a minor chord. If the chord was a seventh chord before, it's still a seventh chord etc.

Capodaster chart

	C	C♯/D♭	D	D♯/E♭	E	F	F♯/G♭	G	G♯/A♭	A	A♯/B♭	B
1	C♯/D♭	D	D♯/E♭	E	F	F♯/G♭	G	G♯/A♭	A	A♯/B♭	B	C
2	D	D♯/E♭	E	F	F♯/G♭	G	G♯/A♭	A	A♯/B♭	B	C	C♯/D♭
3	D♯/E♭	E	F	F♯/G♭	G	G♯/A♭	A	A♯/B♭	B	C	C♯/D♭	D
4	E	F	F♯/G♭	G	G♯/A♭	A	A♯/B♭	B	C	C♯/D♭	D	D♯/E♭
5	F	F♯/G♭	G	G♯/A♭	A	A♯/B♭	B	C	C♯/D♭	D	D♯/E♭	E
6	F♯/G♭	G	G♯/A♭	A	A♯/B♭	B	C	C♯/D♭	D	D♯/E♭	E	F
7	G	G♯/A♭	A	A♯/B♭	B	C	C♯/D♭	D	D♯/E♭	E	F	F♯/G♭
8	G♯/A♭	A	A♯/B♭	B	C	C♯/D♭	D	D♯/E♭	E	F	F♯/G♭	G
9	A	A♯/B♭	B	C	C♯/D♭	D	D♯/E♭	E	F	F♯/G♭	G	G♯/A♭
10	A♯/B♭	B	C	C♯/D♭	D	D♯/E♭	E	F	F♯/G♭	G	G♯/A♭	A
11	B	C	C♯/D♭	D	D♯/E♭	E	F	F♯/G♭	G	G♯/A♭	A	A♯/B♭
12	C	C♯/D♭	D	D♯/E♭	E	F	F♯/G♭	G	G♯/A♭	A	A♯/B♭	B

Made in the USA
Middletown, DE
26 September 2023

39467257R00110